ADAIR T.M. GASPARIAN

Threads

A Memoir

ISBN: 1-4392-3661-5
ISBN-13: 9781439236611

To order additional copies, please contact us.
BookSurge
www.booksurge.com
1-866-308-6235
orders@booksurge.com

DEDICATION

To Barbara, always my daughter and best friend, frequently my sister, sometimes my mother. Because of her, I am.

To Greg and Larry, my sons, my joy, my fulfillment, my future.

And to the force behind those *Threads* that unwound through decades and across continents to bring together Norman and me; a miracle.

TABLE OF CONTENTS

FOREWORD

What I have found during the decades I've been living and teaching abroad is courage:
the courage of those Chinese students, who stood and died together in the Tiananmen Square Massacre because they believed in a future of freedom and democracy;
the courage of the young students in the Middle East, who asked the forbidden questions because they believed it was their right to know;
and the courage of the Armenian people, not only to survive, but to celebrate life, even though faced with the onslaught of disasters wrought by the collapse of the former Soviet Union.

What I also have found is that sensuality and sexuality, and the multiple facets of love as they are expressed and demonstrated in maturity, are of a more multidimensional and broader scope than I had ever imagined. To paraphrase G.B. Shaw: youth is a glorious experience, as a prelude to life.

INTRODUCTIONS ALL ROUND

My youngest picked up his last box of belongings, hoisted it onto his shoulder and bent his six-foot-six frame to kiss the top of my hair. "I love you the most, Mom," he said, and strode out. I didn't close the door, but held on to the moment. Now Larry was joining my daughter, Barbara, and my other son, Greg, as each moved into his or her own independence. This was an ending. I'd heard about this moment, read about it, and now it was mine. It was the first time I'd been without children in the house since the age of nineteen, and for many of those years I had raised them as a single parent. There had been no sympathy, no empathy, no attempt at emotional support or even tolerance from their father. How could there have been when, to his mind, I was the cause of all problems; not only those of the children, but his own as well. And, when the psychologist had said that the root of the difficulties was his abusive ways, he'd simply denounced us all in four-letter words and moved out of the state. My youngsters' stormy encounters, the late-night telephone calls for rescue, the unnerving maze of emotional peaks and troughs had been mine to handle and had taken their toll, but the tempests of adolescence had been outlived. I expected there could be relapses, but they would be handled and they would pass. My story was no different from that of thousands of other women.

I stood watching with pride and sadness as Larry wedged that last box into his older-model car, turned to wave, collapsed his length into the front seat and drove away. I closed the door and turned to accept the emptiness of my apartment. I had hoped I was prepared for it. I wasn't. Truthfully, I was ill prepared for the world I lived in. Why?

Girls born after the onset of the women's liberation movement have no notion, nor should they ever have, of the restrictions we of the previous generations lived under. Those restrictions were an escalating repressive force. My life can well serve as an example of those of us who had special gifts and were not allowed to use them. I was able to complete the first eight years of my education in seven years and went to high school at the age of thirteen; too young both physically and socially to be there...a miserable experience in all respects. Mathematics had been my strong subject during elementary and middle school, but when I went to high school I was not allowed to pursue any further math classes. Instead, I was diverted into home economics: cooking and sewing. I didn't cook at home. That was my mother's duty and she didn't have time in her busy schedule to train me. In my cooking class I learned to make chocolate fudge. My mother didn't sew, and I had never held a needle and didn't particularly care to. I paid a classmate to make my class project, got caught and received a D for the class. This was not some small backwater school system, but city schools in a major metropolitan area. During these years, my complaints and rebellion were responded to by my parents' unquestioning bows to authority figures. The school administration knew what was best for its students. They knew the life we would be entering and were preparing us for that life, for our own good. That future was described to me in clichés such as "A woman's place is in the home." By the year I was born, the ratification of the nineteenth amendment was only a dozen years old. Centuries, millennia of one basic belief system predominated; in order to command and maintain a society's position in the world of nations, power belonged in the hands of the male population. To thwart any threat to that power base, it was therefore essential to keep the *little woman* out of sight and hearing. Approval of one's place in society was secure for those who stayed at home, married, bore children—many children—and didn't make waves. How much better today's T-shirt wisdom proclaiming, "A woman's place is in the house...and in the senate and the Oval Office."

Whatever our talents, as youngsters we were encouraged to learn the womanly crafts, to stay at home and if one had a special aptitude she could be assured that success would come calling: "If you build a better mousetrap, the world will beat a path to your door." Right! Actually, if you do build a better mousetrap you may catch a bigger rat, but no one will come beating a path to your door, unless it is to put you out of business.

Then there was always, "What will the neighbors say?" Well, I never really knew the answer to that one, but

4

today they'd say, "You go, girl!" But not then, clearly! Not then.

   Those were my formative years, and the formative years of my peers. My peers, though, did not seem to be having as much difficulty in adjusting as did I. It became clear to me at a very early age that I was "different" from other youngsters. Shy to begin with, I became more and more withdrawn in public situations. At home, though, during adolescence I questioned everything...every tradition, every value, every institution. The more I read and thought, the more my curiosity about the rest of the world unfolded. The more my mother recited scripture to me, the more nonsensical and irrelevant it all seemed. My attempts to unravel contradictions and convoluted thinking were quickly squelched, no discussion allowed. It made no difference what the subject matter was, the results became predictable. I recall clearly how, on one occasion, I questioned a particularly problematic political situation, trying to understand its meaning to the American public. My mother placed her hand over her heart and began to sing the national anthem at full voice, drowning out my question. My parents were distressed and embarrassed by my behavior. During those high school years, questions became more forcefully restricted. Activities more carefully guided. Dreams of world travels and a nontraditional life were relegated to the privacy of my room, unresolved; curiosity and imagination confined to my journals, diaries, and daydreams—where they churned away, unabated. There were some especially raging times when I became particularly outspoken, argumentative, and rambunctious. Those rages were interrupted by threats to send me away...

somewhere. But, of course, that never happened. After all, if I had gone missing from the neighborhood, *what would the neighbors say?* And this from parents who were educated. My mother was a schoolteacher and principal and my father was an accountant for a major lumber concern. They were, though, both old enough to be my grandparents; no doubt a contributing factor to the disconnect.

We, too, were children of the media, and the old clichés were reinforced, mirrored back to us as American values through the carefully controlled movies and radio shows of the thirties and forties. The Hayes Code was in full swing, guiding and directing the mores of American society. The joy of being female was to be found behind the white picket fence, in the well-stocked kitchen and the twin-bedded boudoir. These were powerful influences. But the power was not in the images or the words. The images and words were so much pap, parroted by quiescent parents and a regulated media; today they're laughable. The power was in believing them—in accepting that there was nothing out there to escape to, that the best of everything in the world was contained within our borders, that beyond them "there be monsters" out to destroy us all. But, that belief system was slowly becoming a festering boil rumbling to a head, the toxicity epitomized by McCarthyism. Senator Joe McCarthy and his cohorts destroyed the lives and careers of countless of America's most talented men and women through challenges to their patriotism. He denounced our biggest and best and any who challenged him as enemies of the state; all of which was glossed over by the all-American sitcoms of the fifties. This festering boil was finally lanced by those few restless, creative mutants who initiated the revolutions of the sixties and seventies. Too late for me.

The white picket fence and well-stocked kitchen were the American dream. Other cultures and their generations were far different. Such dreams were well beyond the scope of those living in that country against which Senator McCarthy and his cronies broadcast their form of terrorism into a propaganda machine that fed escalating xenophobic American fears. Unbeknownst to us, the targets of our fears were also hearing the ravings of their version of the same type of propaganda machine. Fear had to maintain a balance on both sides of the planet. There were visionaries, though, both there and here, none of whom were able to express an alternate opinion in public.

The family of one of those visionaries *over there* lived in one small room in what had been for generations the servants' quarters for the three-story mansion that stood in a grove of trees on an estate that bordered the river. It had been the home of the visionary's wife since her birth. Her maternal grandfather and great-grandfather had been successful land developers; her paternal family line had been vintners, producing the finest wines in the country. The wedding of her grandparents had been the merger of two of the city's five wealthiest families, a ceremony "not seen before" in the country, according to the family archives. Their first child, the young girl's mother, died during the flu epidemic that ravaged the world; her father had been murdered, an unsolved case. The young girl was raised by her grandparents, who adhered to the same formulaic standards for her as were in place for all wealthy children raised in their part of the world. She was educated in a French-speaking school and trained in the higher matters of etiquette that were expected in her social class. She had been quite young on the night that her grandmother had come to her room and told her to quickly help gather up necessities because they would be moving into an area of the house the young child had only visited on occasion. They selected just the fewest of the family valuables. They rolled up two of their most prized Persian carpets—they could be used for warming the floor on the frigid Soviet nights; took two samovars from a glass-fronted cabinet—the hot tea service was as much for survival as for maintaining their cultural tradition; and scooped out silverware and a half dozen silver tea-glass holders. They collected the art books and family photo albums as they passed quickly back and forth through the many rooms and along the lengthy corridors. Bed linens and deep, soft quilts, as many as they could balance, were piled on top of anything they could carry. Salvaging clothes was kept to a minimum. They had very little time and no help. The servants were gone. Some older aunts and uncles had recently left the family home and migrated abroad. Grandmother was not sure where the other menfolk were, only that her husband had awakened her with the instructions, and then was gone again. As they were struggling to roll the upright piano down the hallway and into the crowded room, he returned and helped give it a final shove. It was the smaller of the two pianos in the mansion. The other, the concert grand, would be forfeited. So, this was to become their lives, without kitchen or private bath, while the rest of the mansion was divided up among the homeless poor of the city. All must be equal in this tiny republic that was being consumed by the USSR.

The years passed, the grandparents died, and soon after the young woman met and married the visionary and bore him two sons. During the years while we in America were listening to the propaganda and building underground bomb shelters to protect us from the possibility of annihilation from the dreaded Bear of the North, the visionary and his wife were raising their sons to appreciate education, the arts, and literature. They also began to speak quietly with their youngsters about the world they lived in. The visionary didn't believe the propaganda and feared no annihilation from the imperialists across the sea. Instead, he counseled his sons that one possible way to escape the inevitable decline of their degenerating political regime was to learn the English language. If they would promise to study, he would find an authentic English-language tutor, someone who had traveled and lived in England in earlier days. The older son opted for sports and to follow his father into the field of engineering. The younger chose the new language. At the age of eleven, it would be his fourth. All was settled, and the eleven-year-old picked up his beloved violin and continued to practice. It was to be forty years before the visionary's advice opened the doors for the son.

My culture's traditions and mores were the diet of my upbringing. Success was measured by appearances. Position within the social milieu would stay predominantly the same as one generation succeeded the previous. If one were to move up the ladder, it would be through a good marriage or good luck. Professions open to women were primarily secretarial, nursing, and teaching. There were the favored few who could make a socioeconomic leap by means of writing or the theater arts, but the odds were against anyone trying to make a career out of anything so unpredictable. My parents were not visionaries. And when the time arrived, my parents said, "As long as we're paying your university fees, you will major in education. You will be the fourth-generation teacher in this family, and you will make us all very proud. If the time ever comes when you need to support yourself, you'll thank us." No choice in the matter. I loathed the idea of being a teacher. I despised the thought of being a fourth-generation anything, but forced down my yearnings for...something, anything, else...and entered that course of study. I went off to school in San Francisco, that wicked, wicked city—which is my favorite in the United States. I was far too immature for that transition, and within a few months boys and I had discovered each other and I flunked out. Within a year I was married, and within another year I had a baby and was divorced. (Having Baby Barbara was the best thing that could have happened to me.) With an infant in tow, I wanted to go to a particular private college in my home town, but that was not allowed because it was considered too liberal. They chose a different private school; this one church affiliated. One would suspect that sending me to a religious institution would be the worst possible choice, and one would be right. But I'm sure they thought it would have a strong positive impact on me. Wrong. I was expelled before the year was out! A third university was chosen and this one was a proper fit; the University of California at Los Angeles.

So, they eventually won out, and they were right. I did become a fourth-generation schoolteacher and truly did try to do all the socially correct things. Often failed, but crept back onto the road most taken. I married a second time and bore my two sons. I stayed in that dysfunctional marriage, mostly out of fear that no one else would ever want me, until the abuses began affecting my offspring; then, I stepped into the role of single parent...determined to give my children a freedom I'd not known, to raise them to be independent, analytical, sensitive adults —while always keeping my personal churnings at bay. Child support payments were regular enough, but too small to contribute much and I learned to budget on his pittance and my schoolteacher's salary. Does it all sound too, too familiar?

————

In the sixties, the repressions eased up somewhat and those in the Soviet Union were getting a glimpse of life outside of their extensive borders. Music from the West became available and some very old Hollywood movies were shown to the populace. The visionary was able to move his family to another city and to purchase a private apartment. However, he had overworked his frail body by carrying two jobs over the years, just to give his family something on occasion that was a bit above the base level. Regrettably, he wasn't able to enjoy their new life for long. In 1964 he suffered a massive heart attack and died. Before the funeral, the visionary's wife removed his wedding ring from his finger and secreted it away in a small velvet-lined box. She put it among her most cherished belongings and didn't open the box again for another twenty-eight years.

———————

By the early 1980s, most of us believed the world was in pretty good shape; the social revolution of the '60s and '70s had seen the rise of new ways of viewing ourselves and our place in the world, had renewed interest in Eastern philosophical doctrines, and the Vietnam war was over. As for me, I was not in such good shape. My children were gone from my home. I was left alone to languish in a teaching position that no longer demanded much from me. Those lifelong yearnings acted as an irritant. Granted, the social revolution had opened the doors of opportunity and they were swinging wide through women's liberation, but I was too old to walk on through them.

I was a social introvert and lived in a town which had been chosen for me by others, and in which I had always been a misfit. I was at a loss in any obligatory social gathering, becoming shy and mute and retreating into the wall until I could make a graceful exit. I had long been a complex mix, intensely spiritual and critically irreligious, avidly interested in some things and apathetic toward others, passionately in need of a man with strengths greater than my own, though I'd sworn myself to a life of celibacy. I could cry over the miracle of a blade of grass, and laugh at bawdy stories. I had no middle of the road, and I knew it. And those churnings intensified. I wanted out.

It would be simplest to say that Larry's departure was the cause of the following year, but that isn't right.

It's not so simple. The death of one's parents, divorce, the independence of the children, all are endings, and with each ending another tentacle of one's identity is severed. You're no longer so-and-so's offspring, so-and-so's spouse, so- and-so's mother. The empty nest was not to become a transitory phase relieved by women's groups and volunteer work, but an emotional quicksand whose sucking action was swift and thorough.

It's the accumulation of the paring back coupled with the calendar that brings on crisis. With Larry gone, the tentacles of my persona had finally been cut back to the core, and what I found in that core was a wealth of experience, education, love—and those damned yearnings—all with no challenging means of expression. My home had always been a sanctuary for me and for my family. But, as the months began to blend together, that refuge began to change. It was transforming itself into a sepulcher. I slept to the drone of the TV test pattern, and awoke to deal with one more day's routine while pacing my classroom. Words of encouragement spoken to my students were responded to as expected, but it was all ritual. I'd been doing it for more than twenty years. There were still occasional accolades from my colleagues, but those had long since lost meaning. Their pleasantries became irritating, grating, and I escaped the congeniality of the teachers' room, welcoming isolation. The windows of my classroom overlooked the grandeur of the Sierra Nevada Mountains, but the spectacle of their changing seasons no longer touched my soul. They stood before me as prison walls and I stood before them, vacant-eyed. I read somewhere once that it isn't the months and years that are so long, but the hours and the days. That describes it: hours and days of watching the hands of the clock until they finally completed their journey to three thirty, signaling my legal commitments were over and I could return home to hide in my place of entombment. Repetitive, life-draining ennui. Burnout.

Spring was still an eternity away, and I was sliding into despair. Visits with my family were intermittent and focused on their lives. Thanksgiving came and we congregated at Barbara's house. But it wasn't the same as previous years. Christmas passed, again with my daughter. And again, I was a guest. During the times we were together, my sons were usually involved in some horseplay or sharing information about their latest conquests and didn't pay too much attention to Mom. Mom was a fixture in their lives, a problem solver, a rock. Barb, now a single parent herself, was always intuitive. She had sensed my restlessness and growing melancholy, and spoken of it more than once. New Year's Day she brought her own two youngsters to share dinner with me and, over a late coffee, mentioned it again.

"You're not looking so good these days. Too stressed around the eyes. What are you doing with your time?"

"Not much, Barb. Still trying to think of something new to do with my life. Can't come up with anything of interest. Must be menopausal."

"How about transferring away from here now that Larry's moved out? Have you thought about looking for anyplace else? How 'bout somewhere on the Oregon or California coast...you love the ocean so much. You need a change of scenery."

"Sure. I've though about it. But I'm really too old. School districts aren't interested in hiring doddering ol' menopausal has-beens. Anyway, I'm too high on the salary schedule here. Would lose too much money trying to transfer somewhere else."

"Hadn't noticed you doddering too much lately. What difference would less salary make if you could move somewhere you liked, and maybe find some friends?"

"Taking a big dip in salary would be important at my age. I've got to think about retirement coming up in a few years."

"Retirement! Seems you've already 'retired' by the look of your life. How about going back to school? Are there any courses at the university you haven't taken?"

"Maybe a few in brain surgery. No, Barb, what's the use? I've already got too much stuff in my head. That sounds like busywork."

"Yeah. But you've gotta do something. You can't just sit in this apartment and vegetate for the next thirty years. You look pale. What don't you join a health club? No. You'd hate it. Why don't you just go out for walks every day?"

"Barb! Look outside. It's snowing, for God's sake. Go out and walk in this? Come on...," I said, and we both glanced out the window. I grimaced and shook my head. "I don't think so!"

"Don't be a wimp. Do it anyway."

"Never!"

The roadway behind my apartment complex was a narrow strip that wound up a gently sloping hill and out into the undeveloped fields beyond, where it gradually petered out. There was a thin layer of snow on the ground the next morning. It wasn't even six o'clock yet, still dark out. The sky was clear and the last stars spotted the canopy. I stood, peering out the window. Shuddered at the dim, white glaze. Pushed open my door and stepped out. The air was quiet and crisp. *I must be crazy. This is ridiculous.* And crunched off toward the road. *Why do I listen to her? I'll probably get shin splints.* Jammed my mittened hands deep into my pockets and turned uphill.

Thirty minutes later I unlocked my door to hear the phone ringing.

"Did you do it?"

"Barb—how did you know?"

"Do I know my mom, or don't I? Have a great day. Love ya."

I'd been going over it and over it, and in my mind there was no question but that it would take a miracle to transform my life. After a few mornings passed, I began to enjoy the brisk, energizing air, and as I walked I initiated a game with myself—pretending and imaging that I was traveling away from my environment, each step taking me into a new and exciting existence. I gratefully saluted each rising sun and promised myself it was going to bring with it a rising opportunity. As my muscles became attuned, jogging replaced walking, and running replaced jogging. I reasoned with myself that if I moved faster, results would come faster. Since there was never anyone else out at that pre-dawn hour, I added a quiet, rhythmic mantra—humming, *"I'm on my way out of here. I'm on my way out of here."*

While chugging along one Sunday morning I decided to go to church. I hadn't been to religious services since the children were young. And even then it really had been to give them a religious education. I'd pretended. But maybe now I would find some new insights or awareness within myself, or within the dogma, that would speak to me. And also, maybe I'd find some new people there with whom I could become friendly. Physical exercise was for the outer person. Perhaps it would not be life-changing. I needed more. With hopes and expectations lifted, I went—and continued to go, for a while.

As the weeks passed, my puffs of breath no longer created little disturbances in the chilled air and the snow gave way to the false spring with its attempt at budding green leaves. I tracked the progress of the struggling buds and thought of the symbolism. But the symbolism did not manifest in my life. Nothing changed. The false spring passed, and with its passing my attempt at church services ended. I'd found no new insights or awareness either within me or in them. New friendships? The effusive greetings began and ended at the church doors.

Late snows came again and I crunched along the roadway, humming my mantra and thinking. If I couldn't find meaning in Christianity, I'd turn again to my earlier studies in Eastern mysticism. Long before, I had accepted both karma and reincarnation as truths detached from "religion." Avidly, I reread from my volumes that had been sent into hibernation years earlier, then put them back on the shelf. No. It wasn't quite right, not quite enough. Didn't quite fit. I had my own philosophic beliefs, but they seemed to be for others' lives, not for mine. Solace didn't come. I once again put spiritual guidance behind me as a cruel hoax. Snow gave way to rain. Disillusionment took hold. I told myself that my pretenses were ridiculous and that I was childish. I was ashamed of my foolishness and vowed never to tell anybody what I'd been doing. Discouragement brought mental fatigue, and some mornings I was too tired to exert the interest in exercising. Those mornings became more frequent. At last, I gave up

During those few months there had been periodic visits and talks with Barbara, often on philosophical subjects, and occasional visits and chats with my sons, but a growing dread of any outside contact other than my family had set in. For the first time in my career I began missing classes. I called in *sick* and stayed home doing...nothing.

Depression deepened. I had nearly stopped eating. The sight and smell of food repulsed me, and there were times when I scraped prepared meals into the disposal. By mid-March the period of decline had spiraled down, sucking me into the abyss. I awoke early one Saturday morning to a pillow damp from my tears. Hollow. Desolate.

Thirty, forty more years of what, Barb? Ten, fifteen more years in the classroom. The classroom. I hate that classroom. Hate it. Ten, fifteen more years. I can't do it ten, fifteen more days. And then what? Twenty, thirty years of what? Of this. No. Can't do it anymore. Can't pretend. Not anymore.

Can't, don't want to. A hundred years of nothing. Of wanting.

Why do You ignore me? When I've tried so damned hard. You and Your empty promises. Why don't You help me?

Don't know what to do. Nothing to do. Just want somebody to touch me. It's been so long since anybody's touched me. Somebody right here beside me. Somebody I can reach out and

touch. Nobody's here. See? Nobody's here and nobody's out there. Face it, Adair. You're alone.

What kind of a loving parent are You, anyhow? I would never do to my children what You're doing to me. You don't care. Care? You don't exist. Damn You for not existing.

Can't do it anymore. Can't do it alone. Can't...it's got to end.

My conscious mind forced its way into wakefulness. *What am I doing? Who am I talking to? I gave up that nonsense years ago. What am I doing? Stop wallowing. It's all up to you. Get up. Get out of bed. Make some coffee. Clean the apartment.*

An hour or so later Barbara walked in. She found me mindlessly scrubbing the baseboards of my apartment with a toothbrush. I was unprepared. I had neither brushed my hair nor washed my face, but was sitting cross-legged on the floor in my pajamas searching out minuscule grains of dirt from between the carpet and the wall. The scene of her mother hunched over on the floor jolted her.

"What in the hell are you doing?" she gasped, echoing my own question.

I looked up at her and my unexpected tears began to roll. "I don't know, Barb."

She calmed herself and lifted me to my feet. "Get dressed. I'm taking you to breakfast."

I obeyed, and over breakfast I told her. Confessed to her about missing school and all the things I had been thinking and doing. She listened patiently, lovingly, but didn't commiserate. That wouldn't have been in her character. Rather, she took me to her home at the lake and we spent the weekend playing with my grandchildren and walking through the pine trees, talking, talking, talking about everything...about nothing.

The revitalization was short-lived. It was less than a week before I was once more hiding in my apartment, despair engulfing me. I sat for hours staring into a void. The next time Barbara phoned I was in such a depth I was hardly coherent, couldn't focus. Everything seemed disconnected from me. She must have changed her tone, or something. I'm not sure. But her words came through to me, softly.

"Mom, where is Larry?"

"I don't know."

"I want you to hang up the phone, Mom, and stay right where you are. I'll locate him."

"OK, Barb."

Obedient as always, I sat quietly, staring at the door, waiting. I don't know how long it was, but after a time I was aware of Larry's tires squealing in the parking lot. I must have realized that deliverance was at hand, because as soon as I recognized that he was in the room I allowed myself to slip away, and he caught me as I passed out.

He carried me to his car and then into the hospital emergency room as I vacillated between semiconsciousness and unconsciousness, only attentive to the safety and strength of his arms protecting me. I couldn't answer the receptionist's questions, couldn't count backward from ten, couldn't even tell her my own name. From some remote state of consciousness I knew that I was being wheeled into a cubicle and attached to machines. From a great distance I heard the urgency of the duty nurse's voice saying that she couldn't get a pulse. Emergency care was immediate. I remember opening my eyes and seeing a battery of specialists moving quietly and quickly in and out of the curtained-off space, and wondering who they were. Voices were murmuring, fading away and coming back into my awareness, but words were without meaning. Two intravenous drips were started into my arms. Blood tests were run and later, x-rays taken. As the magic potions moved through my veins I began to recover my sensibilities. Larry was hovering near the foot of my bed and someone shooed him away. I could hear him, and knew that he had remained near the emergency room doors and had edged his way in from time to time—and that he was being sent back with assurances that everything was being taken care of.

When I was fully awake, they allowed him to come to me. He told me he had made call after call to his anxious brother and impatient sister, telling them it wasn't necessary to make the trip from the lake, that he would stand by and keep them informed. Over the next hours results of the tests came back. There was nothing wrong with me. They monitored me overnight and discharged me in the morning, prescribing some antidepressant medication. Larry took me to my apartment where Barbara and Greg were waiting. She telephoned my supervisor, requested an extended sick leave for me, and we went as a family to her home at Lake Tahoe. She didn't allow me to fill the prescription for the drugs.

For the next days they treated me to favorite dishes and little surprise gifts. We walked through the trees and beside the lake and talked, endlessly. They were courageous about my life. I wasn't. But my energies and spirits gradually picked up as the time went by.

My sons had been coming regularly and as I strengthened they began to play with me, as they had over the years, chasing me, tickling me. During one such escapade, Larry swooped me up in his arms, saying, "Who wants her? I don't want her. Here. You take her!" and tossed me across to Greg, who feigned a theatrical balancing act as we collapsed onto the floor. No one remembers who first spoke the words, and they compete over taking credit, but it was while they had me pinned on the carpet that one of them said casually, "Mom, why don't you just join the Peace Corps?"

Startled, and wanting to stop what could become a fatiguing barrage of concern, I got to my feet, dismissing it with a giggle and, "Yeah, right!"

Barbara overheard the comment. "That's it! Do it, Mom. Call them."

"Now? Or can I wait till morning?"

I returned to my teaching duties without heart, but with renewed physical strength. During the next few days I performed a lukewarm investigation into the possibility of the Peace Corps and was told that it normally takes from a year to a year and a half to be placed. As I had suspected, the well-meant suggestion had been useless; a year might as well have been a lifetime. But, to appease my family, I went ahead and applied, expecting nothing and resigned to that nothingness. Routine continued. My family made more and more of an effort to involve me in their lives, not to allow me enough time alone for my feelings of futility to escalate. Seeds of possibilities were planted, but we didn't discuss any particular future for me. I told them of the delay in obtaining any Peace Corps assignment, and that idea was allowed to fade without further comment. We speculated about summer vacation sites and it was my assignment to start collecting travel brochures. Busywork.

The days passed, one indistinguishable from the other. I participated in our holiday planning, but, when by myself, it was an ongoing, hour-to-hour struggle to stay in control of my depressions. I would fight them, though, would try anew, battling dolor. I forced myself to start my morning walks, chanting that earlier mantra, consciously trying to detach myself from the anguish of what I privately saw, but no longer discussed, as the reality of an impending and menacing oblivion.

It was exactly six weeks after applying that the telephone call came—at seven thirty in the morning. Because of the hour, I thought it would be one of my offspring; but it wasn't. When the caller identified himself, I had to suppress a rising panic, disbelief at the suddenness. His unexpected words of salvation came through: "And if you're still interested and available, an unexpected vacancy has occurred and we would like to send you to Jamaica as a teacher-trainer. We'd like you to report to Miami for orientation." I bit my lip to get control of my attention. *Flatten your voice, Adair. Don't let too much excitement show. Sound businesslike. Friendly, but professional.*

"Yes, of course. Thank you. What do I need to do? What are the steps?" I was taking notes. My hand was unsteady. I had trouble forming the letters.

My mind had shifted to another level; it was some disconnected part of me that spoke, accepting the invitation, calmly overriding my torrent of relief, overriding the tears welling up, overriding any thought about the multitude of preparations which would be necessary and the limited amount of time to get everything done. The date he had given me was only days after the end of the school year. It didn't matter. When I hung up the phone my eyes were burning and my mouth had gone dry.

Jesus, Joseph, and Mary! An unexpected vacancy! Un—ex—pec—ted vacancy! It's my friggin' miracle! It's not just in my mind. It's real. I'm going to get out of here! I'm Out Of Here!

I was gripping the telephone to my chest as the surge of adrenaline charged through every cell, and the tears and laughter rose up inside of me. I could scarcely see and my fingers were trembling as I fumbled to dial my family. I said, "You'll never guess what has just happened...," and I heard their shouts of joy.

The school year was in its closing days; end-of-year details had to be completed. I would need a release from the intent-to-return agreement which I had already signed. I went to the school district office with apprehension, but they were enthusiastic, envied me, and processed a two-year leave of absence in record time. Events began to gel. My energies soared. I gave up my apartment. My family and a colleague or two came to my assistance and helped pack up and store my belongings while I sped from office to office, completing all the remaining details and obtaining the endless documentation needed to close out one segment of my life and open up another.

Right on schedule, the small group accompanied me to the airport. When the announcement came, the hugs and kisses were exchanged with excitement and a touch of nervousness. I boarded the flight for Florida. As the plane lifted off the ground, I leaned my forehead against the coolness of the window and watched Reno, the site of my despondency, coalesce into an unrecognizable blot and disappear from sight. I thought of the symbolism and smiled at my reflection. I had direction. I was fifty-two years old.

———

There was no way for anyone to even imagine at the time, but that suggestion to enter the Peace Corps, which had been made so offhandedly by one of my sons, was the key to my destiny; a destiny concealed within strands of threads which had been wound decades—perhaps life-times—before, in one of the earth's most remote regions, far removed from the western hemisphere. What had, in my extremity, appeared to be the end of the rope was, in truth, only a knot. The season had come and destiny had spoken quietly through my son. After listening, no matter with what hesitation, I did accept. It was acceptance that untied the knot and allowed those threads to begin to un-ravel, and they would continue to unwind through a series of seemingly unrelated incidents—of coincidences large and small. Threads which, over the next several years, would lead me across the world many times, to experiences only read about or seen in a theater. Threads which seemed to be somehow attached to the top of my head and under which I jiggled along like a puppet, without questioning, only doing. Threads which were always leading me along the way toward one particular and paramount symbol, and then beyond, far beyond. The tapestry was taking form.

In a city I had scarcely heard of, in a country only a few people ever think about, a small velvet-lined box had been secreted away, lying unopened for more than two decades—and it was waiting, and would continue to wait, for me.

JAMAICA

This cannot be a real place. It's far too beautiful. The foliage is too rich and vivid and dense, and the colors are all too intense. It looks like a Hollywood movie set which has been cast with extras who tote heavy burdens balanced on their heads, who wear their long hair in dreadlocks, and who are too tall and thin and attractive. Here and there among those extras are interspersed minor actors as well as principals who are too well dressed, and soldiers whose weapons are always at the ready, all of whom are wandering about the streets and neighborhoods, chatting and enjoying music throughout the cooler hours of the evenings and nights, all awaiting the director's call to action.

But after a few days of unbearable heat, swarms of flying cockroaches, noise that defies known decibel levels, untreated sewage flowing through the gutters of poverty-stricken villages, and men urinating in the public streets, it became unquestionably real.

Each morning, after dueling with the scorpions over use of the bathtub in my temporary domicile, I showered in cold water and ate breakfast, then left for our in-country orientation. By the time I had walked to the bus, the sweat was dripping, my clothes were clinging to me in an embarrassing fashion, and I longed for another shower. The orientation facility was not air-conditioned and, except for one tall oscillating fan, there was no ventilation. While the in-country indoctrinations were being given, I sat squirming on my metal chair to keep from sticking to it and trying to observe whether or not the second hand on my watch was moving. After days of lectures on cross-cultural understanding, I was directed to my assigned school. It was a residence facility for nineteen abandoned or abused boys, most of whom had never been inside an educational institution until they were placed there. For those mere nineteen students there were two fully qualified teachers and one teacher's aide. These educators' first words of greeting to me were, "Did you bring any soccer balls? What sports equipment can you get for us from the United States—free?" Teacher training? I wasn't too sure if that was exactly what the administrators of this school had in mind when they requested the Peace Corps to send someone to upgrade the teaching skills of their staff. I mentally questioned the administrator's motivations, but reacted to the teachers' smiles.

Concurrently with being given my assignment, I moved into what was to become my permanent home for the duration of my tour of duty. I was more than lucky to find it. *Lucky* is not the appropriate word, as this particular locale was to become the site from which the next step of my reentry into life would take place. Nowhere else would have provided me with the same precise combination of circumstances necessary for that to come about. The house was situated in one of the wealthier districts of Kingston, and had all the amenities of life which I, as an American, was used to. When I would later describe my living accommodations to other returning PC volunteers, they would laugh and shake their heads. Impossible! As I say, I was *lucky*. The owner of the house was a woman with dual residency in Jamaica and the United States. She would be spending the next several months in America and wanted someone to house-sit for her. She provided me with a large room that had a private entrance off a patio, and a spacious adjoining bath, as well as freedom to enjoy the rest of the house. There was a live-in maid and a weekly groundsman to tend the luxurious gardens surrounding the residence. If this was Peace Corps *roughing it,* I could suffer through!

I visited my assigned school daily and observed the teachers in action as I acquainted myself with the students and the general environs of my new situation. I attended the weekly PC meetings and socialized with my counterparts on the weekends at one of the five-star hotels, where we submerged our steaming bodies in the swimming pool that the hotel had given the PC permission to use. As the weeks slid by I became ever more aware that my Jamaican teachers didn't need a teacher-trainer. They were very capable professionals. What they did need was someone to provide them with remedial educational materials and someone to tutor several of the boys who were far below grade level, both socially and academically, and who needed special help speaking and understanding standard English rather than their native Creole dialect. I could create a needed place for myself, and did so. I contacted people at my school district in the United States and asked if they would send me a variety of textbooks which would serve my school's purposes, but which were obsolete by American standards and were stored in a warehouse awaiting the recycling of the paper. They responded that they would be happy to do so. All I needed to do was provide the funds for shipment to Kingston. I scurried around and found sources for funding. Then, one of those quirks that separates developed from developing countries happened. Overnight the Jamaican government devalued its currency. The result was that it would cost more to ship the American texts to Jamaica than it would to buy new ones in-country. I had wasted a great deal of planning and energy. I began to think again about how to procure materials for my students. Not knowing what else to do, I decided to write them myself. The problem was that there were no raw materials available with which to develop booklets, flash cards, and practice sheets. Undaunted, I contacted the local office of the IBM Corporation and requested the computer printout sheets that were then state-of-the-art and would be shredded or thrown away; I could use the backs of the pages. I explained my purpose, and they were agreeable. I collected reams of printout paper. When completed, the sheets would be mounted on cardboard, if I could find some. I was able to purchase colored pens and set up a place at home to work. I also went from café to café asking for caps from the soda bottles which they sold and opened for their customers. They were glad to oblige. I collected hundreds of bent caps, sorted them according to type, and attempted to clean and straighten them. My thought was to use something concrete for the students to manipulate as I taught them simple arithmetic. My days could easily be filled with meaningful work. What I was not prepared for was the lax attitude toward an academic calendar that was a part of the culture.

It was a twenty-minute bus ride from my home to downtown and a fifteen-minute walk to the ferry landing, followed by a beautiful, marvelously relaxing half-hour ferry ride to reach Port Royal near the tip end of the peninsula, where my school was located. Female PC volunteers were allowed to use this route only during daylight hours. Travel time was more than an hour each way, if and when the ferry ran on schedule. And, of course, I was always weighed down, carrying satchels of materials. I knew there would be transportation difficulties when I agreed to house-sit, but believed that I could survive any and all inconveniences if I had a lovely home to return to. After all, I was in the Peace Corps! What I found was that all too frequently I would arrive at my school only to find that it was closed up, classes having been canceled for the day for some obscure reason, or no reason at all. There was no telephone at the school, and the idea of someone walking to a local store to phone me about the cancellation had occurred to no one. (Cell phones would not become a part of people's lives for another twenty years!) After I suggested to the teachers that I could be called if and when classes were to be cancelled, they were most apologetic and assured me that it would always be done in the future. That never happened. I didn't keep a record, but memory tells me that I arrived at school more often to find locked doors than to find students. But that probably is an exaggeration. Step-by-step, I adapted to the cultural difference. Changed my expectations and slowed my pace. I spent four, or five, or six hours each day preparing the various materials, making them as understandable, attractive, and reusable as possible. I enjoyed the challenge of creativity and took pride in my accomplishments.

In the late fall, my landlady returned from the United States laden with an assortment of American supermarket specialties. She and the maid—or *helper*, as they preferred to be called—spent a couple of days preparing her homecoming banquet to share with her extended family. The table was decorated with expensive silver, and great platters heaped with steaming food were displayed on the sideboard. When the hour for the feast arrived she knocked on my bedroom door. She was carrying a small plate of scrambled eggs. She explained that she didn't want me to miss my dinner. I hadn't expected this, thinking that she and I had a congenial relationship. Perhaps I was naïve, but I had assumed that she would invite me to dinner and introduce me to her family. Introduce me she did, but not until the meal was finished and coffee was being served. She brought me to the main living area and introductions were made. I was not invited to sit down. Dozens of people paid no attention to me. Except for one. There was a young man, one of the most handsome I'd ever seen, standing in the doorway to the veranda. He looked across at me. I smiled. He sauntered over and my landlady introduced me to her nephew. We exchanged a word or two, and I excused myself, feeling thoroughly uncomfortable in these surroundings—like the proverbial sore thumb. I had been back in my room only moments when there was a tapping on my outside door. I opened it, and there stood Victor.

"My aunt isn't much of a hostess, is she?"

I laughed and tried to think of something diplomatic to say. He saved me the trouble. "Don't worry; I don't like her, either. She's an insecure snob whose sole purpose in life is to show off what she has and pretend she is still the wife of a political bigwig."

I began to relax and we laughed. He touched my hand. "I'd like to take you to lunch. Where do you work?"

I must have blinked and swallowed. I don't know. I was surprised. More than surprised. Here was this marvelous, tall, athletic, handsome young man asking me for a date. If there was ever *eye candy,* he was it! I had to be old enough to be his mother! I think I said something like, "It's a long way from here," or some such. I hesitated.

"What time can you leave for lunch?"

I gave him the name and location of my school and asked him if he had a car. He laughed, "My dear, I have three cars. Which one would you like me to bring to pick you up?" and he named them. I told him how erratic my school schedule was and again he told me not to worry, that he'd find me. He then returned to the family gathering.

I stood in the middle of my room and began to snicker. *What's happening? Why me?* I slid onto my bed and picked up a magazine, but couldn't do more than randomly flip the pages.

Lordy, I'm such a dolt! He'll never show up. What if he does? Good God! What if he does? What should I have said? Why me? Why does he want to take me to lunch?

A dolt, perhaps, but not so naïve as all that. I was playing another silly game with myself, momentarily postponing what I knew to be true. I knew damn well what he wanted; it was behind his eyes and in that fleeting touch. And there were something seductive about the way he'd come round to my private door to speak to me. He wanted a rendezvous, and I was...curious. It had been a long time. A very, very long time.

I got up and took a look at myself in the mirror; certainly no stranger to my own appearance, but wanted to see what he had just seen. Fifty-two years old...yes, according to the calendar. Five feet eight inches, 115 pounds, and, except for a few laugh lines, a clear and smooth complexion, muscles taut from months of Kingston walking, skin moistened by the high humidity and a deep bronze tone—the result of my long weekend hours at the hotel swimming pool—a bronze that nearly equaled his own Jamaican *clear* coloring. Short cropped hair still retaining its own natural color framed my features usually described by others as *striking*. All the stressors of the past were history. I looked like I had looked years before, like a model...a matured model, I grant you. But still, a model. I appreciated what I saw. My self-confidence, and my curiosity, escalated. Gone was my resolve of celibacy. I ran admiring hands down my torso.

Come on, Victor! Come on along and 'pick me up' for lunch... why not? I smiled the whisper under my breath.

The shining new, deep blue jeep pulled into the school area as I was crossing to the office. Gravel spit from beneath the tires and I glanced around to see who it was. Victor stepped from the cab and stood beside the open door. Perhaps I flushed. As he stood there in his nearly translucent white shirt, unbuttoned almost to the waist and a simple gold chain around his neck, I though to myself that he looked like Harry Belafonte had looked in his younger years. Nearly too handsome to be real. I walked over to him and he smiled and said, "I told you I'd find you. Come on; let me take you to lunch." He opened the door wider so that I could slide across.

I hesitated. "I still have another class."

"Cancel it. How often do they cancel without telling you?"

He had known without my telling him. One of the teachers and some of the boys were passing across the yard, witnessing without acknowledging. I wondered if this was culturally unacceptable, but didn't pay the thought too much attention.

"At least let me tell them that I'm leaving."

His arm encircled my waist and he indicated the step up. "It isn't necessary. They already know."

We drove back toward Kingston. The drive was sometimes awkward, as I often don't have a glib line of small talk. This was certainly one of those times. I'm sure I must have sounded too much like a schoolteacher, but he didn't seem to mind. I asked him about his education, and he told me he had received his degree from a university in Florida and that he now owned his own construction business. He drove fast, too fast for my comfort. I told myself that he knew these roads well, but the traffic was steady and I was nervous anyway. I mentioned our speed.

"You worry too much. I'm a very experienced driver. In fact, on some weekends I compete in races. I'll take you to one, if you'd like to go."

I thanked him, and it confirmed to me that he intended ongoing meetings.

The restaurant was small, unobtrusive, away from the mainstream. The tabletops were plastic-covered and the chairs were the same kind of metal I had seen so frequently in inexpensive places. There was only a scattering of people, mostly just sitting around murmuring to each other. I was surprised, expecting something far more in keeping with his appearance and social level. It crossed my mind that he'd been lying to me about his cars and his business enterprise, maybe even his education, but I dismissed those thoughts at once. That was wrong. That was not what was happening. No. Obviously, he had a wife. After he had ordered I asked him outright.

"You're married, aren't you?"

He was unruffled. "Yes. It doesn't matter." Then he caught my line of reasoning and laughed. "That isn't why I brought you here. This place has authentic Jamaican food which is exceptionally good. I stop here often."

I accepted that as true, and it turned out to be so. The other reason for his having chosen this particular place, and others like it in the weeks to come, was for my protection. It was culturally unacceptable for me to be with him, at least by Peace Corps standards, and he knew it better than I. Socializing with our host country friends was encouraged. But dating a wealthy, highly placed, married man would have been frowned on. Jamaica is a small island and gossip is the favorite pastime.

As we ate, he told me about his studies in America and his trips back and forth. Other than Florida and New York, he'd seen nothing of the country, so I filled him in on the differences between the East and West Coasts. Conversation became easier. We lingered for an hour, maybe more. When the conversation slowed and the check was taken care of, I wondered what was coming next. Now that we were getting acquainted, was he still interested? Or had he changed his mind? Would he ask me out again? I wasn't sure. I felt about as secure as a sixteen-year-old schoolgirl.

I thought he'd take me directly home, but as we pulled away from the restaurant he said, "I'd like to show you my office." The statement was casual enough, but something in his voice set objections in motion. However, I didn't speak them. He drove to an industrial section of the city, through an area of abandoned and tumbledown buildings, along streets cluttered with debris. His office building was not much of a grade up from its surroundings. We entered through a side door and climbed rickety stairs. Inside, though, all was clean and neat, furnished with state-of-the-art office equipment and comfortable accommodations. Although I could hear activity from somewhere, there was no one in the immediate vicinity. He guided me into his private office. It was hot and the wooden shades were closed. He flipped on the air-conditioning unit, but didn't open the blinds. It was dim in the room and I felt a bit of my nervousness returning. He took me by the hand and led me to a wide leather couch. *Already? Oh, no. No, no, no. This is too fast for me.* But I was mistaken. He sat facing me, but not touching me.

"I think you need to understand some things about Jamaica and Jamaican men." His tone was nonchalant, but the smile was gone. He wanted me to understand, to be able to make my own decision. He continued, "In my society most men marry only when they intend to have children. We choose a wife for her place in society and for her desire to join together and start a family. We are... partners. Marriage doesn't stop men from having other sexual relationships...nor women, either, for that matter. Although that is less frequent. Other men never marry the mother of their children. It has to do with the man's social standing, for the most part. I have girlfriends, several of them. I want you to know that. But I don't have any real feelings for any of them, or for my wife. She is pregnant with our first child, and I am a good husband and will be a good father. I provide her with an excellent apartment and a servant, membership in a sports club, money, everything. She was everything she wants."

My mind was racing. What honesty! I knew that such arrangements certainly existed in the United States. Emotionally, I questioned whether or not she *had everything she wants,* but maybe so. Maybe if one is bred to that set of standards, that is what a woman wants. Maybe it works as well that way as any conventional ideas we, as Americans, carry around about emotional commitment and fidelity. I sensed an element of honesty and forthrightness that is too often missing in our marital entanglements. But how was I going to fit into this? What were my values? More importantly, what had they brought me? I'd have to think about this. Moments of silence passed. Perhaps he misread them, or perhaps he read them more correctly than I did. I really didn't know what I wanted, or what to do. He leaned toward me and tentatively took my face in his hands, tilting it ever so slightly upward, studying it in detail. Slowly, he separated my lips just a fraction with his fingertips. I could feel his soft breath on my face. His fingers caressed my lips, touching them tenderly, molding their shape. I closed my eyes, feeling myself respond to his masculinity. He brought his mouth to mine and took only the merest suggestion of a kiss. He waited momentarily for my response. Uncertain, I returned his small embrace and he kissed me again and again, deeply, with growing intensity. As he reached for my breasts, I moved backward. Not from conscience, but from sudden embarrassment. I was stopped by misgivings. In the instant, I was afraid my body would not please him. What if he should recoil? Even the slightest blink of disgust would be intolerable to me. I cooled.

"Not yet, Victor. Not yet." I put my hand against his chest and pushed him away. He yielded without comment. I knew he was looking at me, but couldn't meet his gaze. I was floundering. Didn't know what to say.

He whispered, "I want you to be lovers with me. I've wanted it from the first. You excite me in unexpected ways. Please come to me. Let me take you."

I couldn't think. His nearness smothered my mind. I didn't answer. Again, moments of silence passed, and then he moved farther away from me and stood. He took my hands and said, "Come. I'll take you home now." He pulled me up from the couch and stood looking at me. He brushed his face close to mine and enclosed me in another embrace, his breath nestling in my ear as he stroked the back of my head, pressing me to him. I could feel his erection. My arms went around him and I allowed myself to cradle my head beneath his chin. His touch was strong and comforting and sent its vibrations throughout my body. Then he pulled back and, taking my hand, led me again through the offices and out to the car. I had said nothing. As we drove away I looked over at him. His handsome face and lean body glistened with moisture...from the humidity, or from the encounter? It didn't matter. My sexual excitement had not been so aroused for too many years.

"I think so, Victor. I think so. Just give me a few days, but I think so." I felt somehow adolescent, quite giddy and yet hesitant about myself. I wanted time. I needed to reassure myself. I was fearful. Did he suspect my insecurities?

He smiled at me. "I want you to think about me. I hope so."

The rest of the trip home was quiet. He stopped at the corner nearest the house and, reaching across, opened the door for me. "My aunt must never know. You are an American living in her home. She is very envious of you. She would not like it and would make your life unhappy, would tell stories to your Peace Corps and would make you move. I don't want you to move away." I nodded my understanding. As I turned to leave the car, he said, "I'll be back here on Friday night at ten o'clock, waiting for you. If you decide to come, I'll be here." I nodded, not with acceptance but with comprehension. Slid from the seat and closed the door behind me. "Right here," he said through the open window, and drove off.

I walked back to my house and entered my room through my private patio door. There was much to think about, but I wouldn't think. Perhaps I should peel off my clothes and look at my body. No, that was foolishness born of fear. Or was it a delay born of propriety? He was surely aware of our age difference and what it would mean. Of course. It couldn't be otherwise. I excited him as I was.

And he was not an insensitive man. There was no decision to be made. I knew I would be there Friday night at ten o'clock, on the corner, waiting for Victor. I needed him.

Late autumn in Jamaica, and the temperatures had dropped into the low eighties. Cool and comfortable. That Friday night there was the slightest fog hanging low over the city. No one walked on my street. The streetlights quivered dimly in shadows created by the barely moving leaves of the ancient, bewhiskered palm trees. The quiet was extraordinary. Trees and shrubs and flowers sheltered their outlines within the mist. The beauty was ethereal, otherworldly, encompassing. The sound of my footsteps scarcely intruded into the silence. I accepted this night as a gift and was calm, moving along slowly with a heightened awareness of self—reveling in this ambiance, marveling at the milieu as though walking through an illusion. As I came nearer to my destination, I became more aware of the few cars parked along the roadway, and could discern the outline of the jeep waiting on the corner. The headlights came on. I put aside my inner musings and hurried my pace to slide in beside him. He didn't move to kiss me, only smiled.

"Look in the back," he said, and indicated with his head. I glanced over the seat and saw a small basket and a sports bag. "I have planned a surprise for you that I hope you'll like." He pulled away from the curb.

"Where are we going? What's in the basket and bag?"

He chortled. "I'll never tell! Are you a swimmer?" He eased the jeep through the nearly deserted streets and picked up speed, heading away from Kingston.

"What? A swimmer?" My voice rose and fell in exhilarated confusion. "Why do you ask that?" Surely there was no pool open at this time of night. He wheeled onto the main highway out of town and headed toward the Caribbean. The fog seemed to thin out. Unusual. I would expect it to be even denser as we came nearer to the sea. But that wasn't the case. "Victor! Where are you taking me?" But I had guessed.

He didn't answer, only chuckled and said, "You didn't answer my question. Do you swim?"

I feigned superiority and chose a cliché. "World-class, of course. How could you not know? It's been in all the papers."

The mist-enshrouded lights of the Kingston night trailed behind us and vanished into nothingness. He sped along, passing the occasional peasant's home, and then left all outlying habitations in the distance. Overhead a few stars had broken through, twinkling away, watching us. He turned on a cassette of soft music and sensations of his nearness quivered inside me. I relished the romanticism and wanted to touch him. Reaching over, I ran my hand along his leg. He cocked an eyebrow and pulled me into the contours of his side. I cuddled close to him as he drove quickly toward the beach—bit on his ear, and he jokingly brushed me aside like a pesky fly. I think I punched him at that point. He turned off the highway onto a narrow lane, maneuvering through the palm trees with his usual dexterity—and speed. No road condition ever seemed to slow him down. We lost the pavement and soon were bumping and grating across the sandy covering of a rocky and rutted pathway. He pulled to a stop under a stand of trees, so close to one that there was no way I could get out, swung open his door, and reached for the basket and sports bag.

"Well...come on."

He was halfway across the sandy expanse by the time I made my way under the steering wheel, stepped from the cab and gathered my wits. *On the beach. On the beach?* From Here to Eternity. *We're going to make love on the beach! Incredible.* I was prattling to myself to cover a fleeting timidity while hurrying to catch up. He handed me the basket and spread the blanket and towels. Chilled beer and wine and a tiny pouch of ganja were in the basket, along with some chips and bread and a couple of glasses. The ganja surprised me. I hadn't expected that. And I wouldn't smoke it; never had, and wasn't particularly interested. Victor was stripping off his clothes and rolling them into the sports bag.

"Take off your clothes." He seemed startled that I hadn't already begun to shed my skirt and blouse, but caught his abruptness as he realized this was a new experience for me and that I felt a bit apprehensive and embarrassed. He paused, smiling, waiting patiently for me.

I peered both ways, searching through the semidarkness; checked the long white beach, and tried to see back into the grove of trees we had just come through which grew along what seemed like miles of beach. It was deserted. I relaxed into accepting that we were alone and raised my eyes to our surroundings. *Look at this. Oh, Lordy, Lordy, just look at where I am.* I reached for his hand and held it in both of my own as my horizon widened to accept the luxuries being provided so abundantly by nature. The spectacular beauty infused my senses and I breathed long, deep breaths, inhaling the magnificence. *I am here.* My eyes moved from the flowing grace of the tall, splendid, slowly bowing palm trees, to the moon's reflected glimmer on the fine, minutely shifting sand, to the rolling Caribbean with its modulating line of foam which rose so easily on the crests of the small swells. I felt wonder and simplicity, *and this is now*—so far removed from any part of my previous existence, a tiny speck in the eternity of starlit nights. Awed and humbled I turned to Victor. Looking at him, I was again filled with the almost unbelievable reality of where I was...standing beside this excellent man, and we were together as a part of this vista that reached out to infinity...and we were being freely granted this unparalleled moment and space. There was no one on this earth but us. *Do you see this panorama as I do?* He had taken both of my hands in his and was holding them tightly, watching me as I celebrated the sight. He answered my unasked question.

"I consider this my own private beach, although of course it isn't. But there's never anyone else here. It belongs just to me. Was created just for me. Do you like it? If you want to stay, please...take off your clothes." His tone drifted away as he said, "I want to see you naked."

His nude body stood straight and tall before me. *You are so perfect. I want to touch you. I need to touch you.* Little by little, I reached out and traced the few strands of hair scattered across his chest. My gaze moved down, appreciating the tautness of his athletic body. I ran my hand across the flatness of his stomach. He was responding to me. He moved around to my back and unbuttoned my blouse, letting it fall. He unfastened my bra and slipped it away, with his hands resting momentarily on my exposed breasts. He leaned over from behind me. He let my bra fall to the blanket and sighed slightly as he watched himself cradle my breasts. Fire was mounting within me, consuming the years of repressed need, and when he kissed my neck I could feel his erection, full and firm, and pressed back against him. He moved his hands down and with a quick tug removed my skirt and underpants as one garment. He turned me around to look at him. He was fully extended and his eyes were glazed with lust. He gripped me closer to him, his breath coming fast and whishing through his teeth, and his fingers gouged into my flesh. He kissed me, tongue frantic to explore my mouth. I was wildly aroused and returned his passion, clutching him to me as he swept me down on to the blanket. There was barely a moment more of foreplay before he plunged inside me, nearly out of control. But I was ready. His thrust was deep and steady and the rhythm rocked us quickly to orgasm. We both cried out with the moment's exultation, and clung to each other as the last spasms ebbed away. As our climax diminished he again touched my face, drawing my features, kissing me. He lingered, and then withdrew, falling to his side but still looking at me. At last he whispered, "You are exquisite." Tears of happiness formed behind my eyes. I had never heard such words before. *Yes, this is right for me. I'm so glad I'm here, with you. Thank you, Victor.* But I didn't speak, and the tears didn't surface. We lay quietly, barely touching, subdued, enjoying each other's nearness.

After a few moments, his mood changed and his deep brown eyes twinkled with pleasure. "I thought you said you were a world-class swimmer. Prove it!" He was up and on his way to the water.

"Energy! Youth!" Chuckling aloud, I followed after him.

The waters of the Caribbean are warm, almost like bath water. The floor of the sea slopes gradually and we waded a distance out from the shore, hand in hand, moving into greater depth. We stopped to embrace and the gentle ripples enfolded us, spraying tiny droplets across our shoulders and faces, and the soft Jamaican air nurtured us. We swam side by side, in long stokes. He caught my hand and we turned back toward the beach, to the blanket, to share chips and beer. He offered me some ganja and drew out a pipe from the sports bag. I declined, but said he could go ahead and smoke if he wanted. He smiled, shaking his head, and put the ganja pouch back.

We made love more than once that night and swam in the warm sea waters until nearly dawn. Morning was breaking when I quietly slipped back into my room. Fulfilled. Enthralled.

My work continued with haphazard results. Without consistency and follow-through, the students showed little progress. I missed no classes, but they did...the school did. During a regular session with my Peace Corps adviser, I described what I was facing. He and I talked at length about the various cultural idiosyncrasies and ethnocentricities that are endemic to developing countries. His advice to me was to do what I was already trying to practice; namely, be patient. And modify my expectations. He was supportive. However, there was no concrete solution, and never would be, never could be. I had thought a great deal about the underlying Peace Corps philosophy and admired it greatly, but had some reservations concerning the over-all program design. Simply put, I questioned why Peace Corps volunteers—by the hundreds—were still needed by such a small area, considering that the program had been initiated on the island more than twenty years before. I had some sketchy ideas in mind and suggested to him that certain changes might be of greater efficacy. He listened to me intently, then smiled and said that many people had complained about the structure during his tenure with the project, but that never before, to his recollection, had any-one ever offered any viable suggestions. Nothing ever came from that discussion; changes such as I envisioned would need to come from Washington, D.C. And that was just a bit out of my scope of influence! Although nothing came of *that* discussion, when I became involved in a program in another developing country, I was able to achieve the position and prestige necessary to expand and implement with success the ideas I had had so tentatively in mind at the time. But that's getting far ahead of my story.

Victor and I continued our relationship on a regular, if somewhat sporadic, schedule. I was convinced he must have had second sight, as he showed up at the school only on days I was actually engaged with the students. He final-ly confided to me that he was able to contact the school by radio—both he and the school having a set. He'd just radio over, and if school was in session and he was free for an af-ternoon, he'd come by to get me. He did schedule his arriv-als later so that they didn't interfere with my duties. Many late lunches and afternoons of pleasure in various locales followed, and he was creative about finding unique places.

His oversized leather chair in his office was especially intriguing, as it was a swivel chair and became unusual fun. Oftentimes he used a friend's empty apartment. Once we even made love in his mother's house...which shocked me. But she was in America and it worked out very well, probably because it was so unconventional and *naughty*. Whatever priggishness I'd brought with me to Jamaica vanished into the wave of a sometimes quirky, sometimes bizarre, but always exciting rendezvous.

A few more months passed before subtle changes began to take place within me. Those changes were somehow jumbled up between my work, Victor, and...something else which I couldn't label—at the moment. The moment had arrived, though, and brought with it a...coincidence. A festive social gathering had been planned for all the Peace Corps volunteers on the island. Being a social introvert, I usually avoided large parties. But this time I was coaxed by a colleague and attended. While there, I had the opportunity to meet others whom I had never seen before. I gravitated toward one particular group and they seemed to incorporate me into their small enclave. We chatted about home, our duties, and the Peace Corps in general. During the conversation they spoke of other experiences they had been involved in, and those of their friends. The names Fulbright and USAID (United States Agency for International Development) were recurring. My knowledge of both of those organizations was minimal and I asked questions. What I learned as a result of that afternoon was that there were active programs in teaching English in developing countries, and that positions in those programs were available and very well compensated. It was an open and expanding market for American teachers who held master's degrees in the Teaching of English to Speakers of Others Languages (TESOL). I'd never heard of that particular university discipline. I had a bachelor's degree in education and another in psychology, with credentials for elementary and high school teaching, plus scores of other accumulated credits. However, I wouldn't be qualified to participate in the programs they were discussing. I stored the information away, but it began to percolate, unbidden by my conscious mind.

Several days later Victor and I were relaxing after an afternoon's enjoyment. As he was pulling on his clothes for our departure, he said to me, "I want you to know that I have given up all my other women. I gave them up months ago in fact, after our night on the beach. I want no one but you. And of course I'm not sleeping with my wife, as she is in the last weeks of her pregnancy. I have and want no one else, just you."

I hadn't even thought about him having other girl-friends since he'd first told me. His wife? From the moment I had stepped out my door on that particular Friday night, she had become his concern, not mine. Perhaps to many women his confession would have come as a compliment. My reaction was immediate and quite different. It sounded to me more like he was saying that he was falling in love with me—which in no way fit into my life; such feelings I did not return. In response, I said, "Oh, really? I hadn't given it much thought, Victor. Thank you, though, for telling me." I was flustered.

It was on my next working day, when I arrived for classes, that the school's message was spat out. I needed to go into the storage room to select some of my materials. I switched on the light, and gasped. The floor was strewn with my carefully prepared charts and worksheets. They were covered with footprints from shoes and dirty bare feet. Flash cards that I'd spent so many hours making attractive had been handed out to the students and they had written the answers to the questions on the front of each card, rendering them useless. The trash can was overflowing with materials I'd spent hours, days, weeks preparing; ripped to shreds. How had it happened? I never asked. Why did it happen? I never asked. Who had done it? The students? The teachers? Both? I never asked. Was it somehow connected to my friendship with Victor? No, I didn't think so then, and I don't think so now. But perhaps I am wrong. That was the last day I ever went to the school.

In the following week I tried to analyze my position and categorize options. I had three. I could request that the Peace Corps give me a new assignment, locate one by myself, or ask for early release and go home. The problems connected with the third option were that I had no home to go to, and because of the sudden devaluation of Jamaican currency many months before, I had lost several hundred dollars when exchanging my Jamaican money to U.S. dollars. In other words, my financial situation was desperate, and it would still be months before I could return to my school in Reno and collect a salary. In addition, I'd be walking right back into what I thought my prayers had lifted me out of. How could that be? My mind whirled, creating a rut. I began to pace my room, and when no one else was home, I paced the interior of the house—circling round and round through the rooms. To stay in Jamaica seemed to me a waste of time. I had accomplished nothing. And Victor? As precious as he was to me, Victor was not enough to keep me there. As I paced I began to hum to myself...*In my Father's house are many mansions.* Mansions? What did that mean to me? I found myself repeating it as I walked from room to room. Then, *one door never closes but another one opens* began alternating with the other phrase. They consumed my mind. I paced, muttering them over and over, endlessly. I did not see Victor at all that week, for which I was grateful.

Very early mornings are my best time. When the world is new, I often do my clearest thinking; wake up with some detail already in place. It happened again. I opened my eyes to see yet another cockroach nearly nose to nose with me. I flicked it away, as I had done so many times before, hoping that the geckoes skittering across my walls would eat it. I picked up a pencil and paper, sat in bed and went over my finances one more time. As I was adding up the numbers it came to me. I had totally forgotten that, upon the culmination of a Peace Corps agreement, the volunteer is given a settling allowance which accumulates for the duration of the tour of duty. I counted the months on my fingers and quickly multiplied by the amount. Together with the small sum I had left, I had enough to last for a while, if I budgeted in a Spartan fashion. The other problem: no home to go to. Without forethought I went to the telephone and called Barbara.

"Have you got a couch for your wandering mother to use for a few weeks?"

"Of course. Need you ask? Mom, are you coming home?" The label was right, but hers was the maternal tone.

"Yes, Barb, I am." I made the decision as I spoke. "I have no idea what I'm doing, and don't know what I'll do when I get there. But it's time to come home."

I pulled on my clothes and took the bus into town. Riding along, I thought to myself, *whatever it is I'm going to do, I don't have a lot of time left in which to do it.* I walked into the Peace Corps office and requested an interview, concocted a quick story, and was granted a release. Out of the original number of thirty-eight in our group, I would be number seventeen to leave. They regretted losing me, they assured me. The balance of the day was spent completing the paperwork and arranging an appointment for my departure physical. When I returned to the house my landlady was in the process of packing. She informed me that she was returning to the United States. I told her that I was also leaving and needed to settle my account with her. She was quite taken aback, since she had planned on my rent for two years. I felt I owed her nothing more than the current amount due. I felt no guilt about leaving early, as she had felt no qualms about snubbing me. We settled the account. It would be several days before I could leave because my physical examination was still in the future. I went to my room and started to organize my papers.

Early that evening she left for her plane, and an hour or so later Victor came by. I was expecting him to do so, but with feelings of anxiety, as I would need to explain to him about my decision. I had gone over and over it in my mind, practicing this explanation and that, but still didn't know what I was going to say.

His arms were around me and his kisses were fervent. I controlled my responses. He backed away. "What's the matter?" he asked. I asked him to sit beside me on my bed.

"Victor, please...this is difficult for me, but I must tell you, and tell you now." I paused and he gripped my arm.

"Tell me what?" He looked into my eyes. "Are you leaving me? Are you tired of me?" His tone was low and intense.

"Tired of you? Oh, no. Leaving?" My throat constricted. "Leaving...yes...not you, Victor. I'm leaving the Peace Corps. I'm leaving Jamaica." His grip was hurting my arm.

He slowly pulled my hand to his mouth and kissed my fingers. His brow creased and his eyes closed. He pleaded against the inevitable. "No. Don't. Don't do this."

I put my other arm around him and pulled him to me, caressing him, caring for him. "I am going, Victor." I whispered the words slowly, softly, holding him close to me.

The tension in his body began to ease. His breath came slower, easier. "When?" There was resignation in his voice.

"I have scheduled a flight for a week from today. I am through here, Victor. I feel I am through here and must move on, now." We separated and he stood.

"I can't handle this all so quickly. I'm going to go now. I'll be back," he said, and walked out my door.

I felt miserable and went to bathe. Turned the water on full force and let its coldness beat down on me, cleansing myself, punishing myself.

I spent the remaining time saying my goodbyes and processing all the documentation. My tickets arrived at the office. My physical showed me to be in perfect health. My suitcases were packed and standing against the wall, ready for my departure the next morning. I hadn't seen Victor since that earlier evening when I'd told him. He had said he would come back. But he hadn't. It was midnight when I gave up and went to bed. *He's not coming. He can't say goodbye. It's alright.* I dozed off and slept fitfully.

It must have been nearly three hours later when a tapping on my door roused me. I let him in. He held me without a word; took me to my bed. We made love as we had time and again, with caring and with passion. When it was over, he lit a cigarette and inhaled deeply.

"I understand why you're going. I, too, think it is time. This island is too small for your talents. You are a very gifted woman, and we are too small." He sat up and started to pull on his clothes. "May I meet you in San Francisco when I come to the States?"

That thought hadn't crossed my mind. I held his hand. The words came, unplanned. "No, Victor. Let's not do that. What we've had here is much too special. It belongs here. Forever here. And Victor, I want to tell you something else. You've given me a gift, a very great gift. You've given me back my womanhood. There is nothing more special than that. You will always be in my heart and in the corners of my mind. No one will ever take that very special place that will be eternally reserved for you. Do you understand me?"

We stood and clung to each other, delaying the inescapable as long as possible. With a gentle indication, he guided me beside him toward the door and reached to open it. We stood in the open doorway. The soft Jamaican air enwrapped us, nurturing us once more as it had so often before, and the hints of the new day were breaking. The first birds of morning were restless in the tree. He held me, caressed me one last time.

"Good-bye, Adair."

With the words spoken, numbness touched me. My breath stopped. There were tears in his eyes as he turned and quietly left my life.

The plane taxied down the field. I again placed my forehead against the windowpane, this time to watch Kingston diminish and disappear from sight. Words came into my head that had been spoken the first day of our orientation in Miami: "You may think, now, that your duties in the Peace Corps will change the world. That will not happen. There will be great changes, but they will all be inside of you." Prophecy. The sun shone brightly over my small island, and as the long beaches of white sand faded from view my tears were falling. *Good-bye, Victor,* I thought, and pressed my fingertips against the window, gently caressing it.

Several transfers and many hours later, I arrived at the Lake Tahoe airport and knew why I had come home. I was going to return to my teaching job, yes. That was essential. But the real reason why I was coming back was to pursue a master's degree in Teaching English to Speakers of Other Languages...wherever I could find a university to train me...and I would follow wherever that degree would ultimately lead.

U.S.A. – FIRST RETURN

My love continues to flow out to the late Dr. Jean Zukowski-Faust, former chair of the ESL Department at Northern Arizona University. She was my dear friend and mentor, and saved me from myself...more than once.

The university that accepted me for training was in Flagstaff, Arizona—Northern Arizona University. It would be a summer program and I would have to go there for several summers, in addition to taking extensive night classes at the University of Nevada. It would take years. But I could do it. And so I started back to school; teaching all day and attending classes three, sometimes four nights each week. The amount of work was staggering. The best possible therapy. There was no time to think of myself, only to become immersed in the fascinating world I was discovering. The studies were opening me up to new ways of thinking about individual personalities and behaviors, about societal identities. We are what we speak. Language doesn't take place in a vacuum. It affects the total being. Are thinking processes in one language the same as in another language? Some say absolutely yes, others say not at all. Even if changes are minute, that would be significant in understanding the impact of English as the Language of Wider Communication. What would be the ultimate long-term result of the rapid spread of English? The number of languages in today's world stands at about 6,600, with language extinction occurring at an alarming rate. Would some remote future produce a global society speaking, say, only a half dozen or so languages driven by the language of business and technology, a world of similar-thinking people? What of the richness of our tapestry of cultural diversity? Is it good, or not so good, or neither, simply natural evolution? The studies were fascinating, yes. But time was passing.

Another of those seemingly unrelated events, a coincidence, happened a few days before I was to leave for my next summer in Flagstaff. Barbara had moved from Lake Tahoe to Davis, California. She also was returning to classes and wanted to enter the University of California at Davis. She had rented a condominium in a large complex. We planned a family get-together and set a time between the end of my teaching year and the beginning of my summer school. Gregory and Larry joined Barbara and me, and my two young grandchildren, for a long weekend at her home. The weather was hot, well over 100 degrees. We decided to go to the pool. Greg and Larry and the youngsters went on ahead while Barb and I put on our suits. By the time we arrived, my sons were both casting an eye at a beautiful young Chinese-American girl sitting beside the pool. Greg seemed the more interested, but was shy. Larry jumped from the pool, walked over to the girl, and said he'd like to introduce her to his brother—although of course Larry didn't know her, either. She seemed amused by the manner of introduction and welcomed them both. Amanda became interested in Greg, and by the end of the day they had made a date. Amanda had just graduated from the university, and as a gift her parents were sending her to accompany several of her classmates to a summer school in China, to help improve her Chinese language skills. She would be leaving shortly and, as a result, she allowed her friendship with Greg to blossom quickly. By the time our family weekend had concluded the two of them were sure they were truly interested in each other. With nothing better to do for the summer, Greg decided to stay on at Davis for a while, bunking in with his sister. Larry returned to Reno, and I went on to Flagstaff. Amanda left the next month for China and Greg began telephoning her regularly. He called me in Flagstaff to give me reports of her impressions of China, and his impressions of her. I jokingly suggested that it might be cheaper for him to fly over and join her than to underwrite the American Telephone and Telegraph Company. He jumped at the suggestion, and a couple of weeks later he jumped on a plane. After her classes ended they spent some holiday time traveling around China.

Meanwhile, an Egyptian man had entered our master's program. He would be coming each summer from his profession as an English language instructor at the American University in Cairo. We became friends, and I confided to him that I was interested in finding a university abroad in which to teach after finishing my degree the following summer. He enthusiastically recommended his site and gave me the name and address of the people to contact. After returning to my duties in Reno and registering for my next marathon of night classes, I wrote a letter of inquiry to the American University in Cairo. It was September, and I knew I had plenty of time to process all that would be necessary, if they had an opening for me.

Amanda, whom we had begun to call Mandy, and Greg returned from China and were in love. She applied for and was given an excellent job in Reno and they became engaged. She and Greg took an apartment. We met from time to time and, together with Larry, enjoyed dinners and outings. I told them about the possibility of Cairo, and they seemed interested enough, although our conversations usually reverted to their experiences in China. Months passed and there was no response from Egypt. My mild anxiety was mounting. By January, nervousness was turning into deep concern. I telephoned the office at the university in Cairo and was told that my papers had been forwarded to their American office in New York, and that I would be notified. Another month passed. In early February I telephoned the New York office. They had never heard of me, had received nothing, and the deadline for applications had passed. My deep concern went straight to panic. Deadlines are deadlines are deadlines. What was true for one university was generally true for all. I would finish my degree and be stuck in Reno for another year, at least. I feared forever. What had it all come to? Nothing. If I had learned one thing, it was not to let my traumas escalate. I called my sons and Mandy. Larry had another commitment, so the three of us went to dinner. With increasing tension in my voice I explained the news I'd just received. Greg ordered a bottle of wine to go with dinner and filled my glass, which I downed quickly. He poured me another.

Mandy asked, "Why don't you go to China?"

Actually, although I'd listened to their adventures with mild interest, China was nowhere in my plans for a future. I tried to make excuses. "It's too late to start another application. Much too late."

They both became insistent. Mandy took the lead and said, "No, it isn't. I'll give you the name and address of the foreign affairs officer. Just write to him. They'll hire you. I'm sure of it."

She was being sweet. She was trying to get me through the evening. She was too young to understand. Again, as I had several years before, I acquiesced to get people to stop haranguing me. To allow Mandy to feel that I thought she had credibility, which I didn't. By the third glass of wine I calmed down and we finished our meal in peace. I had no intention of sending a letter.

By the end of February I changed my mind, wrote a simple note of introduction stating my credentials and experience, mentioned Mandy's name, and asked about their staffing for the following year. I let it sit for a few days, then, surprising myself, I mailed it. And again, the waiting began. March and April passed with no response. I was beginning to harbor old feelings of futility; occasionally, despair tried to settle in. My fears, my terrors, tried to take control. I had to put them aside. Had to focus. No time could be allowed for them, as I had to concentrate on my last three night classes at the university. There were only six weeks to go till the end of the school year, at which time I would hurry back to Flagstaff for my final course work to finish my master's degree. Perhaps six weeks has some significance in my life. I don't know. But, it was nearing the middle of May when once again a phone call came which would change my life. It was an early Saturday morning when Mandy phoned.

"Are you sitting down?" she chuckled.

"No, but I will."

She was laughing. "You're not going to believe this, but I just received a phone call from one of the guys I went to summer school with in China. He lives in California. He received a phone call at two o'clock this morning from the foreign affairs officer at the university. The FAO told my friend to call me and tell me to call you, to tell you to get your documentation in. You've been hired!"

I twirled the phone to the top of my hair and sat unbelieving, dumbfounded, shaking my head. I began to chortle, then to laugh along with her. "Mandy," I said into the phone, "get real. I can't take this seriously. The FAO was probably drunk when he made that call. Surely, no one would expect me to pack up everything and traipse half-way across the world because of a middle-of-the-night telephone message from someone I've never spoken to, never had any response from. Where's my contract to guarantee me anything?"

She became more serious. "Don't worry about it. I'm sure it's a legitimate offer. That's the way they do things. But I'll call the FAO back, if you want. Come on over and I'll make breakfast, and we'll call him."

I was on my way at once. Coffee was waiting and Mandy was searching through her notebook for the phone number, at the same time calculating the time difference.

"He should be in the office by now." As she dialed the number, she asked, "What do you want me to ask him?"

Before I could collect my thoughts she was speaking to someone—with difficulty, to say the least. She was yelling into the phone, "No! No! Don't hang up!" She covered the mouthpiece and whispered to me, "I can hear his voice in the background." She switched to Chinese and yelled again, trying to make him hear her clear across the world through a telephone he wasn't even near. But it worked. Hear her he did, and took the call. They chatted for a few moments and she burst out laughing. They talked a while longer and then she hung up."

"Yes. You've been hired. Get your HIV test; your visa will be processed through San Francisco, and send him your CV. And, oh yes, they'll be paying your transportation, you'll be getting a great salary, you'll be given a large apartment in a new building they're preparing for the foreign experts, and you'll have a 'Western toilet.'"

I stopped midway through a sip of coffee. "A 'Western toilet'? What's that?" Incredulous that such a topic would be important enough to be discussed internationally.

"You'll see!" was all she would answer, but she laughed again.

No problem! I was used to this lifestyle by this time. In slightly more than five weeks I had to finish out my school year, complete essays for three university classes, process the documentation for my visa to China, take my physical and HIV test, and pack: pack for summer school in Flagstaff, pack for a year in China, pack whatever things I wanted to leave with Barbara, and pack the remainder for storage. Easy! I organized the piles in my apartment into four stacks, switching things back and forth from stack to stack as I changed my mind. Wound my way through the mess to find my desk and write my papers, then stepped over the material accumulation of my life's accomplishments on my way out of the apartment so I could run from school to office to office. I had put in the requisite number of intervening years and the school district gave me another leave of absence. Barbara came to Reno to help with the last-minute details. Greg and Larry rented a U-Haul; we loaded up and caravanned back to Davis to unpack in time for me to catch a late plane for Flagstaff. The final weeks of summer school for my M.A. brought a wealth of new materials and I had my degree. I returned to Davis with three days to spend with my family before departing for China.

CHINA – FIRST TRIP

*I've done my best to disguise exactly where in China I was.
It's been two decades, but for some party authorities,
memories are long and vindictive retribution is sure.*

The CAAC plane was late and packed, every seat
taken. I had requested an aisle seat and jammed my over-
weight backpack into the overhead bin, cramming another bulging tote bag under the seat in front of me. I had
only inches for my feet and legs. The flight to Shanghai
was to be some fifteen hours. From San Francisco we had
to make one more stop in Los Angeles. By the time we left
Los Angeles International, we were already four hours behind schedule. The flight to China was never-ending and
my fatigue, mixed with my claustrophobia, was creating a
more than irritable frame of mind. The lights of Shanghai
finally began to tease us through the darkness of the late
night. We'd been circling the airport for several minutes
when an announcement came over the intercom. "The
Shanghai airport is closed for the night. We will continue
on to Beijing and you will be routed to your destinations
tomorrow morning." Unbelievable. The huge Shanghai in-

ternational airport was *closed?* I was furious. We flew on, landed in Beijing about three o'clock and deplaned. We were herded into a holding area. There was no one in Chinese customs or immigration to process us. A crew had been called, but we had to wait for their arrival. Eventually we were shown to the processing area. There were too many of us and too few of them. It was chaos. My passport was stamped without much attention, and I never did go through customs, but followed another crowd of our people into yet another waiting area. We would have to sleep in the Beijing airport on wooden benches until a flight could be arranged for us. Using one bag for a pillow and the other for my feet, I actually did get a couple hours of sleep. A little after daybreak someone came and took us to a cafeteria. We were served coffee and some dumplings I gagged on. I followed others back to the holding area, and we waited. About noon someone came to get us. A flight to Tokyo would accommodate some of us and would take us to Shanghai on its way. I pushed into the group that would be first to go. The weight of my backpack and tote bag was almost more than I could handle and I had no idea where my suitcases had been taken. I'd lost track of them after not going through customs. I'd seen them on an overloaded cart, but that was the last time. I couldn't ask anybody anything, as English was practically nonexistent. I'd have to find somebody in Shanghai to help me with that problem. There was no time, now, to do anything but push on to the plane.

We arrived at the Shanghai domestic terminal. I followed others out of the plane. Domestic terminals and international terminals are a world apart in China. As uncomfortable as the Beijing airport had been, this one was shocking, disgusting. It had been raining, and I followed some fellow passengers to a low building set far across the tarmac from where we'd deplaned. We sloshed through oozing mud. The building we were entering looked like it would collapse momentarily, and I couldn't imagine that it could possibly house luggage carousels, but it did, such as they were. I didn't expect my bags to be there, but went with the crowd because I didn't know where else to go. The interior of the building was congested, with hundreds of people pushing and shoving for a place near the stopped carousel, and dozens of others waiting around to meet arrivals. The din was thunderous. I decided that the Chinese people had never learned how to talk...only to scream at each other. The carousel began to move, squeaking and groaning. To my amazement, both of my suitcases came around to meet me. *How did they know in Beijing that I'd be on this first flight?* How many times in the future would I repeat some form of that interrogative? The Chinese seem to know things without being given any information. They must have a psychic network! I hesitated to set my backpack and tote bag down, but I had to in order to heft my heavy suitcases off the carousel. No one helped. Once I had them all in order, I looked around the room more carefully. My hotel reservation had been made from California, but of course it would have been canceled since we were more than a full day late in arriving. I didn't know what to do, where to go, even how to get out of that building. How would I ever find, or use, a telephone? I wouldn't. I'd try to find a main exit and locate a cab. How would I explain to the driver where I wanted to go? Don't worry.

He'll understand English, I irrationally assured myself. My eyes began to scan the waiting Chinese. Then there he was. I couldn't believe what I was seeing. In the front row stood a young man holding a sign that read "Sheraton Hotel" and had my name on it! *How did they know when I'd get here?* The second time I'd asked myself that question in the first few minutes. I waved my arms at him and identified myself. He took charge of everything. We drove through the broad streets of Shanghai in a small white van and arrived at the lovely hotel. They'd held my reservation and I checked in.

My room was a welcome and glorious sight. I immediately ran a hot bath, loaded the tub with the bubble bath which was provided, and noticed that the gleaming white bath towels were at least an inch thick! As the water ran, I stripped off my clothes and left them in a jumbled heap on the floor, opened the door of the minibar, took out a bottle of wine, swooped up a glass, and, clutching both in my sweaty, grimy hand, dropped into the foamy tub, thanking the powers that be for the Shanghai Sheraton. I'd live. No need to worry about my flight to the university city. I was so fucking late that any connections would have been tossed. I was shocked at my even thinking that word. I had always prided myself that my command of English did not usually necessitate the use of strong expletives. That changed, abruptly and permanently. There come times in one's life when no other word will suffice. However, I should have delayed this first time for a couple more days. I went to bed and slept until early the next morning.

Breakfast in the spotless, cheery dining area was tasty and abundant. I went to the reception desk to try and arrange my flight and was directed to an office equipped to handle transportation. The agent was a charming and friendly Chinese woman who spoke excellent English. I explained my dilemma and she picked up the phone. There would be no problem with the next leg of my journey. There would be a car at six o'clock the following morning to take me to the terminal. I told her that the university had been expecting me to arrive, and that I needed to try and telephone the foreign affairs officer to advise him of the delay. She took the number I offered and tried to place the call. It didn't go through. We would try several more times during that day, but never complete a connection. I returned to my room and finally took time to investigate my immediate surroundings through my windows. A group of probably a hundred people had just concluded its regular early morning tai chi exercises and was disbanding in a square directly across the street. Thousands of bicyclers were weaving in and out among each other, dinging their bicycle bells. A few lorries lumbered along. I decided to go out for a walk. Reception gave me a card with pertinent information in both English and Chinese, in case I got lost. I went out, was immediately overwhelmed by the number of people and the confusion of the streets, took courage and hailed a cab. I wanted to get to the American Embassy to register my presence in China. It worked out and I was taken to the appropriate place. Well, maybe I could learn to handle this after all. I entered the building and felt a sense of familiarity. I was processed and filled out the necessary forms. Afterward, I was told that the USIS library was on the other side of the building, if I'd care to take a look. The librarian welcomed me, and after

I explained why I was in China and supplied her with the name of my university, she offered to provide me with a packet of readings that might be of use to me. I thanked her, but told her I had no way of getting them there. I was already too overloaded. She smiled and said she would be able to forward them to me. I was grateful. (They did arrive, about two months later.) I returned to the hotel with no problem and we tried again and again to telephone the university. I was becoming concerned, afraid I wouldn't know where to go, how to take care of myself, when I arrived.

I was ready at six a.m. and waiting downstairs for the van. The lady from the transportation office came to inform me that she had not been able to connect with the university. I thanked her for all her efforts. To my good fortune, another American was waiting and would be on the same flight. He was an engineer, also from California, and would be training a group of Chinese engineers in the use of some specialized equipment. It was his first trip to China also. The same young man who had accompanied me before was waiting in the van. We drove through streets crowded with bicyclers to the domestic air terminal. Once inside, the Sheraton guide had us stand against a pillar, out of the way of the mass of jostling passengers, while he took care of the details of our luggage. He returned and took us to the passport counter, where he spoke to those waiting in the long line and had them step aside so we could get our documents processed first. He then shook hands with us, wished us well, and left. We went up a ramp, through a security check, and entered a vast waiting hall with windows along one wall overlooking the boarding areas. Our flight was due to leave at ten o'clock. That didn't happen. About noon my new acquaintance bought me some packaged orange juice and we looked for a restaurant, and found one. We picked out something that looked edible and selected some fruit. The "something that looked edible" wasn't, but the fruit was sufficient. We returned to the waiting area and found some space on benches at the rear of the crowded room. Announcements were made from time to time, but in Chinese. By the middle of the afternoon we were both concerned. Perhaps we'd even missed the plane; no, he didn't think so. By six o'clock crowds had gathered together and were sitting in what appeared to be sections according to flight destinations. My companion finally found a man who appeared to be some kind of official and who spoke a few words of English. Our flight had been canceled. We would be taken with the others to a hotel for the night...soon. An hour or so later, seemingly without any information being given, "our" crowd began to gather belongings and move toward an exit door. We followed, not knowing what else to do. A bus was waiting and drove us for nearly another hour through narrow back streets of Shanghai. It was dark by the time we arrived at our hotel. Before we even entered, we looked at each other, knowing what to expect. And we were right. It was obscenely filthy. It was late, we were both exhausted, we didn't speak the language, and it would be another hour's ride back into Shanghai proper, to the Sheraton, if we were able to arrange for transportation. The bus that dumped us had already left.

We walked side by side up to the counter where everyone else stood. After much attempted explanation and gesticulation the receptionist figured out that we weren't married and gave us adjoining rooms. A young girl directed us to our quarters. We followed her through long, winding, dim corridors. She unlocked the door to his room and we nodded good night. She then unlocked the door to my room. She was carrying something in her hand which I had not recognized up to that point. She preceded me into the room and took the pump canister she was carrying, sprayed the room for bugs, and left. I didn't move. Just stood there in a state of paralysis rising out of abhorrence. It had been a long time since the cockroaches of Jamaica, and I was, again, repulsed.

There was a soft tapping on my door and a young man entered with my luggage. He set the suitcases inside and motioned that I was to follow him. Never! Why? But I did. We stopped next door and my new friend joined us. We were taken to an enormous dining area and seated completely apart from the Chinese guests, isolated from everyone. Shortly after, a smiling waitress proudly brought us steaming bowls of noodles...with a half inch of grease floating on the top. She returned with chopsticks, some disgusting-looking bread, and two bottles of beer. The oilcloth covering the table was so dirty we both hesitated to touch it, but touch it we did, sparingly. He offered me a cigarette, which I accepted, and we drank the beer. We returned to our rooms, unescorted, and again said good night. I went in, left both the light and my clothes on, and tried to sleep—on top of the bedcovers.

Promptly at six a.m., there was a knock on my door and I joined my friend. Our bags were carried downstairs and we were offered more noodles, which we declined. It was drizzling rain and we waited on the crumbling veranda for another hour. The bus arrived and drove us back to the airport. Our flight was scheduled to depart at nine o'clock. It didn't. We finally boarded at nearly noon. As we flew, we discussed what we would do when we arrived. He also had representatives who were supposed to meet him. We both decided that there would be no one to greet us at the airport, we would share a taxi to the hotel where he was to stay, and from there I would try and telephone the university.

The plane landed and we followed others across the tarmac to some tall iron gates. Dozens of people were crowded together on the other side of those gates. They swung open. A young girl of striking beauty came hurrying toward me, all smiles, with a hand extended.

"Are you...?"

"Yes, I am," I said, and right then and there we stood, laughing and hugging each other, interfering with the flow of the foot traffic.

I was more than three days late, but the foreign affairs officer had been tracking my journey and knew exactly where I was all the time. In addition, the lady at the Sheraton transportation office had continued trying to telephone even after I left, and had finally made the connection and confirmed my arrival time. How had she known? The engineer's representative was also there to welcome him. We shook hands good-bye and both exclaimed that neither of us could have survived our ordeal without the other. I couldn't imagine that I would meet him again, but I did, many weeks later. I never did come to understand the Chinese communications systems. With the erratic telephone service and sporadic postal system, I am still convinced that they must communicate everything by mental telepathy!

The drive to the university guest house was through lovely areas of small buildings and gardens, which eventually gave way to the city. The city was a "village" of only a few million inhabitants. We arrived at a gigantic beige stucco apartment building. "Angel" escorted me into the newly completed reception area, where the reception desk stood immediately inside the double plate-glass doors. Reception desk is a euphemism for security. A large fish pond was in the center of the immense room, water dripping into it, but no fish—as yet. A broad winding staircase wound upward around the fish tank and into the regions beyond. An elevator was off to one side, but rarely was functional. I signed in, and a couple of loitering young men took all my bags while Angel led the way up to my fifth-floor apartment. She gave me the key and we entered. It was far more than I had expected. Nearly ten-foot ceilings with floor-to-ceiling windows overlooking the busy alleyways below, out over the university grounds and off to the city in the distance. A large living room, an ample-sized bedroom with corner windows and a corner desk beneath, both adequately furnished, a kitchen that would have been serviceable had there been either a stove or a refrigerator, and a large bathroom.

As Angel opened the door to the bathroom, she pointed with pride and said, "See, a Western toilet." I still didn't know the significance, but would find out soon enough. I only smiled and nodded. "Come, we're going to lunch now. Alexander is waiting for you."

I was puzzled. "Alexander is waiting for me?"

She walked me back down the stairs and to a private dining room used only for small business dinners. "Yes, Alexander has ordered a special lunch for you." She went on to explain, "He took that name so the foreign experts and teachers wouldn't have such a hard time with his own. He selected it because he admires Alexander the Great."

The foreign affairs officer, a man about my height, was standing, smoking and talking seriously to another man nearly a head shorter. Angel introduced us. Alexander had a vibrant energy that radiated from him. His smile was infectious and his English was excellent. The shorter man was the party secretary assigned to the university. He smiled a welcoming greeting also, but had neither English nor teeth. The four of us sat at a round table where several bowls of steaming food were ready. Alexander served me while chatting incessantly about the problems I'd encountered on my journey. I was hesitant about the food, but had to be polite. Anyway, I was very hungry. Surprisingly, the food was delicious and I ate heartily.

Alexander smoked as he ate. At one point, he stopped in mid-sentence and chuckled, "I know Americans think it improper to smoke while dining. But it is a Chinese custom." He asked about Amanda, how she was doing, her health, and so on. Then he chuckled again and said, "I think Amanda sent you over here to me because she thinks we are a lot alike and that we should marry." I choked on my rice.

"Oh, really? I never knew she thought such a thing."

We finished lunch in good spirits and Angel walked me back to my room. We finally said our see-you-laters and

I closed the door behind her. I turned to my new home and thought about Angel. What a curious nickname for anyone to take in an atheistic society. But she later proved to be exactly that, an angel in mortal packaging. Alexander's words also came back into my mind. *Why would anyone say such a thing so early in an acquaintance?*

Down on the corner stood a small restaurant with an open-to-view kitchen, a few ill-sorted tables and square-topped stools, and walls on only two sides. The other sides welcomed customers from the intersecting streets. The campus straddled the wider of the streets. Both university areas were enclosed, with a footbridge overpass connecting. Set diagonally between the boulevard and the narrower of the two streets were the tall iron gates to the university proper. If these gates were ever locked it would be difficult for the several thousand students housed on the campus to get to the streets. The entire campus was walled, with those barricades being maybe twelve feet high. But these gates, and a comparable pair on the far side of the campus, were always open, with a few guards standing on either side, chatting and lolling. It was their duty to check the identification cards of anyone who didn't look like a regular student, and they did, from time to time.

The campus area across the street was an addendum to the main area, with lecture buildings that had been erected more recently to facilitate the rapidly expanding student body, and had its own security checkpoint and bicycle paths.

Inside the gates to the main campus a road wound through ancient trees, which protected garden areas with benches for study and relaxation, passed student housing, then meandered between the scores of traditional-looking university buildings, the occasional sheds, and beside basketball courts. On the way down to the Olympic-sized swimming pool it passed by the square in front of the library, where impressive fountains sent a fine mist over the tiled courtyard. Continuing on, the roadway and paths led to scattered eating establishments of different sizes and purposes, skirted various additional gardened areas with their gazebos covering secluded benches set amid glorious flowering bushes and fish ponds, and eventually exited through the second set of gates and down a steep winding hillside. It was to take probably a half hour or more to walk diagonally across the main campus—dodging the hurrying, chattering, dawdling, studying students by day, and offering a peaceful, inspiring stroll in the evenings.

The interiors of the buildings which housed the lecture halls were undecorated, with classrooms opening off long corridors that led to stairwells at either end. There were no elevators and my freshman, junior, and senior classrooms were on the sixth floor, all in the same building, but not consecutively scheduled. *So, Grandma, what did you do in China? I climbed stairs.*

Angel accompanied me to the Foreign Affairs Office, where Alexander greeted and assisted me in completing the requisite documentation, but didn't offer a contract (and I didn't receive one until well into December, after I insisted). Then, she walked me to the English Language Department office. My schedule was set: oral practice for the freshman, intensive reading for both juniors and seniors. My main focus, though, was to be on the handful of postgraduate students who had returned from their own university teaching posts to take master's degrees. Their classes with me would be in advanced composition, socio-linguistics, and educational methodologies. In all, meeting with each class twice, a twelve-hour teaching week, requiring an equal number of preparation periods, it was a heavy schedule for a university lecturer. No classroom had been assigned for the postgrads, but we would meet on the first day in the English office and decide where and when to hold our sessions. Within hours I loved the campus. Within days I loved the students.

The rat-a-tat tapping called me to my door. "Hello, I'm Jane," she said, and the Oxford-English accent was marked. Dr. Jane Hathaway was taller, thinner, and older than I, with flyaway graying hair and piercing blue eyes, and dressed in sensible clothes.

"Welcome to China." Her hand was extended and her strong face showed a wide smile of large teeth. "I have the apartment just below you."

"Well, hello. I'm Adair, and I guess I have the apartment right above you," I said, laughing and inviting her in.

"Your first trip?"

"To China, yes. But I've taught abroad before. And yours?"

"No. This is my third year, but my first year here. I was posted in another city before. Where in America are you from?"

"California. Is there another state?" More laughter. "Where in England are you from?"

"London. Is there another city?"

This was going to work.

"We're to share the postgrads, I've been told. I'll be doing their poetry and classical literature lectures. What are your areas?" And I told her.

"Good! Perhaps we will be able to coordinate some lectures, right?"

"Sounds good to me. Where do we eat around here?" I indicated my lack of stove and refrigerator.

"They'll be bringing you whatever you need. For tonight, I'll take you to the restaurant on the corner, if you'd care to join me. Normally, you'll be able to buy whatever you like and cook here in your apartment. I know all the procedures for bargaining for the foods you want, and will be happy to take you shopping. The food stalls are along the streets, not far. Hungry now?"

"Starving."

"So am I. Let's go, before it gets too crowded."

We went to the corner restaurant where she directed me to check out the counter separating the dining area from the kitchen. There were sample plates of the various foods available that day. She selected and assisted me in selecting our menu, and we sat at one of the tables.

"So, tell me about your trip, your arrival." I did, to the accompaniment of her head nodding in commiseration as I related the horrors of the flight.

"But it was all history as soon as I saw Angel waiting for me. She's a gem. And after we got to the apartment complex, she went with me to have a late lunch Alexander had set up. That was my first real food in nearly twenty-four hours and—"

"Excuse me? Alexander had a luncheon prepared for you? How did that happen? I haven't even met him yet. Are you somehow connected with him—from before?"

"No, not really. Only through Amanda." *Ding.* I wasn't sure if I'd heard an innuendo, but went right on about Mandy and Greg, the late-night telephone call to California, forwarded to Nevada, to Mandy, to me, etc. It was dropped, and I accepted that I'd read something into her tone that wasn't there. Just a part of any new relationship, getting to read one another correctly. My mistake.

And so began an acquaintanceship which would almost immediately bloom into a friendship. She was very much a take-charge woman and I gratefully welcomed her concern for me. Jane became my ever-present companion and the source of my social contacts over the next weeks.

Angel was taking care of all university-connected needs, and as the official liaison between the Foreign Language Departments and the incoming teachers, she was very busy meeting and completing the paperwork for the seventeen of us, foreign experts and foreign teachers alike, as each arrived in our host country. Our corps would finally consist of two from France, three from the Soviet Union, two from the United Kingdom, and ten from the United States. The difference between a foreign expert and a foreign teacher was a matter of the degree held and the years of experience—and was reflected in number of classes assigned and the amount of salary paid. (Foreign teachers were younger and taught more, for a lower salary.)

With nothing special to do for the next few days, it was Jane who taught me to elbow my way onto the public bus system, shop for everything I could possibly need, and introduced me to the several local restaurants and how to order the excellent food. She connected with the proper persons and my minuscule refrigerator was delivered, along with a two-burner hot plate, an antique manual typewriter, and a small radio. Daily, my appreciation and enjoyment of her camaraderie and know-how grew, and soon I was comfortably set for the coming year.

During those days, most of our team checked in. I'm not going to introduce each individually, only mention that the French couple was pleasant enough when accidentally encountered, but opted to live in a separate building and basically ignored the rest of us for the year. The other expert from England had long experience with China, and chose to socialize with our hosts rather than with her follow country-person or with the Americans, except for Roger. There were six American teachers, all in their twenties, who were housed in yet another nearby apartment complex, and who formed their own tight-knit group—for the most part. The Soviets were to be the first Russians to teach in China for twenty-plus years and would be six weeks late in arriving, due to delays in Moscow. That left three American experts, in addition to me. One of those was a liaison between our university and her alma mater in the States, and spent the majority of her free time in business-related matters. Cliques formed, mine consisting of Jane, two Americans, and later one of the Russians. I'll postpone introducing her until her actual arrival.

I'd like you to meet Roger, a thirty-something American man who had lived and taught abroad for more than ten years. Brilliant, tall, handsome, experienced, and a man much in need of female companionship. (No, not mine—except as a confidant.) Roger's expertise was Business English, and he was assigned to that department.

And then there was Jennifer. I'd seen her. Oh, yes. How could anyone miss her? A mid- to late-forties woman of massive proportions who hefted her weight up and down those apartment house stairs with surprising agility. A gigantic woman wheeling her bicycle in and out among the thousands of cyclists like a professional racer. An immense presence in our fifth-floor, glass-enclosed telephone booth, either thundering or whispering into that instrument. Her apartment was at the opposite end of the hallway from mine. But I'd not met her yet, and was a bit intimidated by her bearing. Jennifer was (is) an attorney from California, assigned to the university law department as the English Language expert, having just transferred from another Chinese institution. If anyone had suggested that Jennifer would, over that year and many years after, become and remain my dearest friend, confidant, and support, I would have replied, "Never!" But...

The day came to start climbing the stairs to the sixth floor. This was the first time I'd ever been fully responsible for university-level students and my nervousness mounted as I left first one floor then another below me. *Just be yourself, Adair. There's nothing else you can be.* I pushed open the ill-fitting door. The freshman classroom consisted of wooden benches and desks, a miserable excuse for a chalkboard, chalk dust that was to bring on sneezing attacks, and broken windows. Twenty-some students were awaiting me, sitting silently, hands folded on the desks, all dressed alike, all looking alike, staring at me with blank faces. *OK, Adair. Big smile. Let's get going.* I'd been told that students each took a Western name for convenience—as Alexander had—so in slow, clearly enunciated speech, I introduced myself, then asked them to introduce themselves with both their Western and Chinese names. They stood when spoken to individually—which surprised me—and responded timidly, in hushed tones. They started to look and sound like clones of some laboratory model. This would never do. I began to wend my way through the crowded room, tripping over book bags, stopping by this one and that one, touching one and another on the shoulder and deliberately grossly mispronouncing each Chinese name as I repeated it. The snickering began, and I thumped a desk, frowning, and said, "What are you giggling at? Don't you think my Chinese is perfect? I do! I've been working on it for YEARS!" And then their laughter erupted. The ice was broken and they commenced to squirm like any normal eighteen-year-olds do.

The junior class was a duplication of the freshman except that they were older, far more sophisticated—they thought—and in greater number. I repeated the pretense. They responded.

The senior class? As you've already figured. After the mispronunciations and laughter, I returned to the front of the class, sat on a desk, propped my elbows on my knees, rested my chin on my hands and queried, "So, tell me, what are you going to do with the rest of your lives?" I don't think anybody had ever asked them that question before. Nor had they ever seen a teacher sit on a desk. The teacher belonged at the podium. Shocking! They loved it.

At five o'clock I went to the English Department office to meet with my postgrads. They weren't there. The department secretary tried to explain their absence, an explanation I didn't fully understand, then she told me to set a time and place for their lectures and they'd be there. There were only six of them. I suggested my apartment, the following morning at eleven

Precisely on time, there was a soft knocking on my door. I opened it to see yet another set of six older and wiser clones; five male and one female. I intended no pretense.

"Please, come in," I said. Smiles and handshakes. Each smiled and nodded in return, walked into my living room and stood like robots.

"Please, take a seat, wherever you'll be comfortable," I said, gesturing to the chairs and sofas. I took my own seat at a small table which I'd placed against one wall. They accepted, but none spoke. I was prepared for that.

"We're going to be spending a lot of time together this year, and I think it best if we take this opportunity to get acquainted. I'd like to know something about each of you, and I'll tell you my own story. I want to know about your families, your teaching assignments, and what you want to get from these classes, everything." Pause. Silence. "Who'd like to begin?"

They looked at each other, at me, smiled and nodded. No one responded. They reminded me of those little nodding dogs in the rear windows of some American cars.

"OK. I'll start." I told them who I was, asking them for any questions they might have along the way. There were none.

When my one-sided dialogue was finished, I indicated for one of the young men to share his life's experiences. When spoken to directly, they were willing to answer; answers being rote-specific and unadorned. Each spoke excellent English, and, thankfully, none stood when addressed.

Harold: a single, twenty-eight-year-old, the only child of professional parents.

Mike: a thirty-one-year-old, married, with one child—a son.

Kevin: a thirty-three-year-old, married, with one child—a daughter.

Thomas: a twenty-nine-year-old, married, with a child expected in early winter.

Ray: also thirty-one, married, with one child—a son.

Julie: a twenty-six-year-old, single, the only child of working-class parents.

And so it went. For nearly the full period, answers to all questions were brief, cloaked, and their politeness was palpable. Talking computers. They were making me uncomfortable. This, too, would never do. I stood and walked to the windows, trying to think about how to handle this. Static moments passed. I didn't know what to say. *Just open your mouth. Tell them the truth. The words will come.* Then I turned to face them.

"OK. I'll tell you right now, I can't work this way. I've come over ten thousand miles to help you in sociolinguistics, composition, and methodology. Both methodology and sociolinguistics are going to take a lot of interaction, and in order for me to do my job, I've got to have a workable environment. This is not that environment.

"To me, each of you is a vital, important, pulsating human being, filled with intelligence and experience and emotions. I have to be able to tap into those qualities that are *you*. In order to do that, I have to have your confidence, as I will give you mine.

"I am fully aware that one of you is the class monitor, whose job it is to report every Friday afternoon on everything I have said and done during our times together. And what each of your classmates has said and done. I don't want to ever know which one of you is the monitor. I will also tell you right now that we are going to discuss everything and anything we want to discuss. There is to be total academic freedom. And every word that is said within these walls *stays* within these walls. Trust! I ask...I insist... that you trust each other, and me. I want your hearts and your minds, and in return I will give you mine. That is what I'm here for.

"If you can't provide me, provide each other, with that environment, then let's call it quits, and I'll pick up another class of seniors.

"I want you to leave now, and think about what I've said. If you are willing to continue, on my conditions, be here tomorrow morning at eleven. If you're not here, I'll know your decision, and so be it. Good-bye."

Six sets of eyes stared at me, dumbfounded. Then the students rose as one body and left the room.

There was a soft knock on my door at eleven the next morning. Before entering, Mike said, "Dr. Hathaway has asked us to call her 'Dr. Hathaway.' What would you like us to call you?"

"You may address me any way you are comfortable with. Just don't call me 'Mom.'" Laughter. They came in. Our work had begun.

During the several years I'd been working on my master's degree, the concept of whether or not a person thinks differently in one language than in another had been percolating. I'd hunted for some research, but had found little. I'd mentioned it to my mentor teacher that last summer session in Arizona, and she'd suggested pursuing the concept and recommended some testing materials I might like to use. Those materials and questionnaires were sitting in their envelopes on my desk, nagging for my attention as I prepared for my various classes. A couple of weeks into the semester, I casually brought up the concept to my postgrads during one of our meetings, and they assured me they did think and reason differently in English than in Chinese, and encouraged me to go ahead with the research. I knew it would take an inordinate amount of time and energy; planning, implementing, and evaluating such questionnaires—and they'd have to be translated into Chinese so that the "subjects" could respond to the same question in the two languages—and I'd have to have the agreement and cooperation of the university administration. One afternoon on my way home from class, it was turning in my mind when I saw Alexander pedaling his bicycle toward me, and I hailed him.

"Greetings, Adair. So, are you finding everything you need? Are your classes OK? Do you want to change any of them? How can I help you?"

"Good to see you, Alexander. You must be very busy with everyone coming in. Are we all here yet?"

"The Russians will be late. Everybody else is here. Have you met them all? There'll be a welcoming feast on the weekend."

"Oh, good. A chance to dress up. Alexander, I have a project I'm interested in doing with the students. I'd like to discuss it with you and see what you think about it... when you have time."

"How about five o'clock this afternoon? I'll come to your apartment."

"Five is perfect. See you then." And he wheeled off.

He was late. Always late. I'd get used to it. I'd removed the materials and questionnaire from their envelopes and was scanning the variety of questions. The questionnaire was lengthy and there were the usual assortment of attitude queries. Although there were none on politics per se, there was a section on political philosophy and a section on sexual attitudes. Those two areas might pose some difficulties as far as getting permission from the university to proceed with the project. They were both taboo subjects, especially the latter. However, they were the topics that could possibly produce the greatest variance in responses from one language to the other—if such variance existed.

"Sorry I'm late." It was nearly five thirty when I welcomed him to my apartment. "The Foreign Affairs Office is quite busy, and my colleague...left early. Sorry."

"No problem. Can I offer you some tea?"

"Thank you, yes." He'd removed his jacket and chosen a seat on the sofa, picking up the questionnaire. *Well, he certainly doesn't WASTE time.* "Tell me what this project is and how you want to do it."

Stepping into the kitchen, I added water to the already simmering kettle and at the same time explained my curiosity about the thought processes from one language to another. Cups of tea in hand, I placed them on the table separating us and took a seat facing him. He reached for his, continued reading, and asked, "What will you do with the information you get from our students?"

"I don't really know. If we get some variance, I'll connect with my mentor teacher at my university. Maybe she'll have some suggestions. Maybe I'll pursue a Ph.D. and use this as the basis of my research, although we'd probably have to repeat it again next year, to make any adjustments to my testing methodology so it would be acceptable. I don't know."

"Are you saying the results could be published?"

"I have no idea, Alexander. That's a possibility."

"Good. I want the world to know what is in the minds of our students!" He'd looked up from the papers and the intensity of his statement surprised me.

"There's a section on political philosophy and a section on sexual attitudes. Have you noticed those?"

"Yes. Those are the ones I especially want the world to know about."

"Are you saying, then, that the university will give permission to use our students?"

"I can speak for the university, itself. That is not where you might encounter objections. It's the Ministry of Education that will have to agree. But I know many people over there. I know how to handle this. There are several people over there who owe me favors. Don't worry about them. I'll take care of it."

"Great! There's a lot of work to be done before testing can start. First, of course, it has to be translated into Chinese. If you know someone who has the ability and the time to do the translation, I'll be happy to pay for it."

"I know the perfect person. Me! And no charge."

"You? But you have no time."

"I'll find the time. I want this to be done. You do whatever it is you have to do. Leave the translation to me."

His enthusiasm matched my own. The intensity of his desire to have the results published sent up a flag. Not a red one...just a flag. Clearly, that was his reason for finding the time to translate. Why was that so important to him?

He put the papers down and leaned back.

"Tell me about yourself. Why aren't you married?"

"I was—for too long." I gave him a verbal sketch of what *marriage* had come to mean to me. "But I have a solution to ninety-nine percent of all marriage problems."

"Don't marry?"

"No, no. Marriage is OK. It's the marriage contract that is wrong. The marriage contract should automatically expire at the end of two years, and have to be renewed for another two years, and so on. If the couple knew that the legal commitment was for only two years at a time, each just might work harder to make life pleasant for the other."

"Great idea! I'll support you in that,"—and his laughter blended into—"ah, to live in such a society as America. To be able to freely divorce and live your own life. To make your own decisions. To be American. Lucky. Americans are very lucky people. Most of you whom I've met don't really know...I mean, you are very lucky people."

"Alexander, are you married?"

"Yes. Married. Legally, yes. I will tell you my secrets. But we must have an understanding...a bond. We must trust each other with our secrets." He paused, leaning toward me, looking intently into my eyes.

A bond? Trust? Secrets? Déjà vu. He's sure made a fast character analysis of me. But his command had been no more immediate and abrupt than my own with the postgrads. "Of course, Alexander. Of course. We can speak to each other...with confidence, in confidence."

"Good. We will both need that. In the days to come, we will need to trust each other."

In the days to come? What does that mean? "Tell me about your marriage."

"I married when I was young. A young soldier. We had a child. But she...my wife...she wasn't satisfied...she couldn't, you know...never mind. Anyway, I've been trying to get a divorce for nearly twelve years. But I'm not allowed. I've lived alone, here, on the campus for those years."

"Not allowed? What do you mean, you're not allowed?"

"I can't get permission to divorce. Her parents are very high in the party, you see. They have the power to prevent me from divorcing their daughter. In our society, a woman must have a husband to have status. That is, divorce is possible, of course, and common. But for the old-time party members, it is status if the daughter is married to someone of rank and prestige. My rank and prestige are not so high, but are high enough for them. They don't believe she could marry someone of higher rank, because she...well, they just don't."

"Let me understand this. It is more acceptable, socially, to be married to a man you've not lived with for twelve years, than to be divorced?"

"Yes. For the older members. For her parents and for her, that is true. I have tried again and again. I'm in the process of trying even now. But it won't happen. They won't give permission. I know that."

How long has it been since he's discuss this with anyone? He's too earnest. "That reminds me somehow of the Catholic Church and its stand on divorce. Irrational. Out of touch with the human condition. Actually, I'm beginning to see other similarities between the structure of the Catholic Church and the Communist system. Maybe the early Communists looked at the two-thousand-year success story of the Catholic Church and adapted its infrastructure! What d' ya' think?"

"Interesting. Possible. All repressive systems design their methods of enslavement...for the same end. Power for the few. And they justify those methods in rhetoric that the people will believe. It's all the same. It's simple, and the same. They promise some abstract reward, but it's all for the power for the few." He stood abruptly, and picked up the questionnaire and his jacket as he moved quickly to the door. "I've said too much." He faced me, solemn. "Trust. We must have trust between us."

"You need never worry, Alexander."

"Thank you." And he was gone.

(It was to be two years before I learned the details of his marriage...those he didn't tell me. At that later time, Angel explained to me that his wife had been sexually promiscuous, sleeping with not only those in the military who were his peers, but with his officers also, changing partners randomly. Alexander's wife would discuss with her bed partners her sex life with her husband, ridiculing and laughing. Filling in the blank spaces, I guessed that she was probably incapable of orgasm because he had used the words *she couldn't, you know*...and she blamed him. He knew what she was doing and her behavior became common knowledge, both among the solders and with her parents. Neither she, nor they, cared...even found it amusing. They used it to humiliate him. Alexander was never convinced that the child of their marriage was his, but he had treated the child as his own.)

"There's going to be a parade downtown tomorrow." Jane was sharing a package of cakes and candies she'd just received from London. "Then, after the parade, we're to go to the dinner reception for all of us, together with the officers from the Foreign Affairs Office and the administration. Would you like to go to the parade?"

"What's it for?"

"I'm not sure which one this is. These sorts of celebrations are held from time to time. Would you care to go?"

"Sure. Why not? How are the postgrads doing with you?"

"As expected. Their analyses of the poetry are acceptable, but too flowery. But that is Chinese. All except for Ray. He never seems to understand the poet's symbolism. I'm concerned about his lack of comprehension... he interprets according to some other...it's as though he doesn't understand the vocabulary. How is he with you?"

"I'm surprised to hear that...no, I'm not. Actually, I'm not. In his compositions, in our discussion, he finds an analysis that is uniquely his own. I'd say that he 'hears a different drummer.' I don't have a problem with that. Encourage it, really. I would have to say that he is the most creative of them. Do you require some stock analysis?" I was sorry I'd said that as soon as it was out of my mouth.

"Of course not. But there are certain parameters. He's far outside those parameters. I don't know if I'll be able to pass him."

"Jane, you've already made that determination? Would you fail a graduate student because he doesn't agree with you...not with you, but with some prescribed set of criteria?"

"Have you ever taught British poetry? Do you have a specialization in British literature?"

"You know I don't. Come on...don't get defensive with me. I acknowledge your expertise. I've told you more than once that poetry is my weak link...an empty box in my head. I'm only suggesting that allowances be made for a mind that grasps a different reality."

"That sounds like trendy American methodology to me. There are certain standards to maintain. Would you not agree?"

"Standards, yes. But perhaps we, I, draw the lines differently than you do. I choose not to get into another discussion over British methodologies of thirty years ago with American methodologies of today. In fact, it is my understanding that today's British are at least on a par with American interest in individual student involvement in their own education—perhaps even ahead of us in that. Ray seems to me to fit into that mold. He is a hard worker, a dedicated student, and always prepared. I couldn't penalize him because he doesn't fit into some box."

"As you say, it is better not to get into another discussion over our methodologies. You use yours. I'll use mine. What about the others? About composition?"

"Flowery, yes. I've developed some exercises to reduce that. They seem to be working. Would you like to have me show you, or explain those exercises?"

"Yes, but some other time. I have lectures to prepare, as I'm sure you do, too," she said, and gathered up her things to leave. "I'll come by tomorrow at noon to get you for the parade."

"I'll be ready."

It wasn't the first time we'd clashed over teaching methods. It wasn't important. We disagreed on many topics, and enjoyed the challenges. Laughed them off. Each claiming vast superiority for our own country. It was part of the fun of being with Jane.

The sun was blistering hot as the crowds of Chinese politely made way for the foreigners. The bleachers were already packed, but Jane spotted a contingent from the university and led the way up. There were two possible places to wedge into, one on a row behind the other.

Jane pushed me toward the upper level so I'd have the better vantage point. I made my way to the space beside the attorney I'd not yet met.

"Hi, I'm Jennifer. I've seen you a few times, and planned to come by your apartment. Just haven't had the time. You're from Davis? I'm from Sacramento. You live about fifteen minutes away from me. And we've come to China to meet." She scrunched herself together to give me an extra two inches; earthy and relaxed. Face-to-face, she was in no way intimidating. My mistake.

"Thanks. I'm Adair. Yes, my daughter lives in Davis and I visit her a lot. Actually, I've been living in Reno, but have closed out that phase of my life. All my worldly goods are either in Davis or in storage. I have no home. A homeless American."

"First trip to China?"

"Yeah, but I was in the Peace Corps. Stationed in Jamaica. This is better, for me."

"Jamaica is beautiful. Smoke any of their great ganja while you were there?"

"Offered some once, didn't try it. Maybe I should have. Do you use it?"

"Have in the past. Not anymore. But God knows, you sometimes need it here. You're working with the postgrads? How is it?"

"Great. We had to come to an understanding the first day about academic freedom. I gave them an ultimatum. They accepted. And everything goes well. How about your classes? In law, right?"

"Yeah. They need a lot of vocabulary. It takes time."

"Sorry to change the subject, but how long before this parade starts?"

"Maybe fifteen minutes. They're rarely on time."

"I hate to be so mundane, but I've got to find a bathroom."

"OK. I could use one myself. Come on."

The small stone building stood behind the bleachers and there was a line of Chinese women waiting to get in. When they saw us, they smiled and indicated for us to go first. If you've ever been to China, you need no further explanation. If you haven't, well...they're called squatters for good reason. This one had a dirt floor, a passageway about four feet wide, and a two- or three-inch-high stone ridge over which to step to enter the toilet area. The toilet was a trench running the full length of the building which was separated into stalls by maybe three-foot-high dividers on the sides. You have to find a place for your feet on boards placed across the trench. The smell was appalling and the passageway was lined with ladies-in-waiting.

One woman exited a stall and the woman waiting in front of it smiled and gestured for me to enter. I walked to the front of it and shuddered. "Jennifer, how am I supposed to balance? What am I supposed to hang on to... while I...?"

With raised eyebrows and sarcasm, she grinned and said, "Well, you can hold my hands, if you want."

"I really don't think that will be necessary!" And I squatted while the lineup of women watched and nodded. I finally appreciated Mandy's giggling over the Western toilet that was in my apartment. It wasn't until we were climbing back up into the bleachers that I realized I'd completely ignored—forgotten—Jane. How rude! Damn. Why had I done that?

The main dining room which serviced the apartment complex was cheerfully decorated and the several round tables were beautifully dressed with linens and a colorful assortment of dishes. Impressive. Jane and I had walked over together with no mention of the afternoon's incident; it must have been more noticeable to me than it was to her. We milled about speaking to the experts and teachers as they arrived. Jennifer was standing with a group and gave me a wave. I noticed, with a smile, that the other expert from England, Claudia, was in a somewhat flirtatious, chummy conversation with Roger. The age difference was considerable and I flashed back on my own relationship with Victor. *Good for you, Claudia. Go for it!*

The administrative staff arrived, together and late, with Alexander clearly in charge. He caught my eye, nodded and smiled. With him was a younger man, well dressed in a Western-cut suit. Handsome and oozing self-confidence, this man walked from cluster to cluster vigorously shaking hands with the newcomers and chatting—with a bit too much laughter for my tastes. *Glad-hander?* "Who is that?" I whispered to Jane.

"He's the one who processed my documentation. His English name is Charles. He's Alexander's assistant, was his student in his university days. He's just returned from finishing his master's in the United States."

"Hmmm. That explains it."

"Explains what?"

"His self-confidence. And his clothes."

"Right. I suspect he's competing with Alexander for the chief's job. Speaking of Alexander, this will be the first time I've been formally introduced to him. You've spent time with him. What do you think?"

"Think about what?"

"Don't you find him somewhat...aloof?"

"Not at all. Overworked. Preoccupied. Not aloof. He's a brilliant man. Sophisticated. I like him."

"Really?" The tone carried innuendo. I didn't react.

"I didn't know Mr. Woo's job was coming open."

"Yes. He will retire next summer."

Alexander chattered and huddled us as a mother hen to our designated places, and the wine stewards brought forth the bottles as the servers brought the food. A feast, indeed. When all was organized, Alexander took his own place at the administrators' table, tapped his glass and called for attention. He introduced those at the head table, then each of us. It was Miss This, and Mr. That, and Dr. So-and-So...giving a brief background as the person stood for recognition. I was the last.

"And, ladies and gentlemen, this is...Adair." That was all. But somehow, I'd been given status. How had I gained it? I didn't stand, but laughed and tipped my hand to my forehead. There were chuckles and applause. And we ate.

The last Saturday of the month was payday and Jennifer had come to fetch me. We stopped by Jane's apartment and the three of us walked over to the finance building. A number of our colleagues were already there, cueing for position at the long counter where ledger books lay open and harried clerks handed out stacks of cash, secured with rubber bands. Give your name, show some identification, wait for the clerk's scanning fingers to find your account number and the amount, and receive your salary. All was open for anyone to see. Mandy had told me how much my salary was to be. When my turn at the counter came, the amount listed was considerably higher. Mandy must have misunderstood. I was so confused by the procedure that I paid no attention to anyone else's wages. But Jennifer and Jane both did.

"That's quite a salary you've received. How do you rate?" It was Jennifer's whisper.

"What do you mean?"

"You've just been paid about a third more than any of the rest of the foreign experts. What are doing to earn that money, Adair?"

With a suggestive sidelong glance, I said, "I'll never tell." But neither of my friends thought me amusing.

We walked over to the university garage where Alexander was waiting with our driver and a university van. He would accompany us to the bank. He pushed the sliding door open and stood aside, chatting with me as the others entered. He then indicated the window seat diagonally behind him, so we could continue our conversation easily—which was to become my "assigned" seat for the year.

Preferential treatment. Subtle, but there. Both Jennifer and Jane noticed, as the others did later.

Banking in China, in 1988! What an adventure. By agreement with the government, we were allowed to exchange 70 percent of our pay into our currency of choice. That necessitated a stop at a downtown office to have each name and amount entered into a computer. Time-consuming, but tea was always served. Back into the van and across town to the Bank of China. Endless counters, crowds of quibbling people, and cash reserves in suitcases at the feet of bank tellers as they sat at their desks performing lightning-fast manipulations on the abacuses. I can almost believe the abacus is faster than a calculator, at least in their hands. Alexander took charge of every detail of each of our transactions. He simply moved to the front of any given line, elbowed someone out of the way, offered a cigarette to a smiling clerk, and went about our business. Considering the number of us, the amount of our salaries and the currency exchanges, he was handling vast sums of money—without error. Then, back into the van to return to the campus. The process took a full day. And the money we received was to be kept hidden, under lock and key, in our apartments—no bank accounts. We each secured our own cache.

"But how did they know how much salary you received?" Alexander was sitting in my apartment, having completed a few items of translation and wanting to check with me for accuracy.

"The ledgers were all open for inspection. The amounts were in no way concealed. Everyone could see what their colleagues made."

"Those fools. I gave instructions. Each person's salary is private business. I was explicit. Those fools. What explanation did you give?"

"I didn't...really."

"That is appropriate. Your salary is not out of line. If I had the power, I'd raise everyone's pay. You sacrifice quite a lot to come to teach here in China. I know that. You should all be well paid."

"Speaking of power, I've heard that Mr. Woo is retiring next summer. Do you think—"

He interrupted me with a laugh. "Oh, one never knows for sure about such things. Perhaps. Let us check these questions. I want to be sure that I'm doing what you want me to do." Discussion over!

These sessions for checking translations were ongoing, usually three times a week, at five in the afternoon, and often lasted up to two hours. He was exacting and accurate. Due to the nature of the questions, especially in the areas of family relationships, sexual attitudes, and political philosophy, we spent the bulk of our time discussing the in-depth meaning and framework of each question so that he could capture any and all subtleties when moving from one language into the other. My method for checking his accuracy was to have him read back into English questions he had translated a week or more before.

What was, initially, an exercise in linguistics had soon become a probing into much more than lexical items. We were exploring one another's mind and spirit and culture. Those commonalities which he alluded to during that first luncheon we'd shared had surfaced. On one level, what was interesting to me was that, although we had been born and raised in such diametrically opposed societies, our thinking on most subjects was nearly the same. What was even more startling was that Alexander and I saw and analyzed the world in more the same way than did Jane and I, and I mentioned it. "You and I, Adair...we live in the same world." And as the weeks in that atmosphere of intimacy and sameness slid by, I knew I was being drawn to this man. The trust he accorded me. The honesty of his comments concerning the severity of life under the Communist system touched my soul. The warmth and attention he was giving me touched my heart. Occasionally he brought me small gifts—a pastry, a candy, something—and I knew that his interest in me had gone beyond the professional. I knew that I had already taken a predominant place in his life. I also knew that there were times when his feelings toward me were sensual. He never said it. He never touched me. But desire was sometimes in the room and I knew it. And there were times when he was relating to me some incident of the sorrow and isolation of Chinese life that I was moved by the pathos of such a solitary existence. His phrases were always oblique, sometimes with a small laugh or a shrug, but his meaning was clear. He was admitting me into his soul, his mind, and his heart. Even though his words were in the abstract, I knew he was confiding to me his personal place within that system, his unrequited passions, his unfulfilled human needs. How well I understood those needs. And in those moments, all I wanted to do was reach out and touch him, nurture, him, comfort him. Perhaps to give him a bit of freedom…of unrestrained pleasure…but the rule against university administrators fraternizing with the foreign staff was rigid, so I did nothing more than listen.

Mid-October, and all was regulated and progressing satisfactorily with our classes and social life. Jane, Jennifer, and I had joined others of our colleagues for our scheduled lunches in yet another, smaller dining area adjoining the apartment house. One Monday, there was a commotion at the doorway which caught our combined attentions. Charles was ushering in the three experts from the Soviet Union—two men and a woman. Introductions followed. All three were well into their fifties, and the men had little English. The woman, though…ah, yes, the woman! The first thing that struck me was what she was wearing. She didn't sit, but extricated herself from the company of Charles and her colleagues and glided over to where we were, removing her head scarf with a dramatic flourish.

It's time to introduce you to Tanya. Medium height, voluptuous, a bit too heavily made-up, but glamorous, with nearly white (bleached) hair which swept away from a face that still retained the beauty of earlier years, and a voice which sang the scale as she exclaimed her excitement, in fluent English. She had made her flamboyant entrance and she shook hands all around, pronouncing each name in turn, relishing her good fortune at making the acquaintance of so many English-speaking "comrades."

Amused, I said, "Tanya, I love your outfit." She was wearing a deep maroon-colored jumpsuit.

"Do you really?" She whirled around, modeling it. "It was a gift. It came from AMERICA!"

"Yes, I know. I have the exact same one!"

She squealed, "Do you really? We must wear them both at the same time. Everyone will think we are twins." She shook hands with me again as Jennifer moved her own chair aside to make room for Tanya beside me at the table.

"I want to be great friends with you, all of you," she gestured theatrically to our group. Then, confidentially, she said, "I hardly know my male comrades. They've caused so many delays, and besides, they're Soviets, bores. They don't speak English." She wrinkled her nose, obviously feeling elitist. "My first question to my new friends is, where can I get my nails done? This long trip has damaged them. Just look!"

Great friends? Unlikely, you may think. But you'd be mistaken. Yes, Tanya and I were to become great friends, for a while: a thread with unsalvageable snags.

"Let us talk about opinion versus fact. Propaganda and euphemism." The postgrads were relaxing in my living room. Relaxing? It was a class period, but our lessons were more like in-depth conversations between friends, followed by some academic exercise. A recent edition of the *China Daily* was spread on my little table and I wanted to discuss a full-page article on Chinese-American relations. The author had written a rambling hodgepodge of personal opinions and party propaganda, which he was presenting as facts in order to justify the current number of Western (especially American) specialists coming into

China. As an exercise in composition, I was going to ask the postgrads to rewrite sections of the article. I read a few paragraphs aloud.

To abbreviate and paraphrase: the imperialist Americans were solely responsible for the years of isolation between the two countries, due, in part, to Christian religious beliefs, and in part to the Western belief in the superiority of the Caucasian race. Before the curtain descended, the Chinese had tried to cooperate with American businessmen and missionaries, but the Americans had always treated their host country as inferior. America had finally denounced China and had since treated her as nonexistent. China was now grateful that the American mentality had matured and that America had rethought her attitudes toward the noble peoples of China. There must have been some major breakthrough in Christian mentality which allowed such a transformation. Chinese psychologists had analyzed the depth of that transformation and determined that it was sincere. And now that America was mature enough to live in harmony with the great people of China, she had requested the privilege of sending specialists to China, and they would once again be welcomed.

Sandwiched into the writing were a number of irrelevant, or quasi-related, half-true "facts." The article had initially caused me to blink, and I reread it with incredulity that a professional journalist could write such drivel and that a responsible newspaper would print it.

"Let's start at the end. Am I here—are all of the Westerners here because America, the West, has requested our presence in China?"

They threw out answers.

"It's probably a cooperative agreement."

"Perhaps related to President Nixon's visit."

"It was the American president who came to China, not vice versa." There was a slight edge to Thomas's voice.

They began to speak on top of each other. I interrupted with, "A cooperative agreement? Possible. Are you also suggesting that a part of President Nixon's efforts to normalize relations between our two countries was his stipulation that any future cooperation between our countries depended on America sending teachers to China to teach the Chinese intellectuals to speak English? If that is true, then doesn't it possibly follow that our employment would have been arranged for and our salaries would be paid by the U.S. government? That is not the case."

Silence, as wheels turned.

"Is it not at least equally possible that it's the other way around...that we are here because the Chinese government recognizes that English has become the Language of Wider Communication, and that if China wants to modernize and enter the world marketplace and scientific community, it is essential for English to become a prime requirement? At least until China translates the language of the computer into Chinese, thereby making it accessible to her people? Is it possible that we are here not because America has 'matured,' but because China has her own agenda for inclusion in world commerce?"

A moment more of silence before Kevin spoke up.

"You must realize, Adair, that we—each of us, and all schoolchildren—used to begin each day of our school life repeating together: 'Death to America.' We have been indoctrinated with the concepts that America is an evil, imperialistic society and Americans are greedy, evil people who care for no one but themselves."

"And what do you think now?"

Another moment of silence. Then, it was Ray who spoke.

"Can you appreciate how difficult it is for us to admit to ourselves that our government has lied to us?"

Julie: "If they have lied about Americans, what else have they lied about? Everything?"

There was pain in these young adults. They loved their country. I'd overstepped a boundary. Wanted to get out of the spot I'd gotten myself into. Closed the newspaper, but didn't know how to make a transition. It came.

"Truth. Let's explore. Define truth for me."

Mike: "A provable fact. An unchanging, unchangeable bit of knowledge. A constant, observable, predictable phenomenon."

"Um-hmm, that's nice. Sounds primarily scientific. Have scientific facts, 'truths,' changed over the millennia? How about consensus? Science is not my strongest subject, so let's talk about the domain of the human condition. If you think about it, historically, is it possible that truth doesn't exist—that there is no such thing—and that what we label truth is really only consensus and is relative to time and place, and is a dynamic phenomenon that does, in fact, change according to whatever people agree to believe? Is it possible that your truth is different from my truth? And that we are both...WRONG?"

The momentary tension was diffused—or defused. The smiles came, and an energetic discussion ensued.

When the end of the period arrived, I said to them, "You guys have given me a lot to think about. I want you to go home and leave me alone to cogitate." I stood.

Harold was the last out of the room; he stalled, and then referred back to my discomfort. "I know that our government lies to us. My father has told me since I was a child. We all know it, Adair. We just don't talk about it. And we get defensive if somebody else talks about it. But please don't feel bad. It needs to be talked about." And he shook my hand.

What was I going to do about this? What was my role? So far and no further? Or all the way? Being an educator carries too much responsibility. Walking a tightrope. I wanted an American sounding board, and a drink, so I walked over to Jennifer's apartment. She wasn't home. The sounding board and drink would both have to wait.

"Are you going on the weekend trip?" Tanya had made Turkish coffee from a blend she'd brought with her. "I'm nervous about going. I'll go, but only if I can share the hotel room with you."

"Why are you nervous about going?"

"I'm always nervous about everything. I'm a rabbit. But I want to go. Please, my friend, say that you'll share a room with me."

She was asking me about a trip to visit some caves, an excursion which had been arranged for any of us who were interested by the Foreign Affairs Office—by Alexander. The caves were far from our city and the trip would take many hours on the bus, then overnight at a small hotel. And, of course, the hours returning. I was interested in the caves, but dreaded two full days on a crowded bus. Was wavering in my decision. And now she wanted me to room with her. It was not my favorite prospect.

Nervous? Yes. She seemed to be frightened by everything. Whenever we shopped, or went to see the temples, or whatever, she always clung to my arm. In the restaurants she'd run her fingers under the tabletops to check for listening devices. Paranoia. I have to say that Tanya was not popular with the other foreign experts. Too overstated and theatrical for most tastes. At first, I was also somewhat resistant, but she was waif-like, and I'd had a lifetime of feeling excluded by my peers so I knew well the feelings of being alone and isolated from companions. She ignored her Russian counterparts and they ignored her. Tanya was Russian by heritage, but she was Armenian by birth. They felt that she should not have been chosen; that the post given to her should have gone to a native Russian. As a result, the two men shunned her and did not acknowledge her as their colleague or their peer. I guess I'm sympathetic to the underdog and gravitate to those who need me. *Earth mother.*

"Oh, well...OK." To be honest, though, my decision was maybe 20 percent influenced by Tanya. The other 80 percent was because I wanted to spend time with Alexander, away from my apartment. I envisioned exploring caves with him, to allow what he had begun to define as our "special friendship" to blossom. I knew we wouldn't be exactly alone together, but it would be an enjoyable, maybe even slightly romantic opportunity, within parameters set by...who? Anyway, Tanya was my justification.

Backpacks slung over our shoulders, our group stood waiting for the larger of the university vans. It pulled up to the front of the apartment complex and Charles stepped out.

"Oh, hi. Are you joining us, too?" My smile and voice couldn't have been more sincere and enthusiastic, I hoped.

"Yes, yes, yes. I'll be going with you."

Tanya asked, "Where is Alexander? We thought he had arranged this. That he would be accompanying us."

"Yes. He has all in order for us. But he has been sent on another assignment. Alexander is out of the city. I promise to show you a good time, an even better time than my colleague would have. It's a promise! Let's go, everybody in."

Damn! Ass-kisser Charles. A weekend cooped up with his inane chatter. Deflated.

There were ten of us, plus Charles and the driver. Tanya and I would be rooming together, as would Jane and Claudia—much to their mutual dissatisfaction. They had grown to loathe each other. "I wouldn't have been friends with Jane in England, why should I attempt a friendship just because we're both in China?" Claudia once had confided to me. Roger, whom I suspected would find a way to sidetrack Claudia, and the young teachers made up the balance of the group. Jennifer didn't go. She'd already been there, twice.

What can I say? The trip and the caves were the experience of a lifetime. My photos and journal entries consist of volumes. That's an exaggeration, but what is important to my story, though, is the late-night conversation with Tanya in our zero-star hotel room. There was no heat or electricity. We huddled in our twin beds, with our coats on, and conversed by the light of a candle.

"Why aren't you married, my friend? Your children need a father. You need a husband to take care of you." I'd heard that question before, more than once in China.

"Tanya! My children are grown. They certainly don't need a father. And I can take care of myself. Having a husband means having someone else for me to take care of—not someone to take care of me."

"No, no. A husband is to care for you. Aren't women in America married?"

"Well, of course. Some are, probably the majority are. But it isn't a necessity. Many American women are single—single parents."

"It isn't proper for a woman to be unmarried and have children. Husbands are essential. The children need to have a father in the home."

"But what about yourself? You are a single parent."

"Ah, yes. It is my great shame. But my husband...left. I did not leave him. It has been so difficult. Pascha hardly knows his father. I have had to be both parents. It has brought us very close. But it is not right. It's a shame for me in my society. I can have no one. No male comrade. It isn't allowed. Pascha doesn't allow it."

"Excuse me? *Pascha* doesn't allow it? You ask your son for permission to have a male friend?"

"Oh, yes. It must be. Pascha would never allow it. I have had opportunities, but Pascha always answers the telephone, and if it is a man he says I am not there. If he comes in and I'm talking to a man on the telephone, Pascha hangs up the receiver."

"Tanya, that is outrageous! You are the adult. Pascha is the child. You allow your child to dictate your life? How could you permit that?"

"But he is the male child. And a young man now. He has the right to do so. No man could ever become lovers with me, or a husband with me. Well, perhaps a husband. But no man wants to marry a woman with children by another man. It isn't acceptable. Anyway, Pascha is my life. I need no one else."

"I don't believe that. Don't believe that you need no one else. We all have our needs."

"We learn to live without a man. It is difficult, but it is our way. What do single women do in America? What do you do? Do you take lovers?"

"Actually, no. But that is my choice. I am free to take a lover, if I want one." I opted not to tell her about Jamaica.

"What would your children say? Your sons?"

I chuckled, thinking about my offspring. "They'd probably say, 'Go for it, Mom.'"

"Don't your sons have any pride? What would they think about their mother doing that with some man who wasn't their father?"

"That isn't a matter of pride. They are proud of me because of who I am, whatever I do. No, it's a matter of choice. They know I am free to do as I like. There's no stigma in the United States about being a single mother. There's no stigma against a woman having a companion, a lover. It is her choice, and his. In fact, a single mother has status. She is looked on as a courageous woman because she needs to provide for herself and her children. It is generally recognized that that is a very difficult thing to do. She is respected—if she does it well."

"It is different with us. A single mother has no status. It is a great shame. You are very lucky to live in such a society. Do you think you could help me to get to America? I could teach Russian in an American university. What would I have to do?"

"It isn't so easy to immigrate to the United States. There are many restrictions."

"I thought that America welcomes immigrants."

"In the past more than now. We have a large population, and there is a shortage of jobs. We don't feel it's fair for foreigners to come to our country and take jobs that should go to Americans."

"But couldn't you help me? You are connected with a great university. Ah, it's only a dream. My dream. But you, Adair, my dear friend. I feel you are a sister to me. The sister that I always wanted. And I believe a woman such as you, so alive, so beautiful, must have a husband. I will find you a husband, a wonderful husband. And he will be Armenian."

"Tanya, hear me well. I don't want a husband. Any husband. That is not something I see as a possibility in my future. I've had husbands. Lots of them. Well...two of them. I don't want to get married. Not again."

She didn't laugh at my attempt to lighten the conversation. "But you must. I will find him. And he will be Armenian. They make the best lovers and the best husbands. I give you my oath." An Academy-Award performance, complete with closed eyes and the hand at the breast.

"Right, Tanya, whatever you say."

And the subject was dropped as we went on to discuss the rise of the women's liberation movement in the United States and its effects on both males and females. We talked until daybreak; we'd sleep on the bus ride home. After all the words, though, I didn't think she really comprehended the right and the honor of individual choices. Cultural biases are too often carved in stone.

"Did you enjoy the trip to the caves?" Alexander had ridden his bicycle up so close behind me that his wheel nearly nipped my heels.

"Watch it, buster!"

"Buster? What is 'buster'?"

"Slang. For 'guy.' Out of date, though. I thought you were going to take us."

"Mr. Woo sent me to meet with some representatives from the United States who are interested in having their students come for a summer program. Sorry. Did you enjoy the trip?"

"All except for Charles. There's something about your colleague that upsets me. I probably shouldn't say anything, but I somehow don't quite trust him. He's too... accommodating."

"This is his first year in the Foreign Affairs Office. He may be trying a bit too hard. He's young, you know." Alexander was making an excuse that I didn't quite buy. His eye contact wasn't right. I let it go.

He changed the subject. "I like riding up behind you. I like to watch the way you walk. Your body is so...compact."

I laughed. "Compact?" But it startled me. In all these weeks, two months now, he'd never made a personal remark.

He lowered his voice to a whisper. "You know, Adair, anything that happens between us...anything...is private and confidential."

Alexander, are you coming on to me? "I haven't discussed you with anyone. Other than a comment on what an excellent job you are doing with the translations. My colleagues know about that."

"Yes, of course. That is as it should be. There are spies everywhere."

"Spies?"

He chuckled. "I'm being dramatic. We just must be careful about...what we say, do. What about the trip?"

And I told him. We had talked for maybe fifteen minutes when I looked at my watch. "Alexander, I'm late for class. I must go." I waved good-bye to him as I hurried up to the lecture hall. Two security guards had been standing, talking together, and had watched me coming toward them. One smiled and pulled open the door. I took the stairs as quickly as possible, but six floors are...six floors. When I entered the classroom, it was empty. That seemed strange. Almost eerie. I turned and started back down the steps. I felt guilty, unprofessional. I'm rarely—never—late for class.

Rounding a landing, the senior teacher was coming toward me. Lips were smiling, but eyes were not. "Adair. The dean had come to observe your class. He missed you."

"I'm so sorry. I was...delayed. Can we schedule another time? I was surprised to find the students had left. I'm really very sorry about this. Please convey my apologies to him."

"Certainly. These things happen. I'll try to reschedule his visit." Her acceptance of my words was...stock. My guilt increased. I was not comfortable about this.

Another month passed and it was again payday; a repeat of the previous, with a small exception. "Small" isn't small enough. Infinitesimal, at first. When Alexander stood at the counter to conduct our financial transactions, he called me over. Asked me, in a voice for all to hear, to please come and double check his figures. Unexpected. He didn't need help, ever. I moved to the counter and he edged closer to me. He said nothing but inched the papers of calculations slowly toward me, at the same time brushing his sleeve against my breast. He pointed at the list of numbers and I placed my hand on the paper. He slid his fingers to mine and barely touched the tips of his to the tips of mine. The gesture was so minuscule, and apparently accidental, that no one could possibly have noticed. But I did. It was a deliberate action. I didn't look at him, but held absolutely still. The vibrations from his body passed across the bridge he'd made. Sexual. There was no doubt. He slid his fingers away and smiled a thank you, sending me back to my chair. It was too strange. I was flustered.

Transactions completed, we grouped to return to the van. It was a several-block walk to the parking area and I strode along between Jennifer and Jane. I wanted, desperately, to say something, to confide what had just happened. But I didn't. Couldn't. I'd promised "private and confidential." Anyway, Jennifer's attorney mind would say I'd imagined it. Jane might overreact. I said nothing.

We came to a stop, waiting for the light to change. Alexander had hurried to catch up to us. With the light green, we all started across. Alexander indicated for me to slow my pace and walk beside him. I did. When there was sufficient distance, he whispered to me, "I have to go to a village this evening. I'd like to take you with me. I have a driver I trust. We'll need to take two of your colleagues as well. If you want to go, just nod your head. No one must ever know. I've never done anything like this before. It is forbidden. If you want to go, nod your head."

I did.

"Which of your colleagues do you trust the most...to keep a secret?"

I chose the two I'd been walking with. Jane was experienced with the ways of China and trustworthy. Jennifer, as a lawyer, knew well the importance of keeping secrets. I'd make some excuse to Tanya later; anyway, we'd already had our trip together.

Alexander nodded. "I'll take care of it. Call them to walk beside us."

I did.

The words he chose to invite them were so innocuous there was no way they could suspect what was happening, he thought. He advised them to say nothing about the invitation and reiterated that administrators were not encouraged to socialize with foreign staff. Jane accepted that he was giving us a special treat, and he let her think it was because he hadn't spent an appropriate amount of time welcoming them when they first arrived. She bought it. Jennifer didn't believe a word, but agreed and said nothing. It would be an overnight trip. We were to pack just a few things in our backpacks and meet him under the footbridge overpass. He'd be there with the car fifteen minutes after we got back to the apartment complex.

It was dusk and the driver blinked the car lights. Alexander stowed our backpacks in the trunk and the three of us took places in the backseat. I sat in the middle, by Jennifer's arrangement. Did she not want to sit by Jane, or did she want me to have easy access to talk with Alexander? He would be "riding shotgun," with space between the bucket seats. I suspected that Jennifer intuited the truth of this escapade, and that was her reason.

The atmosphere in the car was light with merriment and filled with laughter and jokes about doing the forbidden; searching for imagined university police with machine guns at the ready. "Watch out! Duck! Ah, missed us this time." Rocking from side to side. Checking each other for bullet holes. What great fun to party with compatible friends. The driver sped through the darkening city, and on the outskirts Alexander indicated for him to stop at a restaurant for our dinner. We trouped in and were served a wonderful meal, drank a considerable amount of beer, except for the driver, then went on our way again. We stopped once more at a corner so Alexander could buy fruit to be shared for our dessert—to be eaten in the car.

The city was left far in the distance, and the two-lane road became a chuckhole-filled route winding through the villages and on into a forest. The sky was cloudless, and the light of the moon and bright stars shimmered through the occasional break in the treetops. Chatter continued. It wasn't long, though, before Alexander announced that he had to relieve himself. Too much beer. And the driver stopped beside a stand of trees. We each found our own tree to answer nature's call. I don't know why it came to mind, but I thought of dogs marking their territory. Strange, Adair.

I was the first of the women back to the car. Alexander was standing beside the hood, looking up at the brilliant sky. I don't understand much about the tricks that atmospheric conditions play on sight, but on this night, in this place, those stars appeared much too close to the earth.

"Why is it that the stars over China are so much larger than those over the United States?" I asked, and snuggled close.

"I had it arranged. Just for you," he replied with raised eyebrows, moving away a bit. The others were returning.

We were on our way again and I was leaning forward between the two front seats. Alexander broke open the bag of fruit and began feeding me bites of the bananas and oranges he'd purchased. Jennifer and Jane carried on their own conversation, speaking across my back. The conversation between Alexander and me dropped to whispers, though we were speaking of nothing of importance, nothing even personal. Just...talking. Eventually Jane and Jennifer both dropped off to sleep. We hardly noticed. As the night deepened, the surroundings continued to play tricks on orientation. The car seemed transformed into some voyager on an unending sojourn through time and space. The trees breaking up the sources of light marked the direction as our secure little capsule wound upward toward those stars, which always seemed to be just beyond reach. I mentioned the illusion of our trip as I touched my fingers to Alexander's ear, to his neck. He didn't pull away. Didn't respond, except to close his eyes momentarily and breathe deeply. Once, he ran his fingers across the back of my hand. That was all. And thus it went, for nearly four hours. After the first hour or so there had been no other highway traffic. To be so alone, secluded, in a country of more than a billion people, was too uncanny. I had no sense of time. Gradually, our murmurings became less frequent. There was less and less need to talk. Less to talk about. I was braced comfortably forward, resting my chin nearly on his shoulder. Faces no more than inches apart. Intimacy was thick. Sexual tension tangible.

The sensation of being detached—of traveling though some time/space continuum of our own—yielded to reality only as we left the last trees behind and crested a hill, and the few late-night lights of the village appeared.

"How do you want me to arrange for the rooms in the hotel?" He'd turned his face to mine, lips nearly touching my cheek as he whispered the question.

"What do you mean?"

"Shall I book one single and a double, or a triple? What is your pleasure?"

"Three singles."

"And so it shall be." We pulled into the hotel parking lot.

I roused my sleeping partners and the driver retrieved our bags from the trunk. Alexander maneuvered so that we could walk alone, together, through the blackness of the night, across the wide square in front of the hotel. Side by side, I linked my arm with his and matched his stride.

"Why did you even have to ask me about how the rooms were to be booked?"

He didn't answer.

I snuggled closer. He fixed his eyes on the entrance to the hotel and stiffened.

"Alexander, why did you have to ask?"

Again, no answer. Eyes straight ahead. Inching away from me.

I stopped abruptly and withdrew my arm. Faced him. Doubt flooded. Humiliation. I'd misread everything. But I couldn't leave it at that. He'd arranged this. He'd gone against all the university rules to do this. He had to give me an answer. I had never before invited any man to my bed. But I was going to do it, now.

"Alexander, don't you want to spend the night with me? Don't you want to make love with me?" Ten years old and pleading.

His answer was so long in coming that I closed my eyes and bit my lip. Swamped by feelings of foolishness. I turned from him and began to walk on toward the hotel, to escape. Rebuffed and degraded by my own weaknesses.

He was again beside me and touched my arm, momentarily detaining me. "Yes, of course I do. More than anything. I want to love you. But I can't." Words. Just trying to be polite. Placating, to save face for me. Disgrace and anger propelled me away from him. I didn't believe him.

The lights of the reception area were garish. I stood slightly apart from my companions, needing room for my wall of self-protection. We submitted our passports for identification and were handed registration cards. My hands were trembling from the dishonor of rejection.

With the receptionist's attention on Jane and Jennifer, Alexander moved to my side. His voice was so low I couldn't hear him properly, and his eyes were rimmed with some emotion I couldn't even recognize. "You see, Adair, they would come and get me. The police would come. They would take me away to the countryside for rehabilitation. They would imprison me, maybe for years. It could even cost me my life."

"What? Don't exaggerate. I don't understand what you mean. How would the university police even know you are here? Why would they even care?" Sarcasm. My whispers matching his own.

He indicated the desk personnel without moving his eyes from mine. His tension was volcanic. "Not...university...police." As his syllables penetrated through the filters of my culture into the realities of his, the veils of my naïve American mind were ripped open. It wasn't university rules he was breaking. Those guards standing at all the gates, they weren't only university security. The class monitors were not reporting just to the university. All the conversations Alexander and I had had, all those with my postgrads—they were more than intellectual gloss about abstractions. They each had been trying to tell me something else. In a microsecond I understood it all—with a wrenching of outrage that threw my stomach into spasms. There was little sound behind my voice as I said, "I can't believe...you're saying that for one night...that you could be..."

"It is possible. It has happened before...to too many, too often, for too little reason—for no reason. You cannot know how...and the world doesn't care." His voice trailed away to nothing more than breath. That emotion which rimmed his eyes...it was his mortification at having to tell me. It was hatred of a system that forced him to admit to me that the manhood of this "Alexander the Conqueror" was controlled by some anonymous, obsequious creature whose job it was to watch every move, to make a simple report that could end his life. To speak his hatred of a regime that imposed a life-threatening sentence of impotence designed to keep "power for the few"; an impotence political, not personal...that had no reprieve, no cure.

"Even this is too dangerous. But I wanted so much to be with you. As for you—you would only be sent back to America. But for me, the risk is...great. Please understand; forgive me. I'll be here to get you in the morning. We'll have breakfast. I have a small gift for you and I'll show you some ancient temples. It will be OK. Good night." He turned and left us.

Without comment, I followed my companions to our rooms. I could say nothing. Was sworn to say nothing. Then, as the attendant turned the key in my door, Jennifer sidled up to me and said, "And now you know the way it is. We'll talk. Later."

My mind in turmoil, I slept little that night, but the early morning sun had once again healed the world, as is its wont every morning. When Jane and Jennifer and I pushed open the hotel doors, the square was alive and bustling with humanity. Alexander was standing and chatting with the driver. When he saw us—me—his smile lifted his countenance and he spread his arms wide, arcing them upward, hands and fingers poised to receive the blessings of the new day. Oblivious to an audience of surprised villagers, he held the pose, and then slowly began a dance. Captured by some inner rhythm, his steps broadened as his body followed the music within, and he choreographed a celebration of internal freedom as he ran and leapt and turned in the air, scarcely returning to the earth as he circled the courtyard. Leaping to a close in front of me, he bowed deeply then smiled at me. Droplets of sweat stood on his brow and his breath pulsed with exhilaration. "Good morning, my special friend." His was the face of unshackled joy. Of liberation. He had vented his torturous truth. My heart soared at the sight. *Yes. This is Life, Alexander the Conqueror. It can never be taken from you.*

"Come. We'll have breakfast and then I've prepared a great day for you." He led the way—his body, his spirits, his soul bounding forward, rejoicing to a freedom within.

Peace Corps: "There will be great changes, but they will all be inside of you." *I wish to God I'd never heard those words! The way the world is. I don't understand any of this: barbaric, sickening. I loathe it. So do they, at least some of them... maybe only the educated? They're held captive against every code of humanity. Why don't they stand up? Why don't they fight it? I don't know.*

No. I've gotta get my notions, my expectations out of the way and make room. But it hurts. It hurts a lot. Or maybe I should just go home and stay there after the winter break. No.

That's running away. I'm not that weak. Am I? Maybe my students need me. Maybe Alexander needs me. That's ego. Or am I doing more harm than good? That's ego talking to me. I don't know anything.

I don't know anything. Those were the most profound four words I'd ever thought, up to that moment.

It's always astounding; the human capacity to pigeonhole entire theaters of life in such a way that they permit the other theaters of life to proceed, seemingly untethered.

November, and all of the foreigners became supercharged with excitement and enthusiasm. Thanksgiving was coming. We Americans made connections with the university chefs and detailed the traditional feast day menu, made our own lists and shopped for personal favorites to be shared with our friends and coworkers. Christmas was hurrying along, too. We all went our separate ways, secretly devising amusing gifts to be distributed within our community and searching for any and all decorations that could be substituted for the customary adornments. Winter break was coming. Travel plans were made and changed and made again. Jennifer would be meeting some colleagues from her previous university and they'd be off trekking somewhere. Tanya concealed her feelings of being left out. She would be unable to travel, but participated vicariously in our pleasures. Jane invited me to join her for a river trip. Tucked in here and there were classes and lesson preparations, and the few final relaxed and happy translation sessions. The atmosphere was pulsating with anticipation and my delight showered down on my world. The weeks tripped over one another.

The night before Thanksgiving, Roger made his first visit to my apartment. I was a bit surprised to see him and welcomed him with a bubbling cup of tea. I'd known him only from a distance and thought him to be something of a playboy. That he could have a serious thought wouldn't have occurred to me. So his request came as a mild jolt.

"Adair, it seems to me that some words should be said at the dinner tomorrow. What do you think?"

"Words? What do you mean?"

"You know. Thanksgiving kinds of words. We have so much and they have so little. It just seems to me that somebody should say something. We've invited all these Chinese. They need to understand how we feel about who we are and why we're here. Something. I don't know how to put those kinds of words together, and I've only talked to Claudia, but she's a Brit and doesn't want to get involved in that way at an American festival. Doesn't think it would be appropriate for her to say anything. What about you?"

"Well, I don't know, Roger. I hadn't thought about it. How would I do that? I mean, what we're thankful for are our freedoms and our rights. How would we convey that—to them?"

"Couldn't you think of something that would include them? It just seems...necessary, to me."

His sincerity moved me. "OK. Let me think about it. If I can come up with something, I'll do it."

That became a challenge. I fussed with it that evening and until afternoon the following day. Went to discuss it with Jennifer, only to find she was coming down with the flu and didn't want to talk about anything. Just wanted to go to bed. No, she wouldn't be able to go to the dinner. I went back to my apartment and sat at my little table, thinking about my postgrads. Finally, inspiration tapped me on the head and I wrote:

> More than three hundred years ago, a small group of people left their homelands and all that was familiar to and beloved by them, and journeyed far away to a land that was strange and mysterious to them. This small group carried with them a great dream. That dream was to participate in life, each according to his and her own abilities. But when they arrived in their new land, they found they had little knowledge about how to survive the challenges they found there. During that first year many died. What that small group learned in that first year was that they couldn't do it alone. They needed help to make their dream come true. There were other people, the native Indians, living in that land. Those people knew how to survive the challenges. Those people saw that the newcomers needed help. And they offered their assistance. The newcomers welcomed that assistance, and the others taught them all they needed to know to make it on their own. By the end of the year the seeds which had been planted came to harvest. Not all the seeds grew, of course, but enough matured to yield a rich harvest. To celebrate that harvest, the newcomers and the others sat down together for a great feast of gratitude.

In these days, a small group of Americans has left their homeland and all that is familiar and beloved to come to another land, a land that is strange and mysterious to them. The people living in this land also have a great dream. Their dream is to live life, each according to his and her own abilities. These people also know that they cannot do it alone. The small group has offered their help, and the people in the land have welcomed that assistance. The seeds of a new harvest have been planted. Not all the seeds will grow, of course, but enough will mature to yield a rich harvest. To celebrate this future harvest, this small group stands today with the people of this land to share together in a feast of gratitude; gratitude that our assistance has been welcomed so warmly.

Happy Thanksgiving to us all.

I wrote a second copy. I would read phrase by phrase in English, pausing for the translation into Chinese for those invited guests from administration who spoke no English. Now I had to find someone to translate it into Chinese. Find Alexander. But he seemed to have left the planet's surface. It was only an hour before dinner, and I was racing down the stairs one more time to check for Alexander when I nearly ran into Charles. *Well, damn...he'll have to do!* I explained that Roger had asked for an opening message and I had tried to put something together. He raised a sarcastic eyebrow and smiled a smile I instantly distrusted.

"Why are you asking me? Why not Alexander?"

Whoops! "It doesn't matter who translates. I've only just this second finished writing it," I lied.

He took the copy, scanned it, and agreed, taking the copy with him.

The younger Americans had overseen the details of the feast and the dining room was an amazing sight. It looked like a marvelous home set up to welcome an immense extended family. All had dressed in their finest and the room was vibrant with jubilation. Alexander arrived... late and edged toward a chair beside me; a chair empty by design. I asked him to tap his glass for attention and to request that the attendees stand behind their chairs. I murmured to him about the translation, and he smiled it off. I then spoke to the assemblage, telling them that this was a "family" gathering, and that in my family we always begin our Thanksgiving dinner by joining hands in a circle of friendship while a benediction is spoken. The Americans were dotted throughout the room and took the cue, which was picked up immediately by all the other internationals at the tables. The Chinese seemed unused to such an activity, but quickly joined in to the camaraderie. I nodded to Charles across the room and began my salute to gratitude. With each pause, he translated. I watched Alexander's face to ascertain that Charles was, in fact, translating exactly what I'd written. He was. A silence descended as the words were spoken and the meaning took hold. When we finished there was a moment of quiet, then applause began, escalating and reverberating throughout the room. All had understood and accepted the heart of the message; the spirit of the feast was under way.

The roasted turkeys were brought out by the servers, and the multitude of side dishes crowded the tabletops as the wine was poured and the beer bottles uncapped. Alexander and I sat together, close together, and he served me helpings of this and that. We laughed. We joked. We celebrated our special friendship. Tanya was sitting at a table facing us, smiling and nodding, occasionally glancing in our direction. Jane was beside me on the other side. Seething. Why?

One of the young American teachers was seated next to Alexander. By way of conversation she asked him what had been his job in the army. He told her he was in reconnaissance. She jokingly asked him if he hid behind trees, spying. He lifted his glass in a gesture of acknowledgement and responded, "Yes. It was my job to watch Adair. To always keep her in view." There was laughter at the table. Jane excused herself and went to the other side of the room.

Over dessert, Alexander jostled his Jell-O with his chopsticks, an exercise in refined coordination, and asked me about my plans for the winter break. I turned my head to where Jane had moved, shrugged my incomprehension of why she had done so, and told him that she and I were going on a river trip. He chortled and shook his head. "No, you won't go with her. You'll go home to the United States."

"I have no intention of going home."

"Ah, but you will. I know these things. I know all things. Jane is not your friend...not anymore."

"How do you know that?"

"I just told you. I know all things!" And he chuckled again.

Cameras had been snapping off and on throughout the meal, and when I later received copies of those taken of Alexander and me, I noted on the backs: "The emotions speak for themselves."

Whatever risks were within the society about fraternizing too much with the internationals, especially with me, had been shelved for those hours. Regardless of the fact that the room was filled with the administrative staff, he had allowed himself expression of his inner freedom and had openly enjoyed the company of those at his table.

December, and life was overflowing its cup. Classes with the postgrads increased their numbers from time to time. Angel's schedule finally permitted her to attend on a regular basis, and the postgrads invited colleagues from other universities. Not many. But a few stopped by to participate in our often probing discussions, especially in sociolinguistics. When the topic of women's language came up, I had a room full of female guests!

"I've noticed an interesting phenomenon. Watching television, I've seen quite a number of plays produced in Japan. I've been particularly interested in the one about airline hostesses. Have you seen it?" Nods of affirmation. "Have you noticed the range of the women's vocal scale? Do their high-pitched voices sound like those of prepubescent girls?" Nods of affirmation from the females. Blank stares from the males, turning to scowls. "What is their unspoken message? Why?"

No explanation was ventured, but the eyes of the women twinkled with understanding. Smiles were consciously controlled, but eyebrows spoke volumes. My adored male students were not comfortable. I was thoroughly enjoying their discomfort and grimaced at them. "Tell me, Thomas, why do some women adopt a childlike pitch, especially when speaking in the presence of men?"

"I have no idea, I'm sure."

"Really, now. You don't?"

"None!"

"Hmm. And you, Kevin? Mike? Ray? How about it, Harold?"

Five sets of slanted eyes went to slits. No answers.

"Oh, come now, gentlemen. Is it possible that men find the girlish voice somehow sexually...interesting?"

As a group, "Nonsense."

"I've noticed a contrasting phenomenon that I find at least equally interesting...when I watch the evening news. Have you noticed that Chinese female reporters use a tonal system that is nearly as low and evenly modulated as their male counterparts?"

The female smiles broke into the open. The males denounced me with forced amusement. I laughed aloud.

"There are certain advantages in not understanding one word of what is being said on television. One of those advantages is that I have become attuned to aspects of the broadcasts which may escape those who are focused on the words. Clearly, Chinese women who have gotten themselves into positions of prestige are dropping their tonal systems to be on a par with men. Does that tell us something...something cultural? Does that speak of changes within the society that are subtle; very, very subtle? Are women changing their status? Demanding more serious attention? Tell me, ladies, have you noticed it? And what about university women—students and staff alike? Are you...all of you...consciously and deliberately...dropping your tonal systems?"

Outright laughter. Angel said, "Yes. Yes, we are. That's very perceptive of you."

The men grumbled their discontent. But they'd been outfoxed and they knew it. Their natural humor took over. We continued the discourse, moving from tonal systems to body language, and I entertained them with exaggerated examples of how women use their bodies when in the presence of other women as opposed to when males are present. My charades brought forth peals of laughter so loud that there came a knocking on the door, and Kevin reached over to open it. There stood Charles.

"Oh, excuse me. I thought Alexander was in here."

"Why would you think that, Charles? This is a regular class meeting with the postgrads." A quick afterthought. "Would you care to join us?"

"I'm sorry to have disturbed you. No, thanks. Perhaps another time." And he was gone. Interesting. Had he been hovering outside my door?

Ray missed the next class. And the one after that. Had he been so distressed by the innocuous little lesson? No. Not possible. Probably ill. No one ever missed class. I'd have to ask about his health.

The third day Ray still was not present. "Is he ill?" I asked.

Silence. Then Mike mumbled something that sounded like a yes. A flag went up, and I dropped the question. When the class period was over and we were saying our see-you-laters at the door, they stood a moment too long. It was Harold who finally spoke.

"Ray is leaving the program."

"He's WHAT?"

Kevin: "Ray is withdrawing from the master's program."

"Come back in and sit down. What in the hell are you saying?"

They sat. It was awkward. More than awkward. "Somebody. Say something."

Mike: "Dr. Hathaway humiliated him. In class. In front of us all. She caused him to lose face."

"OK, you guys. Just tell me what happened."

Kevin: "We were discussing Byron. Ray made a comment that Dr. Hathaway didn't like. She glared at him, then...well, she told him it was...stupid."

I waited. Processing. Where does professionalism toward one's colleagues end and loyalty to students begin?

"Has he formally withdrawn yet?"

"No. He'll do so on Monday."

"Tell Ray to come and see me, privately."

"Thank you." And they left.

It took about fifteen minutes before he came tapping on my door. Ray was the smallest of the postgrads, and at this moment he looked tiny.

"Come in and sit down, Ray. We need to do some serious talking."

He sat. Totally wrapped, enclosed within himself. Eyes downcast. Silent.

"I'm not going to ask you what happened. Your friends have already explained it to me. I'm going to tell you what I think. But if you ever, ever repeat what I'm about to say... that will be the end of our friendship. Understood?"

A nod.

"I know you very well. I know how your mind works. I also know Jane Hathaway very well. I know how her mind works. I will tell you that she and I have discussed you before, more than once. Western teachers have a code. Under that code they may discuss their mutual students, usually without names. However, in such a small environment as this one, identities would be easily understood even without names. More importantly, though, they do not discuss a professor with their students; one professional teacher is expected to honor the status of the other. I'm going to break that code.

"Dr. Hathaway is an extraordinarily intellectual scholar in her field. However, she lives in a tight, rigid little world of how things are to be understood and interpreted. She and I have had more than one confrontation concerning the importance of individual interpretation. We are at opposite ends of the spectrum, it seems. Anyway, Ray, you are not inadequate in any way. You have an excellent mind and are an excellent student. What you are planning to do is total self-destructiveness; excuse me, but foolishness. You are now in a win-lose confrontation, and if you do this...if you withdraw from the program, you are handing her the winning ticket. Is that what you want? How will you benefit, personally, from such an action? In the years to come? You may think you will be saving face, but I assure you, my dear friend, you can't take 'face' to the bank...'face' won't feed your wife...your children. Think long-term, Ray. You are preparing yourself for an ever greater position within the educational community. You know how things should be in this country. You will spend your life influencing the elite, the university-educated thinkers and doers of this and future generations. Saving face in this way won't benefit your family, your students, or your society. It is not your highest, best, destiny.

"Think, Ray. Make a different plan of action. I don't know how to advise you about that plan. You'll have to design it. But choose an alternative solution to this problem. Are you hearing me?"

His eyes finally found mine. They were enormous. He nodded, stood and walked to the door, then hesitated.

"Thank you, Adair. With all my heart, I thank you. I'll stay."

As soon as he was out of sight I flew down the stairs to the apartment below. I was furious. Storming. Knocked soundly on Jane's door. I knew she was inside. I could hear her. Knocked again, louder. She didn't answer.

It was the last class period before Christmas and I'd decided to have a discussion with the postgrads on the various forms of love that we each experience in our lives, then have them write a brief composition of comparisons.

"What do we mean by the word 'love'? Whom do we love? How is love different from respect? Affection? Adoration? Worship? And so on. What about sexual love?"

Harold: "Sexual love?"

"Yes...to make love to, or with...your partner or mate."

Mike, laughing: "That's a Western concept, for romantic films. It's a contradiction in terms!"

"A con—tra—dic—tion in terms." Pronounced as though I were a deaf imbecile. They all laughed.

What I had intended as a high-level class analysis into the breadth of human emotions had immediately disintegrated into a discussion of sex. A forbidden subject. How did I always get myself into these predicaments? But their eyes were sparkling. That was what they wanted to talk about. Clearly.

"Ladies and gentlemen, really now. It is not just some Western concept for the benefit of movie audiences. Are you suggesting to me that in the Chinese culture you do not differentiate between some casual five-minute encounter with a near-stranger for sexual release and the emotion-driven, tender intimacy between two who love each other?"

"Of course we differentiate," Mike said. "But both ends of the spectrum you suggest are forms, degrees, of the same act. Sex. Love is an emotion, expressed in its different aspects to different people at different times. Sex is an action—expressed with different degrees of finesse. They are not the same. A person does not 'make like to' or 'make hate to.' No. To 'make love to' is a relatively modern, Western, romanticized concept that has been tied to marriage and fidelity. Check your own literature. When did the concept first come into Western literature?"

"Mike, you are a constant thorn in my side. I don't know when it came into literature. But be assured, I'll check it out!" (I did, and they're right.)

"For now, let's table that point, and please tell me about those different aspects of love that are expressed at different times with different people." And they did, but their conversation became communication between and among themselves. I was the audience, sometimes facilitator. I sat, attentive to them, "loving" to listen to their intra-cultural minds at work. With a half hour or so to the end of the class period, I drew it to closure.

"I'd like you to take the next twenty minutes and write a brief composition for me. Take any one of the aspects you've been discussing and give me an instance, an event that exemplifies that aspect. Your choice."

Pencils and paper appeared and the room became silent.

Julie was the first finished and brought her writing to me. I read her testament of a poignant moment with her mother. She told the event in emotional detail, expressing her depth of sympathy for her mother's decision at a time of family crisis. She ended her composition with the sentence "I wanted to tell her that I loved her, but I couldn't."

I looked up at my dear student and whispered, "Julie, why couldn't you tell her that you loved her?"

"There is no word, no phrase in Chinese that one adult can use with another adult to say 'I love you' in that way."

Again, I was caught off guard. "Excuse me, class. I'm sorry to interrupt your writing, but Julie has just informed me that one adult cannot say to another 'I love you' in certain senses; that Mandarin does not contain that concept."

Kevin: "That's true. We can say that to a child, but to use the same phrase with an adult, well, the adult would think you are...retarded, or something like that...would probably laugh at the usage."

Ray: "Because of the influence of the Western media, our scholars have reached back into classical Mandarin and tried to bring an old phrase that carried a somewhat similar meaning into present-day language. But people haven't really adopted it."

"Please finish up your papers and let me read them over the next few days. You all have given me quite a lot to think about. There's a saying that states that a teacher is taught by her students. That is so true in our class. And I thank you for all you are teaching me. Thomas, you have been very quiet today. Have you no particular thoughts on this subject?"

He looked over at me and smiled. "I'm sorry. My mind is elsewhere. My wife is due to have her baby any day now. I'm going home tonight to be with her. I'll be more attentive when I get back."

"Thomas, be sure to tell her that you love her." And the class laughed.

Christmas Day. Claudia had cooked her specialties and most of us foreigners met in her apartment to enjoy the celebration. I'd gone with Tanya. Jennifer had been invited to her previous university and Jane had not been invited...anywhere. I should have cared, but I didn't. Claudia's apartment was decorated and festive and the food smelled delicious. As I watched her welcoming each guest and performing her duties as a caring hostess, I thought that she and I could have become closer. I knew of her dedication to her students and that she spent time tutoring those who needed special help, and I respected her. But her attentions were engaged by her Chinese friends, and I regretted a missed opportunity. That evening, she and Roger were cozy, and watching the May-December relationship I felt a warmth of remembrance of my time with Victor. But I suspected Roger was a bit embarrassed by her public display. He needn't have been. Tiny, deceptively fragile-looking, and always attractively attired, she presented a lovely, graceful picture. After the meal was finished, Claudia distributed small gifts which she'd taken the time and interest to select for each individual guest. Truly a thoughtful woman.

I was relaxed and happy. But it was to be my last day of unmarred joy for the remainder of my stay in China.

"So, take a look and see what you think." Alexander sat upright and proud, and handed me a most professional-looking, beautifully bound file of the completed and typed translation. He hadn't been in my apartment for five minutes when, as I reached for the file, there was a knock on the door. He answered.

"I have a telephone call. I'll only be a moment."

And a moment was all it took. He returned. His face was pale and the veins in his neck stood out. He was clenching his jaws.

"Alexander, whatever is the matter? What's happened?"

He looked at me and was slow to respond. He opened his mouth to speak, but it seemed his English was gone. He took another moment, then that look of hatred I'd seen that night at the hotel reception desk flooded his eyes. But there was another emotion, also. Fear. Finally, his words began to come, haltingly.

"I've been called...he said that..."

"Who was on the telephone?"

"Charles. Let me put it this way. I've been officially informed that my office is not in your apartment. I've been 'ordered' to report back to the Foreign Affairs office. Immediately!"

He stood. Then sat down again. Then stood. "No. They can't take this away from me. Come on. I'm taking you to dinner." Resolute.

The little restaurant was a couple of alleyways beyond the apartment complex. It was his hideaway, a place he used when he socialized with his own students. Open on one side to the street, it was crowded with young, jabbering Chinese who nodded to him and cleared a tiny table at the back for us.

"Can you tell me what this all means?"

"No. Never mind. I'll take care of it. What is important right now is that you give me permission to submit these translations to the Ministry of Education. We must move along on this project. Time is important."

"Your work is beautiful, very professional-looking. Of course, I can't read a word of it, but I'm sure it's exactly right. You have my unqualified permission to do with it as you see fit."

"Thank you. There may not be much time."

"What do you mean?"

"I mean there may be some temporary delays. There may be some...some small problem which I have to clear up."

"Alexander, are you in trouble? Because of me? Tell me."

"Not because of you. Nothing is your fault. I am a man. I make my own decisions. You, we, have done nothing. Nothing. Don't worry. I'll take care of it. I have great power in this university."

"Then why are you so nervous?"

"I told you. I'll take care of it!"

We had snapped at each other. The first time ever. His tension was increasing. He went to the counter and brought back some fried rice and beer. We ate in silence. He stopped eating and lit one cigarette off the other. He drank my beer and then signaled a student to bring him another bottle. I stopped eating. His tension was making me nauseated. Fifteen, twenty minutes. A half hour. We barely spoke. He had gone off into some other world. Some world that was closed to me. I could watch his transitions. The face that appeared so blank to others had become a road map to me. Rage. Then fear. Then back to rage. He drained the bottle, stood, and dropped some money onto the table. I got up. We walked back to the apartment house in silence.

"It's time." He turned abruptly and strode off toward the Foreign Affairs Office.

"Thank God you're home. Jennifer, something has just happened. I have to talk."

"Come in. What's happened?"

I told her in detail.

"Yes. I've been expecting it. He's too careless. He only thinks he has 'great power.' He has none. No one has that kind of power. Power is in the hands of that party man you met; that small, toothless, smiling party man with his third-grade education has the power. Alexander's being reprimanded. He's in trouble. They can't take *what* away from him? They can take away anything they damn well please. Can take his life. He shouldn't have taken you to the restaurant, shouldn't have delayed. He was being defiant. That was macho-stupid. That won't go well for him. He's in trouble."

"Serious trouble?"

"Is there any other kind?"

"What are they going to do to him? And who are 'they'?"

"*They* are the committee, the party secretary, others in the administration, his colleagues. The authorities. They are probably going to force him to make a confession."

"A confession of what? There's nothing to confess."

"There's plenty. But it wouldn't matter anyway. Once he's on the 'list' it doesn't matter whether there's been an infraction of the rules or not. If he's displeased the authorities, he's guilty. Or, if someone wants to bring him down, he's brought before the committee. They have their ways. Every man is imperfect. Every man has some imperfections. The committee usually starts by some sort of bogus assurance that they're sure the person has only some slight imperfection and that, for the good of the person, and the society, that imperfection should be brought into the light and investigated so that it can be corrected. That it will only be a slight humiliation, for the person's own good. But everybody in the room will know that's bullshit. The committee will interrogate until a point of exhaustion is reached—no matter how long, how many days, weeks, that takes. In the end, the person will confess to anything. Then the confession goes into the file along with the accusations, to become the basis upon which the rest of his life is determined. And then the punishment is decided."

"The file?"

"Yeah. Everybody has a life file. The shitty thing about the file is that it doesn't have to contain even a shred of truth. It can be only unsubstantiated accusations, made by anybody. Anybody who gets a bee up their butt can make a complaint. Maybe somebody who wants to make sure that the person doesn't get a promotion. Then the complaint goes into the file. That file is open only to the authorities. The individual has no right to it. So, you never know for sure exactly what's in your file. And that file controls your life, everything in your life. Everything! That's basically it."

"It sounds like the 'lettre de cachet' before the French revolution, or Orwell's Big Brother, or the friggin' Inquisition."

"Yeah. Precisely."

"And the punishment?"

"Depends. Depends on what the committee is looking for. Depends on the quality of the confession. Depends on the promises the victim makes, I suppose. Maybe depends on whether or not the person will squeal on somebody else. Probably lots of 'depends' enter into the severity of the punishment."

"So that's what he meant that night at the hotel reception desk when he said that people are sent to the 'countryside' for 'rehabilitation,' and that some are killed for little or no reason. What about that rehabilitation? What does it mean?"

"The victim can be sent to some camp to work in the fields, or some menial labor. They stay. Worked to death. Beaten. Whatever is the pleasure of the sadistic bastards in control. No contact with the outside world. Or with their families. No escape."

"How long?"

"They're not told. Until...whenever. A year. A lifetime."

"And the world knows nothing of this."

"Right. Hundred of thousands of them. Millions. Welcome to China. Want a drink?"

Fortunately for me, Jennifer's three years in another Chinese university's law department had made her privy to information the rest of us would probably never acquire. And, she had her ways of getting people to confide in her that would be the envy of many other lawyers.

Grappling. I spent the next four days trying to internalize the information, trying to bring mental order out of emotional chaos. I'd read about the terrors at night, the late-night knock on the door that citizens of Hitler's Germany had experienced, and that were a part of existence in the Soviet Union. I knew about the gulags. I'd read Solzhenitsyn. But those were peripheral. They were words on paper, and the book or article could be closed and put on a shelf. Or they were films on a screen, but the film would end; when the lights came up the theater could be exited. They had not been my reality. Even the night in the village, although cripplingly real at the moment, had been followed by days of normalcy, of happiness. That night's truth had been relegated to the same cubicle in my memory where the closed book and the ended film resided. I couldn't reconcile the smiling faces of my students and the day-to-day business of life around me with Jennifer's words, with what was happening to Alexander in some room—a room that might even be within sight of my windows. I stood looking out those windows at the usual ebb and flow of life below me. The swaying of the ancient trees on the campus. The outlines of the buildings. People going in and out of those buildings. Waving and chatting with one another. Dinging their bicycle bells. Pedestrians stepping out of the way. Those things were clear. Tangible. I watched those things. At the same time I knew that both realities were true. They were coexisting. But how was that possible? How could life appear so ordinary? How could these Chinese people maintain their lives with the appearance of normalcy when such unspeakable horrors were taking place in their midst? Cocoons. They wove cocoons. They had to.

I'd read somewhere that the universe "blinks," like the shutter of a camera. And for me it did blink during those days. And when that shutter opened, my mind would glimpse that other reality and I'd be deluged with abhorrence of the system, with terror for my special friend. But the shutter would close again. Perhaps that is protection. Perhaps we cannot tolerate for the camera's eye to remain open. At least I couldn't. Not yet. And so I waited. Went about my own business. Hoping to appear casual, asked my colleagues if anyone had seen Alexander lately. No one had. Each time the answer came, the shutter opened, and closed. And in the night the opening of the shutter would bolt me to full wakefulness. Then it would close. And so I waited.

The monthly banking day arrived. I went with my friends to the finance office and to the university garages to get the van. Would Alexander be there? I wanted to run, but I didn't. The van arrived and we took our places. No one sat beside the driver. He drove through the campus using the back route and up to the gates that led to the downhill road, then stopped. Alexander was waiting at the security check. He slid the door open and stepped in, taking his place. He did not acknowledge me. Did not acknowledge anyone, but sat staring ahead. His usual presence was replaced by a depth of silence that cast its pall over the passengers. The ride through the city was quiet, with all responding to some ambiance they didn't understand. The walk to the computer office was different from previous walks. Alexander hurried ahead of us and was already performing the paperwork when we arrived. He did not acknowledge me. Nor I him. Back to the van and through the city to the bank, without a word. We took seats on the rows of chairs and he went to the busy counter. Tanya leaned over to me and asked in a whisper what was wrong with Alexander. I shrugged and shook my head.

The only spot he'd been able to crowd into was the angle where the counter met the wall. I sat, staring at his back. My contrived nonchalance left me. I knew I was doing the wrong thing, but couldn't control my actions. I stood and threaded my way through the waiting customers and inched in beside him. He did not turn to me. I let my arm touch his. His muscles were rigid. I spoke only his name. He slid one hand around my arm and gradually tightened his grip. His fingers were gouging into my flesh. He was hurting me. My arm began to throb. He tightened his grip, and again. My arm was aching, the pain shooting through my shoulder and down my back. I nearly cried out, but bit my lip and dug the nails of my other hand into my palm as he again tightened his grip. It felt for the moment like he could crush my bones. His body began to tremble, then shake. He had not looked at me, but stood staring, blindly but with intense focus, at the countertop. His neck muscles were extended and throbbing. He separated his lips slightly and I could hear his breath coming in short spasms. His eyes were wild. Then, abruptly, he released my arm with a gesture of casting it away from him. The pain of the release was greater than when he was gripping it. I stood for only a second longer, then turned and went back to my colleagues. I didn't rub my arm, didn't look at it. And no one had noticed anything, except Jennifer, of course. She was looking at me with a stare that shouted out that I was the biggest damn idiot in the universe. This was to be the last time Alexander accompanied us to do our banking. Thereafter, it would be Charles who went with us.

It was after dinner that night when a visitor came to my apartment. It was the retired dean of the Foreign Language Department. As soon as I saw him I remembered a conversation we'd had on the campus more than two weeks before. Since then, it had escaped my mind. I quickly calculated the date as I invited him in. It was December thirtieth. He had come to remind me that he would be taking Jane, Ruth (the other American foreign expert who was the liaison between her university and ours), and me to an ancient village where the inhabitants had never before seen a Caucasian. He would be around with a car to pick us up at seven the next morning. I scarcely knew Ruth, and to spend three days with Jane would not be comfortable. The trip to the bank had left more bruises than those on my arm. Going on this trip was absolutely the last thing in the world I wanted to do, but I'd agreed to it weeks before—then forgotten it. He'd gone to great inconvenience to arrange this by making two trips ahead of time to prepare everything for our visit. I smiled a false enthusiasm and promised to be ready.

Car ride to the bus station. A four-hour bus ride that was a reenactment of a bad movie about Mexico, then a stop for lunch in a small town where we were followed by throngs of giggling, pointing townsfolk of all ages. The balance of the trip was by...tractor. Well, I guess it would be called a tractor. It was a three-wheeled vehicle. The exposed engine and the driver's seat were on an elongated "neck" with one small wheel protruding in front. Behind the neck was a cart-like contrivance which the driver had equipped with a remnant of carpeting and metal chairs.

This cart was perched over a two-wheel base and there were no springs. There was no covering to protect us from the weather. The roadway on into the village was unpaved, so you can imagine the trip, bouncing along for another three hours at the breakneck speed of about five miles per hour, with the engine spluttering and groaning away. Actually, after the first hour or so, the slow rhythm of the journey became a solace. We were far from all evidence of humanity, the winter's sun was perfect for the occasion, and the low hills through which we were winding eventually made room for an enormous lake—more like an inland sea. The totality became a balm for my troubled soul. Jane and Ruth had formed a twosome and ignored me. My time and attentions were my own, shared only now and then with the gentleness of the dean and his two young female companions who had joined us to assist in any way they could.

We arrived at the site for our night's lodging, a tiny village still another half-hour's ride short of our ultimate destination. We would complete that leg of the journey in the morning. The dean had arranged for our overnight accommodations at a Buddhist temple atop a mountain, and the only access to it was by six hundred irregularly sized and spaced stone steps that wound up the mountainside through a tangle of trees and underbrush. I would venture to say that the last time the steps had been cleared of debris, or repaired, was when the last Buddhist monk had made his way down them, decades (if not centuries) before. It was twilight when we began the climb. The dean had brought one flashlight and led the way. It was to take the better part of an hour, with periodic rest stops to gasp for breath, before we reached the summit.

The temple was on three terraced levels, the lowest being the monks' cells of earlier times, which we were to choose from—individually. There were two levels above consisting of a series of three-sided altars, behind which were grotesque statues of devils and garishly painted gods; the fourth side open to the vista of the lake. Strings of various colored Christmas tree lights gave off a dim illumination. Off to the side was a building which housed the dining and kitchen areas, and the recent addition of a generator for electricity. A common squatter was situated some steps back down the hillside, judiciously placed to diminish the odors which wafted back up the mountain.

Several villagers were eagerly awaiting us and directed us to our cells, waited while we chose, then took us to the dining area where a grand dinner had been prepared for us. After dining, we declared our fatigue and excused ourselves to our rooms. Jane and Ruth had chosen rooms next to each other at the far end of the row. I'd chosen one in the center. I wanted the solitude.

When all was quiet and settled, I opened the door of my cell and stepped out onto the stone walkway. From this angle I could look out through the treetops to the lake beyond. The moon was brilliant, reflecting off the mirror-smooth water. On the lake a scattering of small lights shone slightly, indicating only the faintest outlines of the boats. I stood for long minutes inhaling the solitude, the atmosphere, allowing my mind to take in the thousand-year history, to envision the orange-clad monks in their daily rituals, to hear the drone of their chanted prayers.

And I thought of those prayers and wondered. What had they all come to? Could they even have imagined what terrors and horrors would infest their land in these days? No, of course not. There had been terrors and horrors enough in their own time. Perhaps Buddhistic prayers dealt with something other than relief from man's torturous ways against his fellows. Perhaps so, and I recalled the reading I'd done so many years ago. Readings which I'd not fully understood. Readings about merging one's soul with the endless, timeless flow of the river of life. About nonattachment to the vagaries of temporal human existence.

I walked slowly along the passageway and found the broad steps leading up to the altars. Paused before one and then another. Behind one altar was a statue of a woman, or so it seemed. On the low railing were a few nearly spent candles, a thin cup-like vase holding some incense sticks, and a covered jar which I opened to find a few matches. Beside the incense sticks was a deep tray of sand. I removed one stick, struck a match and lighted both a candle and the incense. I then knelt before the railing and ran my fingers along the smooth wooden surface, grooved from centuries of folded hands. I sensed a calmness which seemed to pass from the railing into my fingers, and I folded my hands in repose. The tiny stream of smoke from the incense stick wended upward in an almost unwavering straight line in the stillness of the late night. I breathed deeply of its aroma. Neither did the candle flicker, but its minuscule flame burned steadily. I raised my eyes to the statue, not knowing who she was or what she represented. I then bent my forehead to my folded hands and allowed the thousand years of prayer to blend into my being. I remained in that attitude emptying my thoughts of all tribulations and easing into a cosmos I didn't know. A peace I'd not experienced before settled within me. And it was in that posture and in that state of being-ness and nonbeing-ness that 1988 folded back into history and 1989 was born.

The early morning sun had brought the birdsong and I awakened on my narrow cot to hear the sound of music from some distant radio. It was so far away that the melody was scarcely audible. I reached over and pushed open the window to permit the somehow familiar strains to enter my cell. I leaned back in my blankets and listened as the music infused my tiny room; Barbra Streisand united time and space as she sang "The Way We Were," and my thoughts went to Alexander, and my tears came.

The jostling, noisy tractor crested a low hill and we could see that the roadway before us was lined with the villagers, and with their dogs, their goats, their chickens. Their entire world was awaiting our arrival. They stared as we approached and then a few timid hands found the air above them. We waved in return and their vigor increased as they added their cheers. The driver pulled to a stop in front of what was the newest and largest of the assemblage of tall, narrow homes. The dean jumped down and shook hands with our host, then turned to give each of us a hand down to the ground. Jane and Ruth were introduced first. Each smiled and shook hands. Standing beside our host was a woman no more than maybe four and a half feet tall and close to a hundred years old. She was dressed in the traditional blue quilted garb seen in pictures of the ancient ones of China. She was being supported on one side by a young woman. I realized at once that she must be the grandmother, or more likely great-grandmother, of our host. My handshake with our host was respectful, but brief, and I moved to the woman's side.

"Good morning, madam," I murmured. Her face turned up to me and I could see that her eyes were sightless. The woman said something, and the young lady supporting her said to me in English that the ancient one was blind, but wished she could see the American woman. I reached out and took her hands in mine. They were the texture of leather and gnarled from arthritis. I moved closer to her and held her hands to my face so that she might see with her fingertips, then I wrapped her in my arms. She slid her arms around me and we clung together, and began rocking back and forth. Her chuckling commenced from the depths of her great, ageless soul and we held each other as our laughter rose, and swayed together, bridging years and cultures in an expression of love.

The day in that village was a miracle writ in peace. The finest chefs from the surrounding territory had been brought in to prepare not one but two feasts for the foreigners. In between the meals, the villagers escorted us up a lesser hillside, stepping across rivulets of water trickling down the eroded slope, and circling around through the jumble of boulders. Our climb brought us to another Buddhist temple. A young lad had run on ahead, and as we approached the temple a series of firecrackers began exploding, popping the air with sound and smoke. The dean told us that it was proper to announce our arrival to the gods of the temple in such a greeting...so that the gods could prepare the aura of the temple to welcome us to their abode.

This temple was enclosed with a series of wooden stairs leading from one altar area to another. The handrails of the staircases were nearly black from age and worn smooth. They felt like satin under my hands. This temple was well tended by the women of the village, and was still used by a few of the eldest ones. I again lit an incense stick and candle, but did not kneel at the railing.

When the last meal of the day had ended and all the talking drew to a close, we went back to our tractor and took our places. As the driver pulled away from the village, the people followed us to where the roadway began its ascent. Then they stood and waved until we had again crested the hill.

We returned to our temple from the night before and climbed the six hundred stone steps. But this time my soul was light and the trip up to the mountaintop was effortless. From the vantage point in front of my cell, I again looked out over the quiet lake and thought, *a pocket of sanity within an insane world.*

"Have you got a few minutes? I need to talk to you." Angel had waited while the other postgrads left for the day.

"Sure." I closed the door and we sat together on the sofa. "What's wrong, Angel? You've been quiet today, and withdrawn."

"It's Alexander." She paused, selecting the proper phrases. "I don't know if you know about what happens here in China to people who...well, to people who fall into disfavor."

It had been a week since that day at the bank, and neither I nor any of my colleagues had seen Alexander. I desperately wanted to know about him, but also wanted to appear as innocent as possible. "You mean about the committees and the confessions?" She nodded. "Jennifer has told me. Alexander was called before the committee, wasn't he?"

"How did you know?"

I told her about the telephone call he'd received and about having to report immediately to the Foreign Affairs Office, and all that had transpired. "Has he told you what happened? What they asked him?"

"No. Not exactly. He wouldn't do that. He did have to go. But he wouldn't tell them anything they wanted to know. All he said to me was that they couldn't get him so easily. He just laughed when he told me that. Laughed and said that they hadn't been able to break him."

"So, it's over, then, for him?" I wanted my question to sound innocuous, but what he had reported to her didn't jibe with the episode in the bank. Why had he been so rough with me?

"No. I don't think so. I think he's going to have to go again. I think that...somebody is trying to get something more against him to take back to the committee."

"You mean Charles?"

Her reaction was quick. "How did you know that?"

"I'm not sure. I just don't trust him."

"Yes, Charles. But I don't think it was so easy for Alexander as he pretended to me. He's changed. He's angry, or maybe frightened. I don't know. He doesn't talk to anybody. He just goes to his office, then to his room. He's not acting right."

"But he talked to you."

"Only for a minute. He's always talked to me, and I to him. We tell each other...things. He's been my best friend. And I think I'm his, maybe his only friend. He treats me as though I were his own daughter."

"So, you don't know any details."

"Not from him. But I do know one. I know that somebody saw you talking with him on campus and that you were late to class the day the dean came to observe you." She was referring to the current dean, not the retired dean who took us to the village. "The dean was very angry about that. That was reported back to a Friday afternoon meeting. I heard it myself. It was said that the two of you were standing too close together and talking in an intimate way."

"Yes. That did happen, although I wouldn't say we were being all that intimate with each other. When I realized how late I was, I hurried to my class, but the students had left. I met the senior teacher on the stairs and she told me about the dean's visit."

"That may have been discussed with the committee, I don't know for sure. But Adair, I'm worried about him. He's acting too strange. I'm afraid for him. He's worked so hard here. He's the only one who knows what he's doing. He's organized with his work and he is the one who keeps things running as smoothly as they do. The others postpone everything and they make mistakes. He's always on time with the Foreign Affairs business, and he doesn't make mistakes. He corrects those that the others make.

And he's had such a hard life. The way he was born and brought up. And his marriage. Everything has been so difficult for him."

"He told me something about his marriage. But I don't know about his birth and his early years."

"Oh, well, he was born in a prison. His mother was in prison. And then he was taken away from her and put with some other family and was lost from his mother for several years. He doesn't even know how old he is. Somewhere in his mid-forties. Not for certain."

"Why was his mother in prison?"

"For no reason." Angel shrugged and gave a short laugh. "Why do they put anybody in prison? They don't need a reason. But it probably had something more to do with his father. I don't know exactly. But it was terrible for him. Those early years. And he remembers it. He's had a very sad life. And he's such a good and honorable man. I'm afraid for him."

"I'm so sorry. I'm so sorry because I'm afraid he may be in trouble because of me. This is my fault, isn't it?"

"No, no. You mustn't think that. I know that he thinks of you as a special friend. Whatever happens, you are important to him. Whatever he does, it's him that does it. He knows the rules. He wouldn't want you to blame yourself. Of that, I'm sure."

"Is there anything...anything at all that I can do to help?"

"No! You mustn't do anything. This is China. It is the way things are done here. You mustn't interfere. You would only make things worse for him. I just wanted... needed to talk to you. Maybe I shouldn't have, but I—"

"It's OK, Angel. You've done the right thing. We each need the other to talk to. Don't worry. I won't do or say anything. I promise you that."

"Thank you. This is a terrible place to live. Terrible. I wish I could leave. I wish I could go to America."

(How many times had I heard that plea spoken before? How many times would I hear it in the future? But for Angel, her day would come. Eventually. And I would be able to help her, a bit.)

She had been gone from my apartment for only a few moments when I received another, quite unexpected visitor. It was Jane. Although we'd gone on the same trip to the village, we had scarcely acknowledged one another. I hadn't really spoken to her since the afternoon that I'd gone thundering to her apartment to discuss Ray—and she'd refused to answer the door.

"Adair, I think we need to resolve this situation. We have made plans to travel on the winter break, and we need to...what's the matter? Are you ill?"

My mind was filled with the sorrow and pain of Angel's visit and perhaps I did look pale.

"No, Jane, I'm not ill. I've just had a distressing conversation with Angel and I'm feeling...sad."

"It probably has to do with Alexander! Right? Always Alexander!" Her eyes glazed over. "I'm not interested in anything you have to say about him. I don't want to get involved in any way in your relationship with him. You made your choice. You live with it!"

"Made my choice? What do you mean, made my choice?" I'm sure my tone was brittle.

"You should know what I mean. You're an adult woman. You chose Alexander over me." Her turn was abrupt and her departure in anger.

Her meaning stunned me. But it was so foreign to my experience that I dismissed it at once. I'd known many gay men in my life. Some had been close friends. But I'd never, to my knowledge, met a lesbian and didn't, or couldn't, recognize the signals. I rejected my interpretation of her words. There was not enough space left inside me to give it thoughtful consideration.

I walked down the hall to find Jennifer. When I'd told Angel that I wouldn't say anything, that didn't include talking to my American friend. She was my sounding board. My strength. I relied on her professional adherence to the laws of privileged communication, although she was not, legally, my attorney. But still and all, I relied on her discretion. She asked me in and shared her dinner of noodles with me while I related Angel's conversation. She nodded in understanding; it was as expected, and yes, he probably would be dragged back to the committee.

"By the way," I said, "Jane just came by. I'm not too sure what she intended, but we'd planned to travel together and she wanted to talk about it. I don't know if she wanted to make 'final arrangements' or to cancel. It didn't get that far. But never mind; I sure won't be traveling with her."

"That's hardly a surprise. What are you going to do for the month? Want to go with me?"

"Thanks, no. I'll go home and see my family." Then I laughed at the sudden recollection. "It's just as Alexander predicted at Thanksgiving dinner. How in the world did he know? Know something, Jennifer? Speaking of predictions...I have the strongest feeling that something is going to happen. Since November, I've had this feeling."

"What do you mean?"

"Something. Strange. Maybe...but I think there's going to be a revolution in China. And I think it's soon."

"Hmm. Wishful thinking, my friend. Wishful thinking."

It was the last meeting with my postgrads before winter break and Thomas had just returned from his village. His face and attitude were as remote as his home. We didn't even try to have class, but I poured tea and offered some pastries.

"Thomas, is something wrong? Is your wife OK? Your baby? What did she have, boy or girl?"

He sucked his tea through his teeth, straining the leaves, the standard method of consuming that liquid. He didn't look up.

"Thomas?"

He didn't answer.

Kevin spoke. "The baby died, Adair."

"Oh, Thomas. I am so sorry. What was the matter?"

He didn't answer.

Mike: "The baby was two weeks old when it died. Thomas buried it."

"Thomas buried it? How is that possible?"

Mike: "He did it himself. He wrapped the baby in a blanket and put it in a small box. Then he took it up to the top of a mountain and dug a small grave under the snow. And he buried it. He did it all alone."

I looked over at my dear student, this young man who'd been so delighted over the anticipated birth of his first child. His eyes came up to meet mine.

"The doctor said my wife had smothered it with too many blankets. Because it was so cold in our home. The doctor said it was my wife's fault. That we were too young to take responsibility for having a baby."

"Did she have the baby wrapped in too many blankets, Thomas?"

"No. Of course not. The doctor just said that because he didn't know what else to say. He didn't know why the baby died."

"I'm not a doctor, but I do know that babies die for what seems to be no reason. It's called Sudden Infant Death Syndrome. Doctors in American are studying this. They're trying to understand why babies die for no reason. Of course, I don't know, Thomas, but I think it would be better for you, and for your wife, to try to believe that whatever happened to your baby was...natural, in a sense. That it was not your fault. Or her fault. It just happened. I am deeply moved by what you did, Thomas. To bury your own baby, alone, on that mountaintop. Deeply moved. You are a very special man. Very, very special."

The slightest smile touched his lips. "Do you really think so?"

"Yes. I really think so."

Two days later I boarded a plane for my winter break in Davis, California.

U.S.A. – SECOND RETURN

There's really not a lot to tell you about this vacation, except that it is always therapeutic to come home. My family listened with incredulity to my tales, expressed their sympathy, and did their best to relieve my anguish. The familiarity of my own culture soon dimmed the ignominious actions of the Communist regime on the other side of the planet. Before the month was over, my consciousness was able to temporarily relegate that police state to the mental niche reserved for closed books and ended films.

Two bits of business were put in motion. I investigated the possibility of extending my yearlong leave of absence from Nevada, was denied that, and inquired about taking early retirement. The finance office calculated the amount I would receive and came back with a figure that was little more than a joke. Oh, well, minuscule as it was, at least it was something, and I requested the paperwork. Of importance, though, was my connection with my mentor teacher and friend at Northern Arizona University. When I told her of the efforts being made to test for differences in thinking from one language to another, she recommended a couple of names that might be interested in such research. I sent off the appropriate letters.

I changed my routing to reenter China. Hong Kong was my last reality check before descending into a maelstrom that would never again be banished to the backwaters of my mind.

CHINA – SECOND TRIP

*To all those courageous young students
who lost their lives during the Tiananmen Square Massacre,
I salute you.
You died according to your dream – as free men and women.*

The day after my arrival, a student whom I didn't know met me on the staircase in the apartment complex. He withdrew from a pocket a folded envelope. I thanked him, and he hurried back down the steps. I read the enclosed note. It was from Alexander, and he stated only that he thought we might be able to meet later to renew our friendship. I felt a sense of relief, thinking that whatever had transpired had been resolved—as he had said—through his own power. I accepted that my tension, and Jennifer's and Angel's, had been out of proportion. It had been melodrama brought on by the fatigue of a long and busy semester. I waited with heightened spirits for him to come by, or to contact me. I didn't mention the note to anyone. But the days passed and there was no further communiqué.

On banking day in February I added a major entry onto my life's list of witless accomplishments. Jennifer and I were standing at the university garage area waiting for the van. Charles was nearby, chatting with several of the drivers, arranging who would drive us that day. He selected one and they came toward us. He introduced the driver, who smiled and spoke to Charles in their native language. Charles wheeled abruptly and his face reflected glee—more than glee. But his expression didn't instantly register. "The driver says he knows you, Adair. How does he know you?"

"Yes," I said, and stuck out my hand to shake hands with him. "He was our driver when we went to the (undisclosed) village."

Charles: "And when did you go to (undisclosed)? Who took you?"

I froze. Simultaneously the driver realized the error; what could be a deadly mistake. He took a backward step. Paralyzed, my world stopped. Charles' smile became grotesque. I couldn't recover.

"Charles, I've been as patient about the rewrite of my contract as long as I intend to be. You've promised for two months that my retroactive salary adjustment would be in place after the winter break, and as usual, nothing has been done. Now, I want to know just exactly when you are planning." Jennifer's tone of voice was cold, angry, loud, and professional. He was caught off guard. She'd done it. She'd save the moment. How much more had she saved?

February and March initiated new contacts and activities. Several of the students from my other classes started inviting me to their homes to meet their parents and to enjoy family dinners. The winter's cold and gloomy days were brightened when some of those parents began inviting me to the public dances which, unbeknownst to me up to that time, were held often and regularly. Disco dancing. It seemed incongruous to me at first, and my popularity on the crowded dance floor was a welcome surprise. Everyone wanted to dance with the American. I think I must have twirled and jiggled with half the population of the city. Other social outings were arranged, and I went with families to fashion shows and theatrical presentations, to see the Chinese acrobats who have developed their skill to an art form. And to meals, whether in private homes or in restaurants, which were opportunities to communicate with the adult, usually professional citizens of the city. My circle widened as those dinners began to include family friends and other relatives. I was going here and there two, sometimes three times each week. As I looked back on it later, it was as though I were being granted an accumulating storehouse of pleasure to serve as a cushion against which the events that were to come could be measured.

During those weeks I didn't see or hear from Alexander. No one saw him, except at a distance perhaps, riding his bicycle far across the campus. I questioned Angel, but her response was that he seemed to have "gone into hiding." It wasn't only Alexander, though; there was something else that was disturbing me. I couldn't really identify it, but despite all the social activities with my students and their families, the deepening friendships with Tanya and Jennifer, and the successes with my classes, there was a feeling of dis-ease within. It was like wearing clothes that don't quite fit. I mentioned it to Jennifer. She laughed it off with, "You've just got the hots for Alexander. Forget him. If he wanted to see you, he'd find a way." My friendship with her had matured to the place where honesty lives. Maybe she was right. Anyway, she was busy with her classes and with a stream of students from both our university and her previous one, traipsing in and out of her apartment, each with his or her own dilemmas and each believing Jennifer could solve all problems.

It was at the end of March that Charles came to my apartment. I was immediately wary. His smile and greeting were, as always, too effusive.

"What can I do for you, Charles?" I hadn't invited him in.

"How would you like to be a television star?"

"Excuse me?"

"A television star. I'm here to offer you a great opportunity."

"Right. One career is all I can handle. Being a TV star is best left for my next life."

Gushing laughter. "May I come in? I'm serious. Well, actually, I want to ask your help with a television program."

I stood aside as he entered, brushed a bit too close to me, and sat without being invited. I remained standing.

"All the universities and institutes in the city have been requested to put on a television skit as a celebration of education in China. I've been thinking about what we can do, and since Alexander has told everyone how capable you are, repeatedly, I decided you would be the perfect person to organize something for us. You have the right...

energy...to produce something exciting for us." He was sitting on the edge of the sofa, with one hand in his pants pocket. As he said "something exciting," he wiggled his concealed fingers, suggesting a moving penis, and laughed again. I was not only repulsed, but instantly alert to possible chicanery. "You are exciting, aren't you? It's common knowledge."

"Knock it off, Charles. I don't think I have any time or interest in your television program." I hadn't sat and now moved to the door.

"Oh, come on. I'm only making a joke. An American joke."

"Perhaps you've misunderstood American humor, Charles."

"I apologize. Would you please write up a skit which incorporates as many of the foreign experts and teachers as possible, and have it ready in a week."

His tone had changed, his expression was cloaked; not quite menacing...but suggestive of an order. I didn't know what was going on.

"I'll think about it. Now, if you'll excuse me, I have classes to prepare."

Mulled it over. What did he mean that Alexander had spoken of me "repeatedly"? When had he done that? What had he said? Or was it a trick? How was this request connected to him? Or was it? Just in case, I'd better do it.

That evening, I picked up my pencil and created a brief skit adapting the spirit of American cheerleaders to our university. Spent a couple of hours refining it and went to Tanya's apartment. With her natural theatrical flair she'd be my "star." She was delighted with the offer, and over the next days I was able to recruit all the young teachers as well as Claudia and Roger. The French couple and the Russian men were not interested, and Jane—when I finally approached her—informed me that she had no interest in my "cheerleaders" skit, but had prepared one of her own, on Shakespeare sonnets, more in keeping with the status and quality of university education. *Well, the television audience will love that. Are you going to translate it all?* I withdrew my proffered script with a jerk and she slammed her door; two warring junior high schoolgirls. We were both ridiculous.

We were able to rehearse only a couple of times, then were taken to the television studio where we videotaped our "rah-rah" scenario to enthusiastic applause. (Jane's segment was cut from the actual airing of the program, but I won't be small enough to mention that.)

The program was shown the next evening, and the following morning I accidentally met Alexander in the busy foyer of the apartment building. Or was he waiting around for me? No one had seen him in our building for weeks. He congratulated me. I asked why he hadn't been able to meet with me as his note suggested. He laughed a practiced laugh and said that his office was keeping him very busy these days, and that he was no longer in charge of the foreign experts. I had to read behind his laugh. *He'd been stripped of his position! What else had they done, or threatened to do to him?* He then lowered his voice and commented, "But I will always take care of you, Adair. I never neglect my special friends. You will see."

"Alexander, Charles told me that you spoke of me often in the office. Is that true?" I needed to know how much of a role I had in these troubles. I suspected I was the cause.

Again the practiced laugh. "That was before. I'm afraid I may have been too...talkative about your project. I may have spoken of you in a way that I shouldn't have. I may have said too much. But those were different times. It is better not to...if you need anything, just ask Angel." The meager conversation was fast and slow, and over. As he walked away, I knew how much I cared about this man. More than I wanted to. His tone and attitude had been, at the same time, detached and intimate. And there had been yearning. I wanted to hold him and bury my head on his shoulder and comfort him, and receive comfort from him. And cry. My guilt was eating away at me. I wanted to do something...anything. Impotence. There was nowhere to turn.

Two nights later I was walking along the hallway between my apartment and Jennifer's. The lighting for the passageway had been turned off, except for the two tiny exit bulbs at either end. As I passed by the small meeting room opposite the telephone booth I caught sight of Alexander, sitting inside that room, near the door, in the dark. There was no one else around. I paused at the open entry and whispered his name. He leaped to his feet and faced me with eyes red-rimmed and wild.

"What do you want of me?"

"I want nothing. I saw you sitting here, and...what's wrong, Alexander? Talk to me."

"Nothing is wrong. Leave me alone. Don't talk to me. Don't come near to me. Just leave me alone!" He pushed me out the doorway and fled down the stairs. Why had he been sitting there, in my building? On the fifth floor? What did he expect?

On two occasions during that period, I'd left a Post-it note on my door when I'd gone to visit one or another of my colleagues during the evening, notifying anyone who came by of my whereabouts. On both occasions I returned to find the Post-it removed. I searched, thinking it had fallen. It hadn't. I asked everyone I could think of if he or she had come to my apartment while I was gone. None had. At two o'clock one morning I heard a tapping on my door. By the time I roused myself sufficiently to answer, whoever it was had gone. It came again the next night. Again, I was too slow to answer. That was the last time. The date was well into April.

For clarity, the following will be in a modified journal format.

April 15. Spring was bringing buds to the trees and flowers were peeping up everywhere. Tanya and I decided to enjoy the new warming sun and take a stroll downtown, maybe do some shopping. As we walked the city, we noticed people congregating in front of the shops which displayed television sets; all sets were tuned to the same program. We paused here and there to try to catch a glimpse of what it was that everyone was watching. The mood of the populace seemed—subdued. The program was showing what appeared to be a procession of some kind with large wreaths of flowers. Tanya said she thought it was a funeral. Probably a large one, to be televised like this. Maybe some important dignitary had died.

It was the beginning; spring, 1989.

April 22. "Who was Hu Yaobang and what's going on?"

The postgrads were sitting in my living room, distracted. They looked from one to the other. It was Kevin who opened up first. "He was formerly the general secretary of the party and had become a great favorite with the intelligentsia. He was outspoken about the conditions in our government. He had fallen into disfavor, but recently had been back in favor again. Some liberals looked to him for leadership."

Mike: "He criticized the corruption and hypocrisy in Beijing. He criticized the nepotism and the Swiss bank accounts and the family members who live abroad. He called for an accounting."

Ray: "He spoke aloud the truths that we all know. He was a brave man whom we all admired greatly."

"But what is going on?" I asked. "There seems to be... unrest, on the campus. And what about those posters near the gates? What do they say?"

Harold: "They are notices that the students want to organize to honor the memory of Hu. They are announcements of where and when to meet to hold a memorial for him."

Thomas: "The students are going to have a meeting in the downtown square later today."

Kevin: "We've heard that university students in Beijing are holding a memorial in Tiananmen Square. There are thousands of students beginning to mass there. Universities all over China will be doing the same. Students are bonding together over this."

"He must have commanded enormous respect for the whole country to come together for him in this way. Are you all going downtown?"

Julie: "Not the whole country. There were a lot of people in the government who were afraid of him. Who wanted to silence him. We haven't decided, yet, whether or not to go downtown. There is much to consider. Mostly, it will probably be the undergraduates who will go."

The postgrads didn't go and neither did I. There was no reason why I should. I didn't really understand their unrest and I wouldn't understand anything that would be said. Standing by my windows at about noon, I could see the students beginning to leave the campus. Bicycles by the hundreds were wheeling out onto the main thoroughfare. Among the cyclists I noticed Jennifer with several of her students, and Roger. I went to Tanya's apartment.

"They shouldn't be doing this. They are foolish children. They should be in their classes." She poured the coffee and offered chocolates.

"It's only a memorial, to salute a dead hero. I think it's a tribute out of respect for this man. They need to express their sorrow over his death. They need to go through closure for him. I admire what they're doing."

"You're an American. You Americans don't know about these things. They are foolish, foolish children."

"Tanya, don't overdramatize. They'll all be in their classes tomorrow. Let them have this afternoon."

"I can only hope you're right. But I know more about these things. It is not wise for so many people to hold public meetings. Especially students. The security police get nervous."

"They'll be fine. Stop worrying."

The official memorial service for Hu Yaobang was held in Beijing. Three student representatives requested a meeting with Premier Li Peng. The students had drawn up a petition and they knelt on the steps of the Great Hall. There were 100,000 students gathered in Tiananmen Square. Li Peng did not respond. Minor officials offered to take the petition to him. The students refused.

April 23. My sixth-floor classrooms had a number of absences. Those in attendance told me that their classmates were "tired" from having stayed up late the previous night. And the next day, and the next. Over those days the number of students dwindled. The postgrads missed no sessions. I talked to Jennifer and to Tanya. Their classes were the same. Each time I walked past the gates to the university, there were more and larger notices posted.

"What do the posters say?" I asked my postgrads.

"They're telling the students to stop going to the square and to return to classes."

"Are they still commemorating the death of Hu?"

"No. It's become more than that. A group of students in Beijing want to continue the work he had begun. They want the government to make some serious changes. They're congregating in Tiananmen Square and have asked the government to listen to their pleas for greater accountability by the officials. Their pleas have been ignored."

The postgrads were unconcerned, or so it seemed. They were again bringing a few of their colleagues from nearby universities and institutes. Not many. Sometimes two or three, often only one. But they came. We continued our classes.

April 27. Students from all the major educational institutions in Beijing march to Tiananmen Square to support their peers' strike.

May 14. Student representatives are promised a broadcast forum for their grievances. That does not materialize.
May 15. Russian President Gorbachev arrives in Beijing. The planned reception in Tiananmen Square is cancelled.

May 17. The dwindling numbers in my classes suddenly went to zero. As I entered the campus area early that morning the absence of students was eerie. There were a few teachers walking with their heads down, and other adults standing about, talking quietly. I climbed, alone, to the sixth floor and pushed open the door to an empty classroom. Then went back home.

"Jennifer, what in the hell is going on?"

"The students in Beijing have given a list of grievances they want addressed by the government. They have been ignored. They were actually kneeling on the steps of the Great Hall, pleading to talk directly to Li Peng. He refused to acknowledge them. They are on strike from their universities, waiting in Tiananmen Square for someone to acknowledge them, to receive their list. But no one will respond to them. They are demanding attention. There are hundreds upon hundreds of thousands of them in the Square."

"What does that have to do with our students? Are our kids striking in sympathy?"

"Not only ours. It's going on all over the country. This is getting serious. Do you want to go to the square with me today? You should see it. The square is filled with kids every day and every evening. They're making speeches and demanding that the government address the grievances. They want an end to the repressions. It's becoming a movement. A students' movement toward freedom and democracy. It's all being reported on the Voice of America. Haven't you been listening?"

I began to smile, nodding: No, I hadn't been listening to the VOA, but I would from now on. And yes, I was listening to her. I was listening to myself. *There's going to be a revolution.* I'd sensed it since November. *Thank God! Finally, people are going to rebel against these atrocities.* My mind flipped back to being in the student demonstrations and protest marches of the Vietnam era, and I was charged with the memory of the impact we'd had. *And I'm going to be here to see it. Yes!*

"Today it's going to be more than before. Not just kids jumping on their bikes. They're getting organized. Get your camera and come on."

We hurried downstairs to the street corner. The sight was staggering. The usual populace of cyclists was still on the streets, but riding along off to the sides. These were not the students. There were no trucks or cars. Instead, across the boulevard on the narrower of the two intersecting streets, the entire student body of our neighboring institute was grouping into marching formation. Down to the left, on the slight downward slope, the boulevard was blocked against all traffic as another institute was organizing itself in the same way. Up to the right our own students, by the thousands, were forming up by class level. The freshmen were in the foreground, carrying a nearly street-wide banner identifying themselves, standing fifteen, maybe more, abreast. Behind them were the sophomores with their banner, and so on, back through the seniors.

Townspeople lined the streets, waiting and watching. The atmosphere was riveting, excitement compounding as the students ordered and reordered their lines, yelling at each other. Organized pandemonium. "Good God! Look at this! Jennifer! Look at this!" My blood began to pump, and I caught her hand and dragged her behind me across the boulevard, dodging others who were jockeying for position, edging my way to where I saw a few of my junior-class students standing on the sidelines.

Bicycle-driven carts moved into position in front of the massed marchers of each institute and their mounted loudspeakers began to blast with music. The low rumble of deep male voices from the institute down the hill grabbed attention and the chant was picked up by the crowd of students waiting on the side street. The rumble escalated as female voices joined in. The noise grew and the institute below us began to move. With their banners stretched wide, the marchers on the side street swung out into the boulevard and shifted into position behind them. Two carts carrying massive drums came through our gates, positioning themselves on either side of our cart with our loudspeakers. The drum beats began, shaking the very earth, and our own students erupted into the chant as their lines began to move. Waves of thousands of students were on the march as the drums beat and the music blared. I whipped out my camera, at the same time grabbing the shoulders of two of my students standing beside me. "Why aren't you in the lines?" I shouted to make myself heard. They looked at me and began to laugh. "Get into those lines! I'll give you all an A if you get into those lines!" I shoved them into the street. They ran to join their classmates as others who also had been standing and watching merged with them, picking up the chant, yelling and running toward their places in the lines. A cadence was established and the students' faces were dripping sweat in the hot midday sun, and wild with the frenzy of belief in their own power, of impending change, of coming freedoms. Their courageous colleagues in Beijing were standing up to the government. Demanding rights. Students by the millions across China were marching in support of those colleagues in Beijing. They knew what they were doing. They believed in themselves, as we had believed in ourselves. And so the lines moved.

As the seniors passed by the depth of their sound hurt the ears. Behind them, the lineup of hundreds of waiting bicyclers began to jam forward. Jennifer yelled at me that she was going to get her bike and dashed into the melee. I tried to move across also, but was stopped by throngs of cyclists. I saw my postgrads standing on the corner and waved at them. Harold suddenly appeared out of the free-for-all, on his bicycle. "Want to go downtown? Get on." Without a thought, I side-saddled behind him and caught hold of him around the waist. He inched into the crazed traffic, and as we rode slowly by the postgrads I pretended to check my watch, yelling at them, "Not today! Not today!" They waved me on, heads thrown back in laughter.

The cyclists moved into lines on either side of the marching, chanting students and Harold maneuvered his bicycle into the wheeling stream. The bikers picked up speed, and as Harold and I rode by our own university students they saw us and interrupted their chant, yelling, "Adair! Adair! Adair!" I saluted them, laughing and giving a thumbs-up, shouting, "Go! Go! Go!" We cycled on by, passing both institutes, and on in front of them to thousands more students marching university by university. As Harold wheeled by, students I didn't know saw us and started their own chant, "U.S.A.! U.S.A.!" And I waved at them as the lines surged forward in rhythm, the music blaring and the drums beating. We cycled along, fifteen, twenty, thirty minutes of marching students, striding forward, filling the width and length of the boulevard. Townspeople congested the sidewalks to watch in disbelief. We rounded a wide curve and I could see the square ahead, thronged with thousands more students with their banners flying high, pennants tied to pedestrian overpasses, tied to overhead wires, waving from the swinging arms of still more students who had climbed into the trees and up the light poles. The noise was off the decibel scale. Harold slowed; a policeman was waving him to a stop. They exchanged a few motions and Harold told me we couldn't ride double. I slid off and walked beside my student until we were out of sight of the police. Harold gestured for me to get back on, and I did. We rode on toward the square. He looked for an inch to park his bike, shoved a couple of others a trifle and wedged his in, flipping the lock on the rear wheel. He pushed me in front of him, hands navigating me through the unbelievable mobs of students. It was more than a block to the bleachers where I'd first met Jennifer on the day of that other parade. He was steering me in that direction. The bleachers were packed, but he spotted Jennifer on some grass at the base of a speaker's platform and guided me toward her.

She pointed to the bleachers and eventually I saw Claudia and Roger sitting together. Some man was leaning over them, speaking to them. I didn't know who he was. I tried to ask Jennifer, but the crowd around us and the noise were too great. Some students were on the speaker's platform, testing the squawking sound equipment. One of them began to speak. As his words boomed out over the massive audience his tone grew impassioned, and the thousands of students quieted to hear his words. From time to time there was an earsplitting shout, then the cries subsided and the speaker continued. The energy level vibrated the air around us as the students responded to the speaker. Then another took his place. And another. Each was greeted with cheers of joy. The square rang with exuberance. With the vitality of life. With hope. Belief. And the hours passed.

Jennifer and I were sharing noodles in my apartment when Charles came by. He had come only to deliver a brief message to each of the Americans. We were to meet in the small fifth-floor conference room. A representative from the U.S. Embassy was coming to speak to us.

We sat around the oval table as servers brought in the tea. The American representative was an intense middle-aged man who was making the rounds of all universities in the district where Americans were stationed. We waited until the servers had left. Then his message was concise and clear. Don't get involved with the student demonstrations. Stay out of the way. No matter how much we may understand and sympathize, don't get involved. You can never tell which Chinese would defend you should you get yourself into trouble, and which would not protect you. Anti-American feelings are running high in some quarters. America is being blamed, at least in part, for this surge in democracy that is propelling the students in the country. Be careful.

Roger spoke. He had known this was coming from the man who'd spoken to him in the bleachers. "How well do you, personally, know the Chinese people?"

The man's eyes met those of each of us at the table. "I'm ashamed to tell you...not at all. We aren't allowed to fraternize. Whenever we are invited anywhere, we arrive in a limo with its American flags fluttering in the breeze. We have no one-on-one contact, as you do. You undoubtedly know them individually and personally far better than we do. We know only politics and diplomacy."

"Then, sir, don't you think we can make our own judgments concerning the degree of our involvement with our students?"

"As Americans, I'm sure you will do just that anyway. Individually, you will make your own decisions. I'm only sent to tell you your government's recommendations. And to inform you that should it become necessary, evacuation measures will be made available to you. You will receive that information through the Voice of America, if such procedures should become necessary."

As he concluded his speech, we all sat quietly. Each had already committed to the degree of personal involvement. Each according to his or her own individual personality and character. Of course. We were all Americans. Individual freedoms and rights were in our genes. We respected this man who had come to see us. But we had already made our own choices. And would not question each other. Only let it play out.

From then on, I listened regularly to the Voice of America. My students had already tuned in, and when the Chinese jammed the broadcasts, we quickly learned where and how to find them again. Early in the morning, during the day, and late at night radios were turned on in the dormitories, placed on the open window ledges with the volume turned up. Groups of students gathered in front of those windows, listening to every word reported, hearing about the steadily increasing numbers in Tiananmen Square, the ignoring of their pleas, the intensifying of their resolve. We heard of the visit of Russian President Mikhail Gorbachev. I asked my students if they listened to their own Chinese reporters on radio and television. They laughed. "Only when we want to hear the party line. According to them, there is nothing going on in Beijing."

There was one amusing anecdote during those days. It was the regular ongoing practice for party propaganda to be broadcast in China on loudspeakers placed throughout the country—in every city, town, village, and even in the countryside. The loudspeakers would blare at such volume that the sound was often distorted. After the demonstrations started, the loudspeaker in our vicinity concluded each broadcast by playing..."Yankee Doodle Dandy." We Americans chuckled among ourselves. Was some local wit making his own statement?

May 18. The hunger strike in Beijing is in its sixth day. Li Peng promises the student leaders that they will have a televised forum. It doesn't happen. Li Peng is planning to declare martial law.

The VOA reported that there were in excess of one million students amassed in Tiananmen Square, the majority of whom were remaining in the Square throughout the nights. A hunger strike had been initiated by hundreds in rebuttal to government officials who were denying acknowledgment of their request for an audience, and telling them to go home—as though they were recalcitrant children.

In support of their counterparts in Beijing, more than one hundred of the university students in our city united in brotherhood with those distant hunger-strikers. When we joined the marchers that noon, those young men and women were clearly identifiable among the assemblage; they wore white headbands. After the day's march, they would not be leaving the square again for many days. Others of their colleagues and supporters were to remain at their side, spending the days and sleeping at night beside them on the cement plaza. Shopkeepers and cafes in the vicinity of the square would bring food to the attending group, free of charge, supporting the movement.

The atmosphere had lost none of its exuberance, but other qualities were palpable: conviction and tenacity.

Later that afternoon Charles again made the rounds of the foreigners' apartments. The message this time was that all teachers were to report to each and every classroom as scheduled, regardless of whether or not students were present. We were assured this situation was only temporary and that we were to consider that the university was functioning normally. The university was taking the appropriate steps and the students would all be back. Tomorrow.

That evening Jennifer returned to the square, as did Roger and Claudia, and some of the young teachers. I went to Tanya's apartment. I arrived to find that she had a guest. He was a dean from one of the nearby institutes for whom she had been teaching some advanced classes in the Russian language, on a voluntary basis. They had been in serious conversation, but almost immediately upon my arrival he excused himself and left. She told me they had been discussing the absence of students from classes and decided to discontinue her trips to the institute until such time as the students returned. I asked Tanya if she had been listening to the VOA. She shushed me with her finger and whispered that she was able to get the broadcasts in Russian, and that she took her little radio into her bed and covered both herself and it with blankets while she listened. Tanya was very frightened in a way that I, as an American, was not used to.

In adherence to Charles' dictum, I—and the others—did make the regular trips to our classrooms at each appointed hour. The students did not return "tomorrow" or on any future tomorrow. However, my sessions with the postgrads continued as scheduled. The trips I was able to make to the downtown square had to be fitted into that schedule. Consequently, I was not able to go as often as those who were not teaching postgraduate students. But I went when time allowed.

May 20. Martial law declared. The government shut down all live-via-satellite Western television coverage of the demonstrations and ordered the media to leave China. The networks recalled their correspondents. One American newsman asked, "Why are you telling us to leave? What do you have to hide?"

The VOA reported that Premier Li Peng had ordered military troops from the regular army to come and clear Tiananmen Square of the demonstrators. They were being called counterrevolutionaries and were to be removed by force as they hadn't responded to the requests to leave peacefully. One excuse the government used for bringing in the troops was concern about the health of the hunger-strikers. The military moved toward the Square, but the citizens of Beijing had blocked the roadways with vehicles and with their own bodies. They had pleaded with the soldiers not to move against the students, the youth of China, their children.

May 21. The number of our marching students increased as they were joined by a few workers and other citizens. Resolve strengthened. The postgrads shook their heads in disbelief at the inevitable. Mike said, "Our fearless leaders cannot reason. They cannot fathom that it would be much easier and better for all concerned to just give an audience to the students. They wouldn't even have to act on the requests. Just give them an audience. Idiocy reigns in Beijing."

It was Ray who summed it up. "With Gorbachev's visit, it has become a matter of 'face' for Deng Xiaoping and Li Peng. They can't control a bunch of kids!"

I asked my small group of intellectuals, "Are you going to join the marchers, as Harold did that day?"

Kevin clarified their position. "We dare not. We have more to lose than the undergraduates, or even Harold. Our own university posts would be taken from us if we should be identified with the demonstrations. Not only our jobs would be in jeopardy, but our wives and children would suffer the repercussions. We cannot subject them to what could happen to them. I, for one, and all of us who are responsible for families, would not risk years of rehabilitation in the countryside. Harold is single, risking only himself, his post. But you see, they could take not only us, but our loved ones as well...our children."

Mike: "Please understand, Adair. Our hearts and minds are with the movement. But we dare not participate."

As I watched and listened, the turmoil they were suffering was written on their faces and was heard in their voices as they continued to speak openly. Their trust of me, and of each other, was absolute. They told of family members who had been sent away, imprisoned. They told of years of isolation, of suicides and murders. They told it all to me, one by one. My soul was ravaged by their simple reporting of the barbaric atrocities. Tears slipped down my cheeks.

"Do not cry for us. This is our life. It is all we've ever known. The students want change. They are idealistic. There will be no change. Not in our lifetimes."

Thomas asked, "Would you want us to risk so much... for a dream?"

I shook my head no, but I was torn.

May 23. The regular military reacts to the pleas of the citizens, and turns back. (They would be replaced later by Premier Li Peng's private army.)

As the days merged one into the other, I learned that some of the speakers at our square were couriers who had come by train, occasionally plane, from Beijing. Their transportation was provided free of charge by the train conductors. Collections were taken in the square to pay for airline tickets. They came not only to our city, but to all major centers in China. They wanted to make sure that the students outside of Beijing knew the truth about the activities in Tiananmen Square, and especially to report back to those students that the country was supporting them. Those in Beijing were being told that they were alone in their efforts. That the rest of China was not interested in them, had dismissed their behavior as adolescent and dangerously counterrevolutionary; were disgusted with their antics and had divorced themselves from them.

My time was filled with my postgrads and those who came with them. Sessions were prolonged with discussions about the meanings of freedom and democracy.

About freedom of the press and assemblage. They listened and questioned. I answered every query. When possible, I went to the square. During the days, others of my students would come by and invite me to dinners in their homes. I always accepted and cars would be sent to fetch me. Conversations around those dinner tables focused on the concepts for which the millions of Chinese students across the country were demonstrating. These parents had long since stopped listening to their own news broadcasts and were listening to the VOA and the BBC. Neither my words nor theirs were cloaked, but care was taken that windows and doors were securely closed. One never knew who one's neighbors might be. On every such night my host students would escort me back home in a taxi. If I wanted to stop at the square on the way, the taxi drivers refused to take money for the trip. Endless, nameless numbers of ordinary citizens were participating, each in his or her own way, to support the movement. These Chinese would never make the headlines. But their spirits and their blessings were equally as real as those who would.

May 25. In the late afternoon I was called to the telephone booth. It was Alexander. He didn't speak about the students, but went directly to his bad news. He'd spent three days at the Ministry of Education, arguing to allow me to pursue my research the coming year. After all his translating he'd decided at the last moment to submit the questionnaire in English. His thought was that because of the events taking place and the Ministry's limited knowledge of English, he could talk his way through this. He felt they would grant me permission because of his position and because they didn't understand the questions. Unknown to him, a new official had been assigned to the bureau. That official held a master's degree from Harvard University. When he finally made it to that level, the questionnaire was rejected outright.

Alexander explained that he had put himself in a difficult situation, but that he'd done his best. He was sorry. I thanked him for his efforts. We hung up.

I left the telephone booth and walked over to the post office on campus to pick up my mail. In it was a letter from one of the universities I'd contacted about pursuing my research as part of a Ph.D. program. The department was interested in my research and wanted further discussions with me. Kismet!

May 26. One of the students from another institute who'd been visiting my classes came to me excited by her good news. She'd asked my permission months before to use the techniques I was giving them in methodology to write a paper for a province-wide competition in educational methodologies. I had, of course, given her permission. She came running up to me waving a letter in her hand. She'd just won first prize.

May 27. We had all been invited to participate in the annual "Teacher of the Year" festivities to be held in the ballroom of a large hotel. How incongruous. With all that was going on in their country the authorities insisted on no disruption of regular activities. No one felt like attending, but we seemed to have no choice. I walked over with Roger, Claudia, Tanya, and Jennifer. We were late and found chairs near the back. The speeches had already begun and plaques were being handed out for this and that. The time came for the announced name of the recipient of that year's major award. Fanfare. Applause. And the name was given. Dr. Jane Hathaway was Teacher of the Year. She stood to great applause and received a vigorous handshake from the party secretary.

A small change had been made in my daily schedule. Whether the campus dining rooms were closed because of the demonstrations or for some other reason wasn't clear. It didn't matter, though, because our usual luncheon group had already disbanded. There was only one restaurant remaining open. Somehow I teamed up with Roger. We went together every day for our midday meal. I came to know him, and he to confide in me. He was not to be rehired for the next year. He had been caught in what was reported as a compromising relationship with a young Chinese woman. Nothing specific was seen or noted except that she had been observed leaving his apartment late one night. That was sufficient cause. She had been discharged from her job in a downtown office and he did not know her whereabouts. He was worried about her.

One day when we were walking the nearly deserted campus on our way to the restaurant, Alexander came wheeling around a corner in the distance, riding toward us. When he saw us he seemed momentarily undecided about whether or not to turn off the roadway. Roger waved to him and his decision was made for him. He rode closer to us, nodded to Roger and then took another turnoff. He ignored me, but his facial expression was obvious.

Roger smiled and looked over at me. "He's jealous. Why would Alexander be jealous?" I shrugged innocence. Roger laughed. "Are you in a relationship with our brave conqueror?"

"Brave conqueror?"

"Yes, I think so. I think he's more involved in the student demonstrations than anyone knows."

"No, I'm not. Anyway, it isn't allowed. You, of all people, should know that!"

"I think you are." And it was dropped.

May 28. Sunday. Mike and Ray came to the apartment. Harold had been picked up by the police. They had videotaped us the day I had ridden with him on his bicycle to the square. He had been taken in for questioning.

May 29. Early morning, and I'd just left my regular visit to my empty classroom and was making my way back down the deserted stairs in the vacant building. I heard footsteps coming up and was met on a landing by a middle-aged man. He stopped me.

"Good morning. You must be Adair, the American teacher." His hand was extended and he was smiling.

I was wary. "Yes, I am. Good morning." I shook his hand.

"Tell me, as an American, what do you think about what our students are doing?"

Warning lights! "As an American, I understand their desire to have a free and democratic society in which to live and raise their children."

"So, you support them?"

Reserved, but my involvement was certainly no secret. "Yes, I support them."

"I don't mean to frighten you. Please. My name is Kennedy. I've been sent to speak to you."

"Speak to me about what? By whom?"

He didn't hesitate. "By Mr. Han." (He told me the actual name and position of the man for whom he was the messenger. I will not divulge either. Suffice it so say, the name was well-known. He wouldn't have had to tell me the man's position in the society. His rank was among the highest in the province.)

"Why is Mr. Han interested in me?"

"He is in a position of great trust. Because of his rank and authority he has access to all information. He has asked me to advise you to keep a very low profile. You have been put under heightened surveillance. The police are watching every move you make and every contact you make."

"Why is he telling me this?"

"He, we all, appreciate very much your interest in our students. He is the head of the underground movement for this province. And I am his friend as well as his coworker for the democratization of China."

"Underground! But he is—"

"Exactly. This man walks on the razor's edge. He has great power—on both sides. That is what makes him so effective."

"Why do you trust me with this information?"

"Should we not trust you, Adair?"

I didn't answer, was overwhelmed by all of this. He nodded at my shock and disbelief.

"We know you very well. Besides, what would you do with such information? Report it? To whom? Who would believe you? You would probably be questioned as a counterrevolutionary and deported, or imprisoned. I have revealed it to you because it is important that you understand the importance of the message. Be careful." He bowed just slightly and continued up the stairs, turned on the next deserted floor, and I could hear his footsteps padding softly away along the corridor, toward the staircase at the other end of the hall.

Bullshit! I don't believe a word of it. But I did.

May 30. Students in Beijing create a ten-meter (approximately thirty-three feet) statue of the Goddess of Democracy, place her on a cart and wheel her into Tiananmen Square.

The young woman who'd won first prize in the competition met me by accident on the way to the post office. Her face was strained, her eyes swollen from crying. I asked her what the trouble was. Her father had been taken during the night. He was imprisoned. There had been no charges as yet, but they suspected him of being a counterrevolutionary. He was to be interrogated. He had already served nine years in a rehabilitation camp some years before. She was distraught with fear.

June 1. Thursday, and it was raining. The postgrads came by for their lesson at eleven. Harold was with them. I hugged him to me.

"It's OK," he said. "They just wanted to ask me a few questions. I'm OK. So are you."

But they told me of Chinese teachers from the university who had been picked up and were being questioned. In addition, security had been tightened and no students other than those registered for my class would be allowed to come to my apartment. My own had to be security checked before coming upstairs.

The rain was pelting and the mood in the room was sinking into a quagmire of depression. I wanted to give them something, something beautiful and wonderful for their tortured souls.

"How would you like me to read you a story? I have an incredible story, a very short one that may give you something to think about. On the surface, this story seems to be a fairy tale of sorts about a seagull. But it isn't about a seagull at all. It's about something else altogether. Would you like to hear it? Instead of having class on this rainy day?"

They smiled and nodded yes, and I went to my library shelf and took down Richard Bach's book, *Jonathan Livingston Seagull*.

Although the rain poured, the room seemed to lighten as I read. When I finished, they were silent. I wondered if they'd understood the message of the outcast. Of hope and the miracle of the human capacity to overcome. No one spoke, but they rose and began to pick up their belongings. They walked to my door. It was Ray who turned and held out his hand. "May we have the book?"

"I don't know if this book is allowed."

"It will be OK. We'll take very good care of it. We have other friends who also need to hear this book."

The image of Richard Bach's face came to mind, and although I didn't know him at all, I did know his writings. I thought to myself that he probably would be very touched, proud of the impact of his work on these Chinese minds, at this time.

"Yes. You may take it."

At eleven o'clock that night, the great gates of our university were closed and the students were locked inside. For the next three days and four nights the campus was forbidden territory.

Silent.

June 4. Sunday. Early morning. The VOA.
"And there is mayhem in Tiananmen Square. The killing has gone on all night. Blood everywhere. Bodies still lying on the Square. Armored vehicles are moving in the Square at this moment. The students are screaming. You can probably hear their screams behind me."

How can my little radio do this? Talk like this? How does it do it? How strange...

"It is unbelievable. The mayhem. What is happening is beyond what anyone could imagine, the Square is in chaos."

It's a good thing this is only on my own little radio!

"I saw it. I saw it all. The tanks just kept rolling, just rolled over those students as they slept in their tents. Then the trucks were there scooping up the dead bodies, shoveling them into the back of the trucks, so they'll never be able to get a count of the number of students they've slaughtered."

Well, it's OK for me to hear this, but no one else must ever know. If I don't tell them, no one will ever know.

"It is China's worst day of infamy. Hundred, thousands of our students have been slaughtered."

I'll just pull my radio under my blankets and turn it low, like Tanya does, so no one can hear this. I must protect my students. They must never know.

"I saw them. The tanks just kept coming, and the machine guns just kept firing, murdering, slaughtering our children. I saw the students in a line with their arms linked, and they were walking toward those machine guns, and as those soldiers fired their guns, some of the students would fall and other students would just step over the dead bodies of their comrades and join the line, taking the places of their dead comrades."

No, no, no...

"And link their arms, marching on, straight toward those machine guns."

No, No...

"And they just kept firing as those young people walked right toward them, and more would fall..."

NO.

"and others would take their places,"

NO, NO...

"and they kept on coming..."

NO.
NO!
NO!
They've killed them.
They've killed the students.

My pillow was wet and I heard myself screaming and knew I was muffling my screams into the pillow and my neck hurt from my head being twisted so far around and the calves of my legs hurt from where I was digging my fingernails into them as I grasped my legs to my chest and my gut was wrenching and convulsing and I kept on screaming. And screamed until my life's energies were spent and the sobs would come no more. I hid under my covers. I hid for a long while. Or maybe it wasn't a long while. I don't know.

There was a soft tapping on my door. Weak, drained. There were no loving son's arms to pick me up that day. No nurses hovering over my bed. No one trying to get a blood pressure reading. I was on my own. I don't think those thoughts were in my head, but I knew them as real and I eased myself from the bed to the floor. Huddled against the frame, and then stretched my hands and arms along the rug to make sure that the floor was solid. Crawled to the jamb of my bedroom door. Pulled myself to my feet and felt my way along the living room wall. Unlocked and opened the door.

Jennifer's face was white and swollen. She came in and went to the sofa without seeing me. I leaned my head against the wall as flashes of students forging ahead into machine-gun fire passed in and out of my mind, streaks of despair colliding behind my eyes, radiating down my backbone, settling as dull knots behind my knees, threatening. *Don't collapse. Do something...something. But what?* I waited. Then sucked strength back into my body, pushed away from the wall, and went to the kitchen to make tea.

I stood erect, staring at the kettle, waiting for it to boil. Slowly, meticulously, I measured the leaves into the cups and poured the water to the precise level. Turned off the hot plate, picked up the cups, focused on the distance, and crossed to where Jennifer sat. She handed me a cigarette and took her cup. We sat. And in our silence we drank the hot tea and inhaled the nicotine, and sometimes our tears would slide, and sometimes they wouldn't. And I made more tea and we continued to sit. Until noon.

"Get dressed. I'll make some noodles. Come on over when you're ready." I did.

We stayed in her apartment. I sat on her sofa and leaned my head against her windows and watched the streets below. They were deserted. I watched a rat peer out from behind some garbage, look this way and that, smell the ground, smell the debris, scurry out from its hiding place and skitter along beside one pile to hide behind another. I didn't see it again. Or any other movement. Dusk was coming on when the young teachers began to arrive. Nothing much was said. We sat together. A family.

It was time to sleep. I stood in front of my own windows in the dark and looked out over the silent beauty of our desolate campus. Our place of higher learning. Reservoir of humankind's accumulated knowledge. Sanctuary of great philosophic thought. The upper branches of the ancient trees were swaying gently in the night breezes. A few lights on the tall lampposts gave off a meager illumination. The buildings were painted facades on a canvas. All was empty. Still. Without life.

June 5. The early morning sun was blazing hot. Jennifer and I went down to the streets. Clusters of people were standing about, others moving without direction, crossing and recrossing the pavements. On their arms they wore narrow white ribbons with a tiny flower attached. Jennifer asked some strangers carrying handfuls of ribbons for two bands and was handed them. I tied one on my arm. A man was watching and came over to me, shaking his head with the slightest smile. He untied the ribbon and indicated my other arm, then tied it on properly and walked away.

Commotion was beginning on the narrower of the streets as the students from the institute moved enormous wreaths along the roadway toward the intersection with the boulevard. I looked down the hill and saw that students from the other institute were also moving wreaths. I looked over at our campus. The gates were closed and locked. There was only silence from that place.

Out of the corner of my eye I saw Alexander coming out of the small restaurant. He went to unlock his bicycle and straddled it. He hadn't seen me. I walked over to him and he looked up. We only nodded at each other. Moments passed, and then I whispered through my adopted false smile, "Are you with the underground movement?"

His face was expressionless as he shook his head no. "I am much too unimportant." His voice was low, almost inaudible.

"A man came to see me on the steps at the lecture hall. He said his name was Kennedy. He said..." My tone matched his own.

"Yes, I know."

"Was he telling me the truth?"

Alexander put his foot up on the pedal and pushed down. "You may want to stay here in the streets. I think something is going to happen. Something with our students." He accelerated his bike and was gone.

I went to stand by Jennifer, who was talking to a few of her students from her previous university. "Alexander says for us to stay here on the street," I told her. She nodded and went on with her conversation.

Over the next hour students from the institutes began to form into their lines. Agony stifled the air. Those who had formerly been on the hunger strike were among their fellows. They still wore their white headbands, but they had splattered them with globs of red paint; blood. Grief unmasked.

It was shortly before noon when the drums began. The sound was deep and slow and rhythmic.

BOOM.

BOOM.

BOOM.

Booming out across the streets; across the world. Flogging, pulverizing, annihilating the devil-gods.

But the sound was not coming from either of the institutes. The sound was coming from behind our tall gates. Jennifer and I stood, transfixed, staring at them. Slowly, those mighty barricades began to inch open. Groaned and creaked and scraped aside the gravel. We caught our first glimpses through the widening gap and then they swung wide. Our students stood tall, silent, regimented into their lines beyond, a wide banner held high over the heads of those in the front row. Three carts were positioned in front of them. The one in the center carried the loudspeaker. A student turned it on and the blare of the dirge split the moment. The carts on either side carried the massive drums, and the young men attending them swung their arms in slow, fully extended arcs; straining up, pausing, crashing down, pounding the metered, staccato beat. The intense reverberations ricocheted against the surrounding buildings, driving their pain into the soul of the universe. And the carts rolled out onto the boulevard. The signal had been given. The students from the institute down hill commenced the funeral march. Those from the institute on the side street angled into position behind them, strengthening their lines, footsteps falling in cadence. An ocean of grieving humanity was on the way.

Our lines began to move. Row after row of freshmen came through the gates. Rows of sophomores. The juniors. Seniors. Our entire student body. Thousands upon thousands of students, linked together in the common crusade of mourning. Bonded in abject sorrow, in honor of their own so wantonly slain in Beijing.

The last file of seniors passed between the gates. Then, a few steps behind, another very small group, less than a hundred members, strode into view, their own banner held high in the air, proudly, defiantly. It was painted with vibrant red characters to clearly identify who they were. This banner was being carried by Kevin, Thomas, Mike, Ray, Harold, and Julie. In back of them marched postgraduate students from other departments. As my students passed by me, our eyes met. Their faces were set. Resolute. They were marching for their fallen comrades. They were marching for freedom.

I must be with them. I must go. But how?

As before, when the last of the students had passed by, the line of bicycles behind began to move. Once again, Jennifer said she was going for hers. As she zigzagged away from me, two things happened at once. Roger came along on his bike and one stray taxi was moving toward us. Roger yelled at me, "Going to the square?"

"I'd have to walk...or will you ride me on your bike? No, wait, there's a cab!" I ran toward the taxi, waving my arms.

"Jesus Christ, Adair! You're the only woman in the world who would take a taxi to a revolution!"

For blocks around the square the quieted citizens of our city were standing or milling about, without destination, conversation a low drone of lamentation. I made my way through the masses of people and hurriedly climbed the steps to a pedestrian overpass. A couple of Westerners made room for me at the railing, and I took my camera from my bag and held it hidden in the front opening of my light jacket. I began to snap what I assumed would be forbidden pictures of the tide of students as it passed under the footbridge. I wasn't sure what the banners said, but suspected they were, indeed, counterrevolutionary. I would not have these pictures developed until I was back in California. I would not take any chances.

Wedging solo through the populace, I was able to get to the square as the last of the marchers entered the area. The heat of the day had become humid as a cloud cover moved across the sky. I went to the same grassy area when I'd stood with my colleagues before, and sure enough, Jennifer was there. She indicated that we try to get closer to the speaker's platform. As we wended our way upward, the townspeople standing around took notice of us and made way. Drops of rain began to fall. As we climbed the steps an aged gentleman spoke to me in English. "You see, even the gods are crying for our massacred students."

We saw Angel standing with others of our students and went to her side. She saw us and pulled me to her, slipping her arm around my waist, resting her head on my shoulder. "I'm going to speak today. I'm glad you are here."

"Are you afraid?"

"No. No more. Fear is gone. There is only hatred left in my soul. It would be better to be dead than to live in this terrible place."

I held her close. "Angel, who was it that got our gates opened?"

She looked at me and shrugged. "I'm not sure. But I think it was Alexander. Probably. He's always been on the side of the students. He's helped us a lot. Word was passed very late last night that we'd be let out. Some people had turned off our electricity so we couldn't listen to the radio. But a lot of students had battery radios. We could hear it all. We spent the rest of the night making our banners. We had to do most of it in the dark."

Angel did speak that day. She was impassioned. Her audience listened with reverence and was touched by the depth of her emotions, and the emotions of all those who took the podium. I could understand nothing of their words, but translation wasn't necessary. Their messages were clear. They were demanding freedom and democracy. They were demanding an end to the tyrannies of their Communist system.

When we finally turned to leave, a middle-aged man who had been standing next to me gripped my hands. There were tears of hatred and impotence in his eyes. "Please, madam. When you go home to America, don't let them forget us. Don't let them ever forget our students."

I closed my hands over his. "I promise, sir. I promise. I shall never let them forget."

Late that night, the first of a stream of people who were to come to me over the next period of time arrived at my door. Each night, usually midnight or after, one or sometimes two people came. They came only to talk. These were all men, except for one woman. They would wait, concealed, until after the security guards became bored with their long vigil and dozed off; then, they would make their way cautiously up the stairs to my fifth-floor apartment. We spoke in the dark and in whispers. They came to tell me their stories. These were people I didn't know, but who desperately needed someone to talk to. They had been sent by those who did know me. They confided their hatreds to me, told me of their own experiences and those of their families. The woman, a doctor, told me of her seven years in a camp, of the beatings, and showed me her scarred back. They all told me things they had not spoken of for decades. Things held, festering in the bottomless agony of their souls. The arrests. The camps. The beatings, the atrocities, the suicides, and the murders. They told it all. And I listened. Then they'd thank me. Ask me not to forget the Chinese. And they'd leave, slipping quietly back down the steps, waiting to make sure it was safe, then tiptoeing quickly out of the building. And others would come, night after night. I didn't know who they were. It didn't matter.

The evening of the memorial in the square Thomas had gone back to his village to get a gun. During the days, more posters appeared on the walls of the university. Posters asking that the names of student leaders and teachers be given to the office. Promising that those who revealed the names would be granted special commendation.

June 7. Mike and Ray came to the apartment. They told me about Thomas going, but said not to worry, that he'd be back. Then, haltingly, Mike told me what he'd seen on television the night before. A local newscast had been prepared. The gist of it was to show the province that the majority of the people didn't believe the terrible stories that the Western press was circulating about the "unfortunate" events in Tiananmen Square. That those events had been vastly exaggerated, and that the wise and mature people of China were proud that the military had finally been able to clear Tiananmen and send those counterrevolutionary students back to their homes. That even the liberal visiting Western teachers were supporting the actions of the military. Then, a clip taken from that "cheerleader" video I'd done with my colleagues had been included; only a small section, where I was waving my arms over my head in a "rah-rah" gesture had been shown, to prove that the local Westerners supported the government's action.

June 8. The VOA repeatedly broadcast the schedule of flights available to evacuate the Americans, with detailed instructions on how to avail ourselves of those flights. The U.S. government was encouraging all Americans to leave China, at the earliest possible date.

Neither Jennifer nor I had any intention of leaving until we were sure all of our students and Chinese colleagues were accounted for. We would wait.

During the intense days I'd not seen Tanya. She stayed in her apartment, leaving only briefly at midday to buy a few groceries from the street vendors. I made it a point to go to her rooms. She ushered me in with a shushing finger and closed the door quickly behind me.

"You see, as I told you. They are monsters. Devils. I knew what would happen. We have much experience with these things. And it will not end. They'll keep after the students until they've punished every one, innocent or guilty."

"Tanya, it is coming near the time when I must go home. What about you?"

"I must stay. We must serve out our two-year contracts. I will be alone when you are gone. Totally alone. How will I be able to bear it? Before you leave, I want you to make a tape for my cassette. I want to have your voice, to stay with me for this next year and to take home with me when I go. To keep forever."

"Of course, Tanya. What do you want me to say?"

"Just talk about our friendship."

And I did. I found the words she wanted and spoke about how much she had meant to me, we had meant to each other, and about her compassion for all the students. I was even able to joke that we were using the new sound equipment she'd finally been able to order through Hong Kong and to pay for with her dollars acquired over the year. I chided her that she had caused us all such endless head-aches, but congratulated her that she'd gotten everything she wanted: new television set, the sound equipment, two flutes for her musician son, everything. And I ended by saying that she'd have to figure out a way to get it all home, later, without our help.

June 11. One week had passed. The square had been cleared. There was nothing left except a few pieces of tape on light posts where inflammatory posters and announce-ments had been stripped away. As I stood there looking at it, it was as though nothing had ever taken place.

From that time on, the students began leaving the university and going to their homes. My late-night visi-tors decreased in number. Some nights no one came. It was time to start making arrangements to return to the U.S. I knew from the radio and from my colleagues that transportation was difficult to come by. People were going to the airport and waiting, only to be sent back home. I called Barbara. I'd tried to call her twice before during the demonstrations, but the Chinese operator had cut off the calls. This time I got through and was able to tell her my needs. I asked her to try to arrange ticketing from there, and that I'd call her back.

When I concluded the call, Alexander was standing near the booth waiting to use the telephone. We greeted each other, as professionals. I told him about the difficulties of ticketing. He expressed his regret that I was having trouble. He asked when I wanted to leave and I gave him a date.

June 15. I called Barbara.

"Mom, the strangest thing."

"What?"

"Well, I called the travel agent and she said that she knew the planes were all booked, but that she'd keep trying. To call her back. I called a couple of days later and she said that you already had a seat confirmed to Hong Kong. How is that possible?"

I smiled at the telephone and my heart felt the familiar ache. *Never worry, Adair. I'll always take care of you.* "I think I know, Barb. I'll be OK once I get to Hong Kong. I'll be able to get a flight to San Francisco without problems."

I hadn't met with the postgrads as a group for more than two weeks. We'd see each other from time to time on the streets, and joined in two and threes for lunch. Our conversations were quiet with the sadness of departure hovering over us. Thomas had returned, without the gun. All were planning their trips to their families. But they wouldn't leave until I did. Our good-byes were coming.

My last full day arrived. I was to take the plane at eleven o'clock the next morning. They would come with Angel to escort me to the airport. Blocking my emotions, I finished packing.

It was well after midnight when there was a tapping on my door. I pulled on my robe as I went to answer. Quietly, I slid the lock. There were no lights burning in the hallway and it was Kennedy's voice that whispered, "I'm sorry to bother you so late, but I want to say good-bye."

"Please come in."

In the darkness he told me his own story. As an elementary schoolboy he'd written "Down with Mao" on the sidewalk with chalk. The security police had come to his home and told his parents they were taking him for questioning. His parents pleaded that he was only a little child. It didn't matter. Kennedy was taken to the countryside for rehabilitation. His job was to carry buckets of human refuse from the village squatters to the rice patties, on a yoke across his shoulders. When he had emptied the squatters from one village, he had to go to the neighboring village and continue his work. He had to make the trips from sunup until sundown, every day of the week. The buckets balanced across his shoulders were much too heavy for his young body. After a while he developed severe back trouble and couldn't lift the yokes anymore, and was beaten for being lazy. He was banished from the work unit and left to forage in the village for food. The villagers did not acknowledge him. He stole whatever he could find to eat and stole a blanket from a clothesline. He would huddle beside a village wall during the nights. When the winter came he thought he would surely freeze to death.

In the dark of night, a very old man in the village came to him. He'd been watching him all that time. The man brought him another blanket and a tiny clay burner to be used as a stove. Kennedy would collect animal droppings to use for fuel and the man supplied him with matches. One night the man brought Kennedy a book. It was an old and badly worn English language grammar book. Over the next years Kennedy taught himself to speak English. He was kept in the countryside for fourteen years, without ever hearing from his family. He was twenty-four years old when he was reunited with society.

"Do not cry for me. My story is no different from millions of others. But while I was in the countryside, I swore an oath that I would spend whatever years I had left to live fighting against the Communist devils. When I came back into society my English was very poor, but at that it was better than others. I found a position as an English teacher, and I found Mr. Han. I have dedicated my life to him and to the cause of freedom and democracy. We will never, never give up our fight. Until our dying day, we will never give up." He paused.

"Adair, I tell you this because I have a very great favor to ask of you. I have written a letter. A letter to your great president, Mr. George Bush. Our group has asked me to write it. They and I want him to know about us. It would be a great favor, for me and for all my colleagues, if you would take the letter out with you and mail it in the United States. But before you agree to do so, I want you to read it. I want you to read it and to know—to understand—that should this letter be taken from you at the airport...it will cost not only my life, but the lives of my wife and my

children. I know I ask a lot. Please. If you want to say no,
I will understand."

"Have you signed the letter with your own name?"

"Yes, I have."

He had secured the handwritten letter under his
shirt, next to his body, held in place by his belt buckle. He
withdrew it and I took the six thin sheets of paper from
him. I did not read them. "Of course I'll take your letter,
Kennedy. I will be proud to do so."

He stood and took from his pocket another scrap of
paper. "If you are able to get it through and decide to mail
it, please just drop me a note at this address. On the note,
simply say, 'Yes, I was able to purchase Charles Dickens'
A Tale of Two Cities and enjoyed reading it.' We will never
forget you, Adair. You are not like some of the others, who
only stayed in their rooms. You have become one with
us."

He embraced me quickly and his cheeks were damp
with tears. He skittered like a mouse along the side of the
darkened hallway, paused to listen at the top of the stairs,
and then noiselessly ran down the steps.

If you want to hide anything, put it in an obvious place. I
took my wallet, removed the dollar bills and refolded his
letter, placing a dollar upright between the folds. Stored
again in their proper place, it was impossible to tell there
was anything other than money in the compartment.

The van taking me from the apartment house to the
airport was filled with my students and Angel, together
with Jennifer and Tanya. The ride and the wait in the ter-

minal were quiet. When the moment came for me to enter the immigration area, tears were flowing. I embraced each one. We each said, "See you later," and then I left them and went with the line.

It was my turn at the desk and I offered my passport. The clerk checked it carefully, looked up at me and asked, "Why have you been in China?" I explained. She queried, "Where is your work permit? How do I know you are telling the truth? Perhaps you were here for some other reason." I froze. With all the emotions of the past days and the farewells, we'd all forgotten about the necessity of showing my work permit or an exit visa. Fear shot through me. The woman's expression hardened. I felt my knees giving way. She took my passport and went to an office. Another woman and a man came out of the office and the three of them stood looking from me to my passport. The woman from the office said something to the others, and then looked directly at me again. "Adair?" There was just the slightest hint of something in the expression on her face and her tone of voice, which seemed somehow out of place.

"Yes."

She flipped my passport closed and handed it back to the clerk with a nod. The clerk returned to the desk, opened my passport and stamped it. I was ushered on through into the waiting room.

The room was crowded. I spotted only one seat on a bench and went to take it. It was no more than a minute or two before a soldier came into the room, looking at some small document. He announced something in Chinese and the room quieted. He called out, "Adair?" Twice.

I didn't respond, head down, frightened. He saw me and came over to where I was sitting. "Are you Adair?"

"No. Yes. I'm sorry. I didn't understand what you said." My nerves were on edge.

"A young woman named Angel is in the outer area and wants to know if you need this document. It is your work permit. She had forgotten to give it to you."

My long exhaled breath and smile came together. "Tell her thank you. I won't need it. I'm through immigration."

On schedule, I took my place in the plane and we started to taxi down the runway. I looked out my small window and could see my beloved friends standing behind the iron gates, waving. My soul aggrieved, I accepted that I would never see them again, and watched until they were long out of sight.

It was not until I was back in Davis that I read the letter written by Kennedy. It was a simple statement as to the existence of an active underground and a pledge to continue its work until China was a free country. It was a plea to our president to honor the citizens of China and to support them in whatever way possible. I wrote a cover letter with a brief explanation and mailed them to President Bush, and the note to Kennedy. Three weeks later, I received a gracious response from the man in charge of the Sino-American desk in Washington, D.C. He thanked me for the correspondence and promised that President Bush did understand the courage and sincerity of the Chinese people.

I would spend the next month recuperating on my daughter's sofa. I had lost twenty pounds during the ordeal.

U.S.A. – THIRD RETURN

What followed was not so much another part of the threads which were leading me, but rather a clarification—a labeling, a coming together, call it what you will—of the spiritual quest I had been on sporadically throughout my life. I have chosen not to reveal the name of either the city or the university where I went for further graduate study, as my experience was strictly my own and specific to a certain time and place, and should in no way influence another's decision. In fact, I remained in the program for only one semester. That was enough for me. While I was there, though, I met a woman whom I surely was destined to meet; she was the real reason behind my going. But I didn't know that beforehand, of course. Before telling about the woman, I need to explain why one semester in the advanced studies program was enough for me.

I was enrolled in three doctoral-level classes and taught another three classes of English to the university freshmen. The schedule was grueling. I'm not going to say anything more about the classes I was teaching, other than that they went well. From the opening meetings of my three academic classes I had an inkling that I might be in trouble. To explain this, I should give a brief description of my attitude at that time.

From childhood, I'd been told that the letters Ph.D. behind a name tell the world that the carrier of those letters has spent a vast amount of time specializing in a particular field and is therefore due a degree of credibility far beyond ordinary mortals; not only in the field of specialization, but in all things. I had bought into that belief as a youth and carried it with me during my life. I'd always felt just a bit inadequate because I didn't have those magical initials, and an equal amount of intimidation when in the presence of the mighty doctors of this or that. I was usually—always— reluctant to speak my opinion when one of the chosen was within hearing range. That belief, coupled with the world experience I now had acquired, were the prompters that led me to enter a doctoral program. It was ego.

During my summer recuperation period, I had told myself that the advanced degree would make me more marketable. At my age, that was not true; however, I accepted it for myself. What I discovered in those first classes, and what was confirmed and reconfirmed over the ensuing months, was that there is a great gulf between world experience and academic theoretical studies.

I will speak of only one particular class. The doctoral program consisted of reading multitudes of essays and texts by world-renowned experts in the field. Our responsibilities were to read, digest, and discuss the findings of these experts, and make comparative analyses *between the experts*. The reason I knew I was in trouble was that it seemed clear to me that the experts' expertise came from other books and essays written by other experts, who in turn...well, you have my inference. I finally knew the meaning of the phrase "ivory tower mentality." To compare solely to each other seemed a waste of my time. What I wanted to do was to expand that exercise and compare them to the realities of the role and importance of literacy in developing countries, realities I was finding were far different from the theoretical essays we were assigned.

From the first week, I questioned just exactly how long the expert had researched in the field, and what was the scenario among those being researched toward the expert. It wasn't that I felt I knew so much more than the authors, but that what I knew from experience contained a human dimension, a global reality, that, had it not been ignored, would have yielded conclusions different from those in the reading materials. But we were considered too immature in the discipline to question the authorities. Another—and to me, serious—problem was with the apparent ethnocentricity of some authorities. I'll give you just two quick examples; the first being a reading on the evolution of the Chinese writing system.

Concealed within this reading was a subtle suggestion by the coauthors, neither of whom was fluent in Chinese, that there was a cause-effect relationship reflected in the Chinese writing system which somehow questioned the Asian ability to reason...rationally. A Chinese man in our group was hypersensitive to the reading and quite offended. As was I. While the section was under discussion he whispered to me, "They're saying we can't think!" I'd had discussions related to the effects of the different writing systems off and on with my postgraduate students. They had noted that the differences between the Western and the Eastern minds in analyzing do appertain to writing. Because of the writing systems, the Chinese analyze vertically; that is to say, in depth. The Western writing system is horizontal and we analyze laterally; that is, from point A to point B, etc. The sequencing is different. Any hint of Asian irrationally is preposterous. Their application of logic is different, not missing. I spoke up, but my comments were dismissed. My Chinese colleague remained quiet when he heard my remarks being put down with such condescension.

Another reading was on the rise of literacy in the Western world; specifically, the value—real or ascribed—of the addition of the vowel system—real or ascribed—by the Greeks. The text was lengthy and the bibliography consisted of several pages of names. In the text there was quite a lot of questioning coming through suggesting that what those ancient Greeks had contributed to Western literacy had been vastly exaggerated. That's OK. Maybe yes and maybe no. Whether or not their contributions have been overrated was not my immediate problem. I had a different objection and questioned the professor.

"Excuse me, but as I search through this lengthy bibliography of readings from which this author has culled his information, I find one interesting omission."

The professor puffed up, a little defiant perhaps, and queried, "What omission is that?"

I smiled my sweetest. "Sir, I don't see one Greek name on the list. Is it possible that Greek historians are unable to write? Or is it that what they have to say relative to their contribution to the development of the Western alphabet is of no importance to Western European and

American scholars? Or can the Western European and American scholars not read Greek?" He stumbled for only a moment—obviously such omission had never crossed his mind—then answered, "The Greek academicians of today are not focused on that particular subject." I nodded, silenced for the moment.

Interestingly, one of my office-mate's students was a doctoral candidate in another field, and was Greek, having transferred only that semester from his university in Athens. He came by our office later that afternoon and I questioned him. His response was, as expected, that Greek academicians are deeply involved in the study of the development of literacy and the alphabet, and have highly trained and qualified scholars using the most sophisticated methods of investigation in the field. He proceeded to relate to me research which was current and ongoing. Perhaps my sort of mind-set is excessively nit-picking. But to be an expert in anything requires complex investigation, over time, utilizing all relevant information that can be obtained, from all quarters, in order to reach an objective and justifiable conclusion—or better yet, to pose a question worth asking. What I was finding in my studies was an international network of certain Western European and American scholars involved in research to challenge and impress each other, not to obtain understanding of the world in which we live...in other words, an international circle jerk. My sincerest apologies to those professors who are outside of that framework. I have known a few outstanding scholars who epitomize academia in the highest sense. Those types of scholars, unfortunately, were not represented in my classes. I will end this diatribe by saying that the professor with whom I'd had the above discussions did, on the last day of class, say to the group at large that he had begun to rethink conclusions he had reached long ago. These particular confrontations were only two of many. I won't further belabor my reasons for leaving. Doctoral programs in the humanities are better left to the young. Once more, I simply didn't fit, and left.

What was important to my life during those months was meeting a lovely African-American woman who was pursuing her master's degree at the same university. Our paths crossed frequently and we soon became friends. I admired her calm demeanor and her inner strength. It was in the university cafeteria that she questioned me as to my religious beliefs. *Uh-oh. I hope she isn't some weirdo who is going to tell me that God is married and lives on the sun, and that if I don't believe that I'm going straight to hell without passing Go and collecting my two hundred dollars. I like her and I don't want to cope with some attempted conversion.* I told her that I'd spent many years of study in Judeo-Christian beliefs, which I found to be a quagmire of contradictions, and in Eastern thought, some components of which had personal disciplines I could never adapt, and consequently that I had not subscribed to any one belief system and was not a churchgoer. She baited me with questions which I answered forthrightly. We discussed and, yes, argued—debated—for more than an hour. Her eyes were sparkling as she began to gather her belongings.

"Would you be interested in joining my husband and me at our home this evening? We are Buddhists and there will be a small gathering with others who are on the same path."

I looked at her with surprised interest, little expecting to be eating a hamburger with someone who shared esoteric beliefs similar to my own. I shook my head and clucked my tongue at her, recognizing that she had been baiting me, driving me on, for her own amusement. She bowed her head in acknowledgment. I asked her, jokingly, about what restrictions were applied, what prohibitions were expected from those in the membership. What would I have to give up?

She laughed softly, "Nothing. Nothing at all. Giving up something doesn't contribute to one's spiritual growth, unless that giving up is the result of the growth itself. Then it comes about naturally." I accepted her invitation.

That evening I experienced a philosophy which I would soon come to adopt as my own. I learned to chant, and was taught the philosophic truths revealed in the *Lotus Sutra* and which have been passed on to humankind from some three thousand or more years ago. I was able to accept the fundamental principle that our own spiritual nature—our divinity, or Buddhahood—is always present and available in our highest level of consciousness and will manifest itself in all aspects of our daily lives, if we allow that transformation to take place.

I met with the group regularly, and before leaving the city to return to Davis, I attended a ceremony given by a Buddhist priest who had come to America for the purpose of initiation. As I stood before that priest, my thoughts went back to kneeling at the railing at the Buddhist temple as 1988 became 1989. This was right for me, at this time.

During the spring semester I lived with my daughter in her condominium, slept on her sofa, and taught English to incoming international students in the Intensive English Department at the University of California, Davis. A series of letters from Tanya and my students in China were arriving regularly and were filled with passion concerning the tight security under which they were living, the misery of their existence, and pleas for me to return to them. Of course, their words were carefully cloaked, but I knew them all well and the meanings were clear. I decided to make another trip—not to return to teach, an offer I had already refused due to the political situation—but to spend a brief holiday with them. We had not been able to go through a satisfactory closure we all needed, and it was clear to me that they were reacting to that lack, as was I. I made arrangements for the trip to coincide with the first anniversary of the Tiananmen Square Massacre, and notified my students of the details of my arrival.

CHINA – THIRD TRIP

The flight was uneventful. I routed myself through Hong Kong, with an overnight in that flamboyant city, then a connecting flight to mainland China and my destination. As the plane rolled across the tarmac I squinted through the window, scanning the waiting crowds. Then I spotted them; my students were huddled together, waving at the plane. Harold had shinnied up one of the fence posts and was wagging his arms over his head. It was good; normal and good. I was delayed for some time at customs while security checked the videotapes I'd brought for the university, to make sure I hadn't packaged triple-X-rated films with innocuous-looking jackets, which caused me to be the last person in the area. I was annoyed and impatient with their dallying and I guess my voice began to rise. Heads peeked around into the forbidden zone and my students and Tanya started inching forward, with Angel leading the way, then backing up, then inching forward again, jostling one another. The couple of guards on duty warned them once or twice, then threw up their hands in a gesture of resignation and quit trying to control us, laughing with us as my friends broke through the barrier and ran toward me. We all ignored the Chinese social constraints of not touching and hugged and pounded one another on the back. The customs official gave up; laughing, he slid the videotapes back into my suitcase without further inspection. Mike and Kevin picked up my bags and we all left the terminal. Alexander was not with them, but had provided one of the university vans for them to come and pick me up.

The ride back to the guest house was chaotic, with everyone laughing and yelling simultaneously. I sat between Tanya and Angel and we had out arms about each other, hugging and patting. The huge bouquet Tanya had brought for me nearly eclipsed my view of the front seat, so Ray grabbed it away from me. My welcome at the guest house was only slightly less enthusiastic than it had been at the airport. My heart was bulging from the warmth of my friends and acquaintances, but with a twinge of disappointment because Alexander was nowhere to be seen; I would not see him until the third day. Angel had arranged for a smaller apartment, and we all crowded in and our conversations continued. Kevin and Mike had scheduled a short series of lectures for me, which were to be on the subjects of my choice and which would be open to any and all interested students and faculty. Eventually we began to wind down and they left me to rest, promising to be back and get me for dinner. I told them to be sure to keep the evening open, as I'd be giving a small party in Tanya's apartment. They could invite whomever they pleased. Tanya was the last to leave the room, and whispered to me that she had much to tell me and to come to her apartment as soon as I was rested.

Late in the afternoon I awoke and finished preparing the presents I'd brought, attaching name tags to the individual gift bags. I collected a few and went to Tanya's apartment. She helped me with the rest of them and then made coffee, and we finally could sit quietly together and catch up on each other's lives. After the openness of our greetings it took me a bit to re-acclimate myself to realities, to the practice of speaking in hushed tones. Tanya put her finger to her lips to caution me. There was to be no more small talk. As before, her voice dropped to barely above a whisper as she started to relate the unfolding of events during the year, and I had to lean toward her to catch it all. She told of the heightened security, that officers were now permanently stationed in the guest house—even living on the first floor—and that an expanded security station had been initiated on the campus proper. She spoke of the pall that lay over the city...the tensions...the fears. She said that my arrival was the first demonstration of life she'd seen; that normally people were not speaking to each other except on the most insipid topics—the weather being the most convenient. I asked about her "friend" with whom she'd become more or less familiar the previous year. He was that dean in another university who had asked for her help with his department, and to whom she'd given her time voluntarily. The seeds of a deeper relationship had been sown before Tiananmen Square, but during the time of the massacre they hadn't seen one another at all. I wanted to know if he'd come back into her life, if she was still able to see him, and if their friendship had "changed." I expected to get a smile from her in response to my innuendo. But there was no smile. Instead, she moved from her

chair and came to sit beside me. She reached for my hands
and whispered.

"I haven't been able to say anything. It's so terrible,
what has happened is too terrible. I'm so glad you're here; I
need you to help me, to reassure me. I'm so frightened."

"What is it, Tanya? Tell me, what is it?"

She gripped my fingers. "I think he'd dead."

Was this Tanya's love of the melodramatic? I proceeded with wariness. "Tell me, Tanya; just tell me what
has happened."

"After you left, I was so lonely. I missed you, Adair,
and I had no one. I got so sick, you know, I wrote you
about it, and while I was in the hospital no one came to
me. I didn't exist anymore. He found out I was sick, but he
didn't come to the hospital, either. He couldn't. But when
I came back here I was still sick, and then he came to see
me. He was good to me. He'd been good to me before,
but he'd changed. He began to come more often and he
brought me so many presents. I'll have to show you all the
presents. And because you were gone I needed somebody
to talk to. I was so lonely. I can't keep everything inside
of me like these Chinese can. And so I began to tell him
what was in my heart about this place, and about my loneliness. And then he began to tell me what was in his heart.
It wasn't like before, when we'd talk about other things,
about the students and teaching, you know. He told me
that he didn't have anyone, either, that he'd never been
able to talk to anyone about what he felt. And, well, we
needed each other so much and we found a bit of happiness with each other...and..."

"Tanya, did you become lovers?"

Her tears began. "Oh, I wish it had been so; it could have been, should have been, but no. He was too frightened and so was I. You know what they do to Chinese who are lovers with foreigners. We couldn't. We began to love each other, but not the other..." Her tears were streaming and she gulped for breath. "That's what makes it more terrible. Because they thought we were, of course, it would seem to them that we were. But we weren't." She was so intense that I thought she was trying to convince some security officers, not me. "He came here so often and always had to hide, you know, to hide until those devils downstairs went to sleep or something. Then he'd sneak in and come up. You remember how it is. Those devils forbid you everything. They forbid you to live and breathe."

The rest of the story came in bits and pieces between her sobs. He had continued to make frequent forbidden visits to her apartment...his visits always carefully calculated to avoid disclosure. He had been willing to risk anything to be with her, if only for moments. But he was not as careful as he imagined. Just weeks before my arrival, he had written her a brief letter and had been able to get it smuggled to her by a trusted student. She broke off her story and went to the bedroom where she kept it hidden among her supply of Kotex, wrapped to look like another napkin. I complimented her on her inventiveness, but she didn't react. She handed it to me to read. The first thing I looked for was to see if he'd signed it. He had. As I read it, the recollections of the horrors of the past curdled inside me, the memories of what Alexander had told me, of what Kennedy had told me, and all those who had come to my apartment so late at night during that time. As I read, I knew she was not being melodramatic. It was all possibly true. My heart was aching, the old familiar pain. He wrote that the letter itself could have caused his downfall, possibly his death, but that he was desperate to write. The letter was filled with love and passion and longing. It was also filled with fear, and a resignation to that fear. He said that he knew he had been seen, because of a trifling incident that had happened at the reception area that late evening when he was leaving which aroused the attention of the snoozing guard. He knew instantly that the inescapable was coming, and coming soon. He had immediately returned to his rooms, composed the letter, and gone at once to hand it to his courier, fearful that he was being watched even as he was handing it over, fearful for the life of his student who would carry it...but love made him risk all.

I handed the letter back to her with nothing more than the cold nod of accepting the inevitable evil. She told me that her friend had disappeared from his rooms in the early hours of the morning following the sending of the letter. He had not been seen or heard from since. He had been quick enough to get it to his courier and the young man was safe. But her friend's existence was in question.

"Do you think he is dead, Adair?"

"No, Tanya. No. I think he's been taken to the countryside for rehabilitation. I think he'll be back." What did I know? What could I say? It had happened before, how many times, over how many years? She knew that there was nothing other than that to say. She knew I had no more answers than she.

I told her to destroy the letter; that if he were still alive some authority might still be searching for evidence against him. One never knows about their procedures. But she never did. I probably wouldn't have, either. There are just some things one can't do, and to destroy a love's last words is one of those things. The chance will be taken, no matter what the cost.

(I learned much later that, up to the time Tanya had finished her tour of duty and returned to her native home, her friend's whereabouts were still unknown.)

Dinner with my entourage picked up our spirits and we enjoyed the bounty which the students had arranged to be served. I'm sure they each must have been saving a part of their pittance since learning of my return in order to collectively pay for the feast, but of course that was not mentioned. We returned to Tanya's apartment, acknowledging the security guards as we passed by. One of the students had explained earlier that a welcome-back reception was being given by me for all of them and the names given of those who would be attending. It had been okayed. The occasion was festive, as I passed out the gifts to my surprised friends and offered them glasses of the liquors I'd brought—which none of them liked! Although they didn't say so, I could tell by the half-full glasses that remained. It was nearly time for us to bring our party to an end when there was a soft knocking on the door. It was Kennedy. The network works fast, and he'd heard I was there and waited for an opportune moment, then slipped into the building, scurrying up the stairs. Some knew him, some didn't, but nothing was said. I rose to greet him and in the presence of everyone he embraced me, kissing me on either cheek, a forbidden gesture of friendship. There were only smiles in the room. He stayed just moments, then excused himself and was gone. The incident was never spoken of, by anyone. For those who knew him, it was unnecessary. For those who didn't, they may or may not have asked the others; it didn't matter.

The next day the postgrads came to my apartment. Their enthusiasm was subdued. Kevin spoke. "I'm very sorry to tell you that the schedule of lectures which we'd arranged must be canceled. I'm sure you understand why." I grimaced, but nodded. He lowered his voice and said, "They questioned why you came back on this anniversary." Of course!

Thomas, like his namesake in the Bible, voiced his doubts. "Why did you come back at this time? Why would you come back...to this...at any time?"

I looked at my beloved students for several moments. A fable came to mind that I'd heard on the radio shortly before leaving the United States and I decided to share it with them. They especially loved and understood lessons in the form of stories. I began.

"There was a man who lived along a seacoast. Each night the ocean's tide would wash ashore hundreds of starfish. Those starfish were beached, abandoned, and unable to return to their waters, to their lives. Early each morning the man would take a stroll along the water's edge, picking up the starfish one by one and tossing them back into the sea. On one particular morning, another early morning walker was coming along the strand toward him, watching him. As the second walker approached the first, he asked, 'Why are you picking up these starfish, one by one, and throwing them back into the sea? You fool! Can't you see that there are hundreds of starfish? You can't possibly save them all.' And he indicated with a sweep of his arm the sands cluttered with multitudes of dying starfish. 'You can't possibly think that what you are doing will make a difference to these hundreds.' The first man looked at the second, and then down at his own hand which held one small starfish, and answered, 'No, it won't make a difference to the hundreds, but it will make a difference to this one.' And he tossed it back into the churning waters."

There was a palpable silence in the room when I finished. Six sets of deep brown eyes were rimmed. Ray was the first to move and the others followed. As they had done before, at the conclusion of that other story last year, they left the room without a sound.

It was the morning of the third day and I knew that they would all be back. I was looking out my window when I saw them congregated below on the driveway, talking to Alexander. As I watched my dear, my "special" friend, I felt the warmth of intimacy that I had to admit was a major part of why I had returned. I wished I could run down and hold him just once, but he had made no effort to contact me as yet, and anyway, an embrace was impossible—not only because of his position within the university system and the society, but also because we had scarcely touched. It would be both unacceptable and a dangerous expression of regard. I was hurt because he hadn't communicated with me, but tried to accept his hesitance as being politically motivated, not personally. Nonetheless, it was painful for me. The small group broke up, and he mounted his bicycle and rode off.

The students entered the building and were soon knocking on my door. They came in, all smiles, and took what had already become their self-assigned seats. The previous day was not mentioned. I asked them what they wanted me to talk about. Harold suggested I go over the format for writing a master's thesis, an activity they were each involved in. Mike had managed to procure a small blackboard and some chalk. He balanced the board on the backs of a couple of chairs and leaned it against a wall. They adjusted their chairs and I went to work while they took notes. When the lesson was ended, we scheduled lessons for the remainder of my time with them and said our see-you-laters.

Thomas lingered for a moment and was the last out of the room. As he shook my hand, I asked him the question I'd wondered about so often over the past year, the question that came as a result of his having left the university that earlier winter to bury his dead infant on that mountaintop. "Thomas, how is your wife?"

His face broke into the widest possible grin. "She's pregnant!" he said, and gripped my hand in both of his, shaking it vigorously.

"Oh, Thomas, I am so glad, so very happy for both of you." I clasped him on the shoulder.

He beamed even wider. "Thank you. Thank you," he said, and joined the others waiting on the stairs.

They had been gone for a short time when Angel came back to my rooms. "I've been sent to you with a message," she said softly as she closed the door behind her. She lowered her voice considerably. "Alexander wants to take you to dinner. You are to meet him at the restaurant a few blocks from here, where you dined before. He said you would know the place. He asked that you be there at five o'clock. He wants me to accompany you and to sit with the two of you. Is it OK with you? I need to go back to him with your answer."

Relief passed through me and I squeezed her hand. "Tell him I'll be looking forward to seeing him," I said, and she left. I went to tell Tanya the news, and promptly at five minutes before five o'clock she showed up at my door to make sure my appearance was up to her standards for a date.

Angel arrived at the same time, and Tanya said to her in an almost scolding tone, "Angel, when you're all together in the restaurant, for heaven's sake, don't just sit there. Get up and make some pretense to leave them alone for a little while. Be smart!" Angel laughed and reassured her that she would do just that.

The small, unpretentious restaurant, its street side without a wall, had changed not at all since that late afternoon when we'd sat there before. Alexander was seated and chatting with some acquaintances when we arrived. The café might not have changed, but up close I could see that his appearance had. Small lines had formed around his eyes and at his temples. His look was strained from too much unrelieved tension. That intense energy level was gone; he looked tired, unhealthy. He feigned surprise at our presence, introduced us to the others and invited us to sit with them. He quickly concluded the conversation they had been having in Chinese and dismissed them with a wave of his hand. He turned back to the table and looked over at me. There was no smile on his face. His hands were shaking noticeably as he smoked. He poured more beer into his glass and said something in Chinese to Angel. She nodded and went to the counter to select our meal and to fetch me a beer. As soon as she left he glanced at me again, and there was the faintest curvature to his lips. "It's good to see you. I'm sorry I couldn't meet you earlier, but..." His voice seemed to leave him. I wanted so much to reach out and quiet his trembling hands. Such a simple gesture, but forbidden, so I didn't.

"It is good to see you, too, Alexander. I've thought about you a lot." He flinched at the word. I'd misspoken and was immediately sorry, biting at the inside of my lip.

"Thank you for the Christmas card and the birthday card, but they weren't necessary." His tone was noncommittal, but again I suspected I might have done the wrong thing by sending them. Innocent, innocuous, and wrong. I let it go.

"Tell me about your duties in the Foreign Affairs Office. Did you get the promotion?"

"No. It went to...another..." Again, his words seemed to get lost somewhere. I understood him to mean that the position he'd wanted for so long, worked so tirelessly for, deserved so completely, had gone to his nemesis, Charles. I knew without being told that the reason for his punishment had been his association with me, and my stomach knotted with guilt. Had I said anything he would have denied it, as he had before. His appearance and his demeanor were unsettling me. He'd already let me know I'd made two more "mistakes." This was not going well. He glanced over at the counter as though irritated with Angel's delay. Was he irritated, or was that a ploy for the other diners? Angel was chatting with someone and had, apparently, "neglected" to place the order yet. He gestured to her to

hurry up. But was that, too, a stratagem, and had she understood it as such? Clearly, he was increasingly nervous.
He seemed to be gearing himself to get the appropriate
words collected and arranged. He seemed to be having difficulty with English. That had happened before, on other
occasions. I waited for him to collect himself and I looked
over at Angel. She was still chatting, ignoring the cook. It
occurred to me that he might have given Angel the same
instructions that Tanya had. I waited for him to begin. To
set, or reset the tone.

He leaned back and began to chuckle. That was for
the benefit of others, as had been the whole setup, for
what he had to say was far from amusing. He was a master of cunning, a technique perfected by those who want
to remain...safe. He lit another cigarette, then noticed his
lack of good manners and offered one to me. I accepted
and he lit it, bending ever so slightly toward me. "I need
to speak to you about...something. I want to explain to
you." He leaned back and chuckled, again for the benefit
of some real, or imagined, audience, and to indicate to
me that I was to understand the circumstances, clearly.
What followed came in tones that only I could hear but
which would remain with me for life. He began, "I want
to explain about last year. I want you to know that there
was another reason why we couldn't do what you, what I
wanted to do." I understood the reference to mean that
last year was more than the existing social and political
taboos. I nodded. He continued; his voice plane flat. "I am
Chinese. I will always be Chinese. I am a prisoner here and
I will never leave this place. I will die as I have lived, a prisoner. I have accepted that. Because I am Chinese there are

certain...things that men and women do together, other things...that I have never experienced. These are things I am not allowed. Things that would be shocking, horrible to many Chinese women of my generation. Things that could even be reported by an angry woman. I know about these things, but can only think about, perhaps dream about, what they would be like. If I...if we...you see...you would have changed me. You would have changed me forever. Then you would leave, but I would live here for the rest of my life, a changed man. It is better not to change... to only dream. I couldn't allow you...allow that change to happen. I can only permit myself to...dream. It has been very difficult for me...for me to know you...I hope you understand my poor words."

Yes, how well I understood wishing for a life that is more than dreams and the despair of believing you will die never finding that way out...how small my own despair from so many years ago seemed when compared with his. A sickness born of anger gushed within me. Abhorrence of this unspeakable system clutched at me. The unspeakable arrogance of this unspeakable system...designed destruction of the human spirit...killing of the soul. I wanted to strike out at the fiends, not even knowing which ones were the fiends, the ones who twist and crush and plot to destroy...who would report even a trembling hand.

What did I do? Nothing. Nothing at all. I sat with my hands clenching and unclenching on the table. With the most subtle motion possible, Alexander touched my fingertips with his own, to calm me, for myself, but also to tell me not to draw undue attention to myself, to us. I stared into his eyes. They were blank, their blankness sending me a message. I straightened my back and rear-ranged my expression to match his. Angel returned with some plates of food. Alexander picked up his chopsticks, but his hands were shaking so hard that he dropped the first bite in his lap. He quietly set the chopsticks down and lit another cigarette from the one he was smoking, and poured another glass of beer. I pushed the food around on my plate. Angel reached for my hand. "It's time to go," she said. She nudged me to get up, protecting the two people she loved most in the world...protecting them from each other...from watching eyes and ears.

We left Alexander sitting alone at the table, smoking and drinking. Angel told me later that he had drunk him-self into a stupor that night. I was never to see him again, but that was because of a mistake.

I went to Tanya's apartment. I had to talk and need-ed her very much. She sat with me as I related what had happened, what had been said. I was there for maybe an hour, then was exhausted and wanted to sleep. She walked me back to my rooms. As we came in view of my apart-ment, there was a group of three men standing in front of my open door, Charles being one of them. There were two more inside. They were ransacking it. I stood there, aghast. Charles ignored the investigation which he had ordered and to which I had become an unexpected wit-ness. Instead, he reached out to shake hands with me, all smiles. "It's nice to see you again. I hope you enjoy your vacation." Then he turned and spoke in Chinese, the two men came out, smiled at me, and the entire group went down the stairs. I withdrew my still extended hand. What in the hell had they been looking for?

It was the fourth morning, and I was awakened early by the daily maid who was making her rounds. I reached the door just as she was opening it with her passkey. She hurried past me, laughing an embarrassed laugh and jabbering in Chinese. I watched her, not understanding her arrival, which was several hours ahead of her regularly scheduled time. She went straight to my bed and threw back the cover to inspect the sheets. She shrugged her shoulders, replaced the cover, laughed her embarrassment again, and hurried past me on her way out. I surely didn't have to have that one explained to me. She had been sent to look for any traces of semen that might have been on the bed linen. Charles' determination to destroy Alexander was still seething inside him. What more did he want? Would it never end? Was it all his doing, or were there others driving him on? Bastards! Damn, damn bastards! Loathing swallowed my senses.

There were two weeks left. I didn't want to stay even another day, but of course I would, for my students and friends. I told them about my rooms being searched. They already knew and said it would be better not to meet there anymore. So we met in smaller numbers and walked the campus or the streets where there was no likelihood of listening devices. My hours with them were spent in deep conversation. They told me of the events and the tensions in the city, in the country. They told me of students, dissidents, who had been released from prison as a gesture to the West. However, those dissidents would have preferred to remain incarcerated where they had others to talk to. As it was, they were restricted to their homes, and even their parents and relatives shunned them out of fear of reprisals against themselves. Mostly I just listened. There was nothing to say to them. Encouragement? When it wouldn't sound ridiculous I tried to give it, but attempts at encouragement would sound too much like I didn't understand and wanted to escape from their truth. I kept still and let them vent. Repercussions against them, individually, would be coming later—repercussions that I wouldn't hear about for several more years.

The night before my departure, Alexander telephoned me from somewhere out of town. His tone was again flat as he said his good-bye to me. His last words were, "We will always be special friends, and when I die I want you to come back to this city and pound one nail into my coffin. Then it will end." And he hung up the phone. I went to Tanya and she comforted me.

My last morning arrived and Angel came early to my rooms, as did Tanya. They helped me organize and pack up without much talk. A knock on the door took Angel to the telephone. She came back saying that she'd have to leave for a few minutes, but would return. Alexander was waiting for her on the street. I wondered why he had returned to town. We finished packing and my students began arriving with small gifts. They carried my bags down the stairs to the waiting van. This one was smaller than the other and there would be room for only one student to accompany Tanya, Angel, and me to the airport. I wouldn't make the decision as to who would go; I couldn't do that.

They discussed among themselves and Mike was selected. Tanya and I were ready to get into the car when Angel came running back. She had two small packages in her hands, neatly gift wrapped. She passed them to me and we got into the van. My beloved students formed a semicircle beside the car. All talking had ceased, moments dragged by, and it seemed that each was waiting for the other to speak. Finally, it was Ray who called out, "We love you, Adair," and they all saluted. Those words, so impossible to say in Chinese, had been said by dear friends as they crossed that cultural barrier to become one with me. I was sobbing as the driver pulled away from the guest house and I turned to watch through the rear windows until we rounded a corner.

Tanya held me and gave me a handkerchief to dry my eyes. I fumbled to open the gifts which Angel had handed to me. The first was a lovely double-stranded, interwoven golden necklace. I understood the meaning. The second was a small carved ivory statuette of a woman. I recognized it from the night at the Buddhist temple and from the statue the students had created and wheeled into Tiananmen Square.

"Who does this represent?" I asked Angel.

"She is the Goddess of Mercy. Alexander asked that you think of him whenever you look at it, and to have mercy on him." I clutched it and the tears began again.

Angel turned to the driver and began talking rapidly in Chinese. She seemed to be giving him instructions. He questioned again for clarification, and seemed to be arguing with her. Her voice rose as though she were giving a command. He shrugged and turned the van onto another road which would take a bit longer to connect with the airport road. She turned back to me. "Alexander has asked that we take this route because he will be waiting along the road to say one last good-bye to you."

I gasped, scarcely able to believe that he would do that. But apparently so. There were hundreds, perhaps thousands of bicyclers and pedestrians jamming the streets and sidewalks. We each were looking, searching for Alexander amid the crowds. The driver delayed as long as traffic allowed, then a policeman gestured for him to move along. There had been no sight of Alexander. I thought to myself that he had become fearful and again changed his mind at the last moment.

We arrived at the airport and our farewells were said with few words. As Mike was saying his good-bye, he leaned over and whispered in my ear, "Haven't you ever wondered who our class monitor was?"

I was taken aback for only a moment, then lied, "Many times."

He leaned even closer and there was a smile on his lips as he whispered, "It was I."

I pulled away from him and his eyes were twinkling. I choked back a giggle and punched him lightly on the arm.

I went through immigration without any problem and boarded the flight back to Hong Kong. I saw that my small group was waiting behind the tall gates. A couple of hands waved a bit. I waved back, knowing they couldn't see me, but waving anyway. I grieved over leaving them behind to their own destinies, knowing that I was helpless to change their futures. We could only hope that changes would come in China, and within their lifetimes. But my grief would pass and I would be consoled that I had done the right thing by making this trip. We'd been able to go through closure.

It was more than a year later, when Angel was able to obtain a student visa and come to the United States to study, that I learned what had happened on the way to the airport. Alexander had been waiting to meet me along the roadside. He had stood for more than an hour, knowing by the length of time that we'd missed the appointed place, but waiting anyway. It was never clear to Angel whether he had misdirected her, or whether she had misdirected the driver. It really didn't matter. What would be impossible for me to ever forget was that he had been there. I have long created a picture in my mind, seeing him waiting and watching, keeping vigil, and then, resigned, turning to leave, and I know what he had risked just to speak to me for one more brief moment. And I have thought of the statuette of the Goddess of Mercy and believed that it was for his protection that the rendezvous never happened, and I carry his sadness within me.

Winters in Armenia are cold, deadly cold. In a Yere-van apartment a man lived together with his aging moth-er. In that city, during those days, the food supply was scarcely at subsistence levels, there was little to no elec-tricity, little to no fuel for either the gas stove or for heat-ing. Water was turned on for only two hours daily, start-ing from midnight. Survival had become an unrelenting challenge against the odds since the blockade; since the earthquake of 1988. Everything had converged at once. In the vast areas beyond some were hailing perestroika as be-ing the great opportunity. It was being celebrated by the neophytes as the possible opening of the doors for a bright new future. But for this land it had meant the shutting down of essential, albeit decrepit, lifelines by people who may have believed in that future, but who had no plan to bridge from having everything supplied through a crum-bling infrastructure to having nothing supplied through no infrastructure whatsoever. They'd known for decades that water was being piped through lines that were riddled with bacteria that kill, that the nuclear power plant had been built in the wrong place, and leaked, and that the broken-down rail lines linking them with life-sustaining goods ran through enemy territories and were no longer dependable. *Shut them all down, for the good of the people.* Ide-alists without strategies, or experience had made the de-cisions, while homeland temperatures dropped deep into the subfreezing zones. That was one story, one explana-tion. There were others.

On one particular night, the man was sitting beside his mother on an ancient sofa, their feet cradled in pillows on the floor, pillows to absorb the frigid air seeping under the door and through window frames that didn't fit snugly anymore. They sat with a blanket wrapped about the two of them for warmth. They sat together quietly, each reading some book by the light of flickering candles. The burning of the candles was a luxury they allowed themselves on occasion. Candles were expensive, when they were available. To sit in the dark, speaking of past events or of their daily plans was the more common. On this night they allowed the candles for a short while. It was late when his mother stifled a yawn and the man knew it was time for her to retire. He took her book gently from her hands and nodded toward her room. She smiled at her son. He helped her to her feet and secured the warm blanket around her body, picked up one of the candles, snuffed out the other, and walked with her to her bedroom door. He handed her the one candle and lingered until he was sure that she was comfortably in bed, watched the tiny glimmer of light issuing from under the door and waited for it to be extinguished. Only then did he return to the sofa. On his way, he lifted his greatcoat from the hall peg and wrapped it about himself. The cold of the apartment had already penetrated through him, chilling his very bones. He again cradled his feet in the pillows on the floor and sat, waiting until midnight, until the water would be turned on. Then, as was his duty, he would work quickly and cautiously in the dark. He would take their buckets and go to the sink to fill them, lining them up on the floor along one wall. By daybreak there would be a thin layer of ice coating the water in the buckets. If the gas was not turned on that next morning, the water would be used sparingly for bathing, as well as for their other daily needs. The man sat, as he had sat for countless nights, for countless months before, waiting. This was the measure of his life.

On this particular night there was a small amount of light reflecting from the moon. He looked toward the heavily draped plate-glass door to his loggia and wondered what the weather promised. Would there be more snow? He stood, pulled his greatcoat tighter, and scooted his feet along on the pillows to the door. He inched aside one of the drapes and peered out over the rooftops of the city and beyond to the reason why his father had purchased this apartment. The moon itself seemed frosted as its light filtered down onto snowcapped Mount Ararat. That view touched his soul; always soothed him. He stood looking out through the thick glass, his breath making small disturbances on the pane. He breathed slowly and deeply, staring vacant-eyed at the scene before him. He didn't allow himself depression, despair. Those were also luxuries, luxuries that drained energies required to face the next day, and the next, and the endless time that stretched before him without hope. He had trained himself to put away all dreams, not to think back to other, better days, never to acknowledge that his life was being crushed out of him by the hopelessness. His loneliness was an emptiness inside of him that was beyond calculation. He accepted it.

On this night there was no change. He didn't think of it as a change. But from somewhere in his depths a tugging began again; a yearning always lurking, but which he had consciously not granted exposure for a very long time.

An impossible thought tried to infiltrate and express itself. Will it never end? Is there no one? Is there no one? He squelched it before it could be fully born, but in that seminal moment he ruminated idly; had the thought expressed itself in the English language? No, probably not. He had little opportunity to use that language. But sometimes he deliberately drew on it as an intellectual exercise. Only infrequently, though, and this was probably not one of those times. Anyway, that was of no consequence. He continued to look out at that mountain of history. But he didn't believe the stories. Had never believed them. One could just look at the scene and scientifically recognize that the stories were an impossibility. Stories are for children.

He turned and scooted along on the pillows back to the sofa. He sat and waited. In time, the gurgling and spluttering of the pipes intruded into his near-sleep. He went to complete his chore. When it was done he retired to his cot in that same living room. He held the blanket and crawled between the icy sheets, pulling his greatcoat on top of the coverings. The cot made a crinkling noise under his weight. It was the sound of the cardboard beneath him. His mattress he had long ago given to his mother to make her rest more comfortable. In time he slept his dreamless sleep. It was just one more night.

The man did not know that in the early spring a phone call would come that would change his life. He did not know about the threads which were unwinding; threads which had been wound decades—perhaps lifetimes—before. He didn't think about his father's prediction. How could he? That was more than forty years ago. Long since forgotten. He did not know that the impossible thought was his beginning, and that it was connected to something that was happening not so very far away...just a few hours away...in a hotel by the Black Sea.

U.S.A. – FOURTH RETURN

I had returned to teaching summer school classes at the UC–Davis campus immediately upon my arrival back in California from the trip to China. The schedule was heavy and I needed the work, both emotionally and financially. My financial situation was so dire that I took a second job, teaching immigrant Mexicans in the evenings for a State of California program designed to provide survival skills to the farm workers. The drive out to their site three times each week took me along miles of deserted, dark roadways. Frequently, I was nervous and spent the time chanting. I would arrive to find sometimes a full class of fifteen, and other times to find only two or three. I admired those men and women. They worked the tomato fields all day in all kinds of weather. Backbreaking work. Then they'd return to their homes for a quick supper, shower, dress in their best clothes and come to class, exhausted. Some may have been illegals; I didn't know and didn't want to know. Their work ethic was unquestionable and they were doing jobs that too many native-born citizens feel they are above, won't accept. Even if there were only two or three in attendance, I gave the class. If they could try, so could I. Then I'd drive back in the pitch-blackness, chanting aloud to relieve my trepidation. If I should have car trouble, I would be stranded. Or maybe some crazed drunk would run into me. I felt helpless, often frightened, but the chanting eased the time.

The 1990 fall classes began and I rode my bicycle to the UCD campus. The best possible form of transportation! I felt like a kid, and loved it. Barbara began coaxing me to investigate another foreign site for teaching. UCD contracts were each only of ten weeks' duration, and were iffy, dependent upon the number of internationals requesting Intensive English. I was reluctant to begin thinking about moving abroad again. I carried too many emotional scars from China to be willing to set out for foreign ports; not yet. I developed a routine of biking to classes, driving to my immigrant students, and preparing classes. Seven months passed by, uneventful but satisfying enough. I was gaining in physical, mental, and emotional strength.

Another April rolled around and with it my birthday. Barb and I were sitting together that afternoon on the sofa, having a coffee and a gossip session. The door was open to the spring warmth. A car drew up and a man came to the door, gave it a little tap, and peeked around to see if anyone was there. "I have a telegram for an...Adair? Is there someone here named Adair?" I looked at Barbara, gave a shrug and a grimace of surprise, went to get it, and he left. I sat back down and opened the envelope. I read it aloud.

"Happy Birthday. My friend sends love's greetings. I hope your marriage will be incredible. Love, Tanya." Her telephone number followed the message.

"What?" we both shrieked it at the same time.

"Read that again!" Barb demanded, and I did.

"What's she talking about?"

"I have no idea! Tanya's finally gone round the bend."

"Call her!"

"Call her?! It's...it's three or four o'clock in the morning in Yerevan."

"So? Call her!"

"Oh...OK," I relented, and went to the phone and dialed.

After five or six rings I was ready to hang up when a sleepy voice said, "Da!"

"Good morning, Tanya, I just got your telegram."

"Adair! Adair! Happy Birthday. Did you like it?"

"Tanya...what in the world is this? What are you talking about? What marriage? Who's your 'friend'?"

"I told you, Adair. I told you. Don't you remember? I told you I'd find you the perfect husband and that he'd be Armenian. Surely you remember."

Well, you can imagine...to say that I was flabbergasted would be a vast understatement. Yes, she'd said it—well over two years before. I'd dismissed the idea, forgotten all about it.

"Tanya, you can't be serious," I said, and began to laugh.

She was instantly miffed. "Why are you laughing? I gave my word. Doesn't that have any meaning to you? My vow means nothing to you?"

I stifled my giggling. "Tanya, I didn't think you were so serious. I told you, I don't want a husband...any husband. I don't want to get married...ever again."

"But you must. And I've found him, and he's interested."

"Interested! How can he be interested? He's never met me. How does he know about me? Who is this guy?"

"His name is Norair Gasparian, and I've known him for more than ten years."

Because of her Russian pronunciation of the name I didn't understand it, and wouldn't for a very long time. I just called him "that guy."

"Tanya, what have you done?"

"I've found him. It was very difficult, because of the English. Whoever I found had to speak excellent English. That was difficult. But then...well, anyway, it's a long story and this is costing a lot. Anyway, I invited him over to a dinner party, showed him your pictures and letters, and played the videotape we'd made. He said he's ready to fall in love again, and I told him to write to you...but he said he couldn't do that because that wouldn't be proper without your consent. Can he write to you?"

"Tanya! Great God in Heaven! What *HAVE* you done?" I began to laugh again, but then stopped myself. I could feel her frustration with me through the telephone. "OK. Tell that guy that I will be happy to receive his letter and will answer it." I was ready to end the call, but she had one more thing to say.

"By the way, Adair, I've made arrangements for you to come and teach at the Brussov Institute of Foreign Languages here in Yerevan."

"You've *WHAT*?" I exploded.

"I said, I've arranged for you an invitation to come and teach here in Yerevan. They can't pay much, but—"

"Tanya! I'm under contract to UCD. I can't quit and come to Armenia...for...to..."

"When does your contract end?"

"Each contract is for ten weeks. They end every ten weeks."

"That will be fine. Whenever you can come, you can arrange with your schedule."

"I'll call you back, Tanya. This is all too much...I'll call you later. Bye."

"Bye-bye, Adair. I told you I'd do it! Bye." And we hung up.

I went back and sat on the couch, speechless. I just looked at Barb. She, of course, had heard only my side of the conversation, but it had been enough. She'd caught the drift. We both began howling with laughter.

"Barb. Get me a drink. Make it a big one!"

She popped up and ran to the refrigerator to make drinks, two of them.

"So. You're going to quit your job, go to...where? Lower Slavovia? Marry some guy you've never met...and spend the rest of your life teaching English to a bunch of Russians."

"Yerevan...Armenians. No, I'm not. Of course I'm not. Don't be preposterous!"

"Mommm...I'll bet you do. Betcha!"

"Barbara, you are *WRONG*," I stated, and we drank our drinks, and than a couple more. After all, it was my birthday.

We were having dinner that evening when a neighbor stopped by. "There's a volleyball game at the high school tonight. Davis is playing some team from Russia. Want to go?" We had nothing better planned.

We walked over to the high school, were late, and the bleachers were pretty well filled. Barbara spotted two possible places, one in front of the other. We made our "excuse me's" and I took the first seat. We were near the players' bench which was designated for the Russian team. I was seated next to an attractive middle-aged woman who was leaning sideways talking to the team members in Russian, then to the announcer in English. She was one of the chaperones and translators for the team. At the end of the second quarter the teams took a short break. I began chatting with the lady, asking her about her trip, the usual. She responded to me easily and we were soon talking about ourselves and our families. I started to laugh and told her about the telegram and the telephone call of that afternoon. She listened attentively, but didn't laugh.

"You say he is Armenian?"

"Yes."

"I'd think about that very seriously, if I were you."

Play was about to resume and I turned around to look at Barb. She hadn't heard the interchange, and it would have to wait until later for me to repeat it.

The game ended. The Russians had won. The cheering was brought to an end with the announcement that the Russian team had brought some gifts, and if we would look at our tickets, the winning numbers would be called. Mine was the first called. I was presented with a wax candle in the shape of a champagne bottle, a plastic wrapper around it written in Russian which said something like "Greetings from Russia" or some such.

On the walk back home I told Barbara about my conversation with the woman and handed her my prize, the champagne bottle candle.

"Barb,...you don't think...? No! No way! It is not a sign. Definitely NOT a sign."

"Right, Mom."

By the middle of June Angel had been granted her student visa after a yearlong quest, and had arrived for her advanced studies in the United States. She was to spend the summer with us before taking up her classes. Angel and I sat for long hours on Barbara's patio, drinking iced tea and discussing everything that had happened in our lives. It was at that time she told me about Alexander having waited along the road to say good-bye to me. She told me that during the year since then his physical as well as mental well-being had declined. He was retreating ever more into his shell, and what conversations he had with anyone were usually confrontational. He was angry all the time. When she'd had the opportunity to speak to him alone he had confided to her that he thought he was "going crazy." He was drinking heavily. Angel's compassion for him, her surrogate father, was profound. It hurt to hear her report. Hurt more than I was willing to admit. It was a pain that would dull but never disappear. Had I been in love with Alexander? Was I still? What difference did it make?

I told her about Tanya's telegram and phone call. Angel listened wide-eyed, not comprehending how it could possibly be true. Tanya had sent a four-page letter that had arrived just days before. I went to get it and read it to her.

In it, Tanya had given a detailed explanation of how she'd "found" the man, and also of his family background and of him, as a man.

After returning to Armenia, three months after my last visit to China, Tanya had tried to take up her post at the university in Yerevan. But over the next several months her spirits and her health declined markedly. She had expected to be vital and exuberant upon her return home, but that had not happened. She had tried to tell of her experiences in China, but received no commiseration for what she had suffered. Her scenario about China was not all that different from thousands of Soviet scenarios, and her involvement with me, with her Chinese students, and with her "special" friend was of little importance to anyone. She had spoken of her desire to find a husband for me, but no one had any suggestions nor was much interested in her search. Her family and colleagues had their own problems just trying to survive in a collapsing society. Unable to vent, she had become weaker in both body and spirit. She asked for, and was granted, a few weeks' recuperative time to spend at the Black Sea. She had gone alone and knew no one there. In the hotel, though, she had become acquainted with a woman from Tbilisi, Georgia, who was also at the spa to recuperate from an illness. As two women alone often do, they began to spend all their time together, talking of this and that. During one of their conversations, Tanya casually mentioned finding a husband for her American friend, explained all the specifications she had in mind which would qualify any candidate for such matrimony, and complained of the difficulties she had met. The woman had listened carefully to her and then said, "I know just the man. He was a classmate of mine when I was in elementary and secondary music schools in Tbilisi. I know he speaks English fluently and I think he has even gone to live in Yerevan. He was married, but I've heard he has been divorced for some time now. His name is Norair Gasparian."

Tanya wrote that she had fairly shrieked with recognition, saying, "Yes! Of course! I've known Norair for more than ten years. Obviously. How is it possible I didn't think of him?" She'd gone straightaway and packed to return to her home. Arriving back in Yerevan, she'd started her tactics to interest him in me…and then told again about the dinner party she arranged, and his reaction.

She also wrote that Norair was the son of an old and cultured family who had lived many years in Tbilisi, a family that had been wealthy vintners and of the highest class, but had lost everything due to the Soviet takeover of the Republic of Georgia. They eventually had immigrated to their Armenian homeland. His father was long since deceased, but Norair lived in Yerevan with his mother and brother. Tanya described him in adjectives that were a bit too overstated, but they were her adjectives, chosen to interest me. Norair was an intellectual; a highly educated, multilingual violinist with the Yerevan Symphony Orchestra. He was handsome to the point of looking like a movie star, and there was always a cluster of women seeking his attentions. But he was a man of "noble" traditions and, although he had been married, his requirements for a wife were not met by any of the women in their circles.

Angel reacted to the "coincidence" of Tanya's meeting with the woman at the Black Sea, which certainly had not escaped my attention. She also commented favorably on the qualities as Tanya had described them. I said that I thought he sounded more like a stuffed shirt, which I then had to explain to Angel.

Over the next weeks, Barbara and Angel and I discussed "that guy" several times, but there was no letter from him. We let it cool; we were probably all thinking the same thing, but not mentioning it. He'd lost interest. Or, I thought, more likely he'd sobered up after Tanya's dinner party and come to his senses.

It wasn't until August that his letter arrived. Angel was concluding her visit with us and Barbara had stayed home for the day. She brought the letter to the patio and handed it to me. The first thing I did was check the post-mark to see when it had been mailed. It had taken nearly three months to make the airmail trip. I opened it and a small picture fell into my lap. I picked it up. Tanya's description was not quite accurate. Not a movie star, no. With his dark but graying curly hair, dark eyes, thick eyebrows, and meticulously trimmed mustache, he looked more like the prime minister from some obscure country. I said "hmm" and passed the picture. Then read the letter. Stuffed shirt? That didn't come through at all. A few simple lines saying that he'd seen my pictures and all that, and that I sounded like a "lusty" woman with whom he'd like to correspond. If I were interested, would I please answer his letter? He said that his name in English would be Norman. I passed the paper.

"Well, Mom, when are you leaving?" Barb asked.

"Well, Adair, when are you leaving?" Angel echoed.

"Well, ladies...well..."

I telephoned Tanya to have her explain to "Norman" that his letter had only just arrived and that I was not ignoring him. I would answer right away, and to expect my reply. She asked me what I thought of him and I answered that he looked and sounded...well...interesting. I reminded her again that I was not looking for a husband, and did not want one. She laughed and said it didn't matter, but to come to Yerevan to visit her and get acquainted with him. I didn't say no, but said I'd think about it. She took that as a yes, and said she'd go ahead and have the foreign language institute send my formal invitation. Oh, well. Why not? I didn't have to proceed with all of this. But it was fun to think about.

The 1991 fall semester began, Angel went off to her university in the Midwest, and I bicycled to my classes at UCD. It was one morning in early November and I was just wheeling out of the parking lot on my way to the university when the mailman came by with an envelope for me. He noted that is was from Armenia. I thanked him and stuck it in my backpack. I didn't have time to open it until I was in my office between classes. It was the formal invitation to teach in Yerevan, with instructions on how to proceed for a visa. I looked over at one of my colleagues and asked when our current contracts ended. She checked the calendar and answered, "December seventh, and the new one starts on December tenth." Five weeks. I thought how often five or six weeks' preparation time had already entered my life. I knew I was going to Armenia. No question about it. The trip would leave me penniless—again—but that was a nuisance, not a deterrent. Sitting at home and accumulating money was no substitute for the life I was living.

ARMENIA

*December 1991, less than three months following the collapse of the Soviet Union.
Chaos dominated life throughout the Republics.*

The decrepit Aeroflot crunched across the icy tarmac and shuddered to a halt at the Yerevan airport, two hours late. The aircraft was full to capacity with Armenians returning to their homes from visits to Paris, bringing with them boxes and crates of impossible sizes and shapes. There must have been no restriction as to what they could bring on board. Several men around me used their cartons as tables and played cards, talking nonstop, cheering at the drop of some winning card. The noise never slackened. The inside temperature had swung between too hot and too cold. I'd asked for a glass of tea and been ignored. I'd had to use the toilet, made my way back to it stepping over boxes in the aisle, and then returned to my seat without using the facility. It was so disgustingly filthy I wouldn't enter it—and this decision from someone who had used squatters! I was uncomfortable.

Standing in the aisle waiting to deplane, my claustrophobia mounted. What with passengers, boxes, and suitcases, there wasn't enough space to move. I was being squeezed and shoved from all sides. The Armenians were excited to be home and the noise level was escalating. I needed to escape to fresh air, badly. The movable stairway was finally wheeled into place and the door opened. When it was my turn on the top step, a gust of the freezing wind grabbed my coat and nearly whipped my heavy stole from my shoulders. I had to be quick to transfer both carryon bags to one hand and awkwardly wrap my scarf securely around my head, covering my entire face, leaving only a slit for my eyes. Anxious, mumbling passengers were pushing from behind and I stumbled my way down the steps, regained my footing, and hurried to catch up while bending into the wind and trying to protect myself from the icy blasts that were pummeling me. The throng moved toward a cavernous building which appeared to be nearly dark. It was two in the morning. The building was not heated and there was but one small bulb burning in the huge, practically bare immigration area. Two officials were on duty to process the plane load. Déjà vu, Beijing! Passengers began pushing in front of me and I ended up near the end of the lines—*lines* isn't exactly right—at the rear of the elbowing crowd. I was among the last to have my passport stamped. After passing between the railings I found myself again jammed in among the throng, waiting to descend a broad stone stairway which wound down, turned a corner and disappeared into darkness. There were two and sometimes three people standing on each step. I didn't want to do so because of the wet floor, but my tote bag straps were cutting into my shoulders and I needed a few moments' respite. I put them down and awaited an opportunity to get closer to the steps. It came, and I hoisted my totes and began what was to become more than an hour's descent into the nether regions. Step by endless step, each step wet with the accumulated slush from the boots preceding me; the cold of the stone stairs and walls increasing with the descent. As we moved, the slush from the step I'd left behind splattered onto the back of my pant legs as those following me took my place. My pant legs were soon wet through, the cold and damp material rubbing against my skin and the moisture seeping into the fleece tops of my boots. The dampness soaked down and my feet began to numb. From below I could hear a grating of doors opening and closing, and could see a sudden burst of light, accompanied by an irritable babble bursting into angry shouts, then subsiding. The sporadic hubbub became an erratic, rhythmic coda to the testy mutterings of tired people. Minutes of silence, near pitch-darkness, and a subzero temperature, then the droning chorus would start again and the next grating of the doors and another eruption of light and shouting. At the end of each coda I moved down another step. Numbing feet and fingers, tote bags painfully balanced on my shoulders and gloved hands shoved into my pockets; the minutes were slowing down. Again the grating doors and another step. It must have been an hour before I rounded the landing and was in a position to see where that sound was coming from. At the bottom of the stairs were two large metal doors leading into the customs area. They were being pulled open and security guards were admitting the passengers in groups of two or three and then closing them again. At the next opening of the doors a blaze of light broke from the room and showed that there were still some ten or twelve steps ahead of me before it would be my turn. On the bottom landing a dozen or so people were jammed into the area, jockeying their belongings and vying for position. Again the grating and the winners escaping into the light, the impatient yelling, then the closing. A cacophony of Russian? Armenian? I couldn't tell. And again, with men's fists pounding on the metal, the doors opened and closed. I moved with the herd. I had another five or six steps to go. The doors opened. I'd had enough, more than enough. I began yelling, "Don't close those doors! Don't close those doors!" I shoved my way through the startled crowd that was packed together and bickering for position. It must have been the sound of the English language, but an opening was grudgingly granted and I thrust my way through and wedged between the closing doors.

The room was busy and brightly lit. Piles of boxes and suitcases still unclaimed were thrown haphazardly along one side, where the passengers who had preceded me were pulling and moving the baggage this way and that. I spotted mine at once. Easy enough to do; they were the newest, most expensive-looking ones in the stacks. I started making a beeline toward them and simultaneously heard a female voice yelling, "Adair! Adair! Over here!" I swung around in mid-pace at the familiar sound. Tanya was standing on some steps near the corner of the opposite wall, waving her arms and shouting at me. Because of the elevation of the entry in which she stood, my view was unobstructed. Beside her stood a large man carrying a bouquet of flowers. He was wearing an ill-fitting, colorless greatcoat that hung to the tops of his boots. A dull, possibly plaid scarf dangled from his shoulders and down the front of his coat. I could tell even from that distance that his clothes had endured years of wear. Though his attire transmitted a quiet message of poverty, he wore it with dignity. In the midst of the noise and pandemonium of the room there was a calm, aristocratic demeanor in his stance, setting him apart from the others. His posture was erect and he had the air of a man of substance. A beret was perched jauntily over dark graying hair, and its tilt added a capricious note. I knew who he was. I grinned and waved, looking from them to my bags, undecided, then shrugged. I'd have to get my luggage first. I wound a path among the arguing throng, released the hand grips of my bags and rolled them toward the customs counters, at the same time trying not to drop the slipping tote bags from my aching shoulders. When I reached the counter Tanya and the man were there to meet me, Tanya's voice punctuating the surrounding prattle. She grabbed me, yanking on me, pummeling my back, kissing my cheeks. Still wrestling with my luggage, I looked up at the man and said, "Here, take these." My first words to him. But he was already reaching for them, having transferred the bouquet to under his arm, crushing it. He hoisted my bags onto the counter and I turned to hug Tanya, clasping her to me, laughing and banging on her back. The meeting was chaotic. I swung back to the man. He was watching the greeting and smiling. I extended my hand and said, "You must be Norman." He took my hand in his, turned it palm down and bent to touch his lips to it. I was a trifle nonplussed. I'd seen it in the movies, but no one had ever done that to *me* before. He straightened, still holding my hand, and looked into my eyes with a directness that was disconcerting. I found myself staring into the most soulful brown eyes I'd ever seen. There was a momentary... something. Recognition? I heard Tanya speaking to the customs official in Russian and turned back to the counter. She was talking fast and he handed her some papers. She turned to Norman and explained something to him. He released my hand and stepped to the counter, took a pen and began filling in the forms. Tanya said to me, "It won't be necessary for you to open your bags, and they are terribly sorry you had to wait in the line. If they'd known that there was an American teacher coming to the foreign language institute, you would have been passed through immediately. They extend their apologies." Because of my fatigue and irritation over the prolonged trek down those stairs, an obscene expletive wanted to spit itself out, but I swallowed it and smiled, nodding at the customs' officers. Norman spoke to Tanya and she said to me, "We need to indicate how much money you have with you. Would you please tell Norman?"

"I've brought two thousand dollars in American currency," I said, and leaned across to make sure he entered the correct amount. He wrote two hundred dollars. I pointed and said quietly, "No, no, no, two thousand dollars, not two hundred dollars." He poised the pen and looked at Tanya. She repeated in Russian. He looked at me questioningly and I whispered again, "Two thousand dollars." He seemed confused, then scratched out the first amount and wrote in the second.

Tanya and I shared the tote bags while Norman pulled my suitcases by the handles. He wasn't sure at first and had lifted them with the handles already extended.

Clearly, this was a new gadget in their lives. I indicated to him their purpose and he put the suitcases down, took the tote bags on his own shoulders, and pulled the luggage along behind him. We entered the parking lot and they walked toward a waiting man. I was introduced to Goga, Norman's brother. Several inches shorter and a couple of years older than his sibling, Goga flashed a smiled that dazzled and complemented his twinkling eyes. We shook hands, the normal way. The men loaded my belongings in the trunk of a twenty-plus-year-old Lada while Tanya and I crawled into the backseat. I was finally handed the flowers, which were now somewhat crushed. I thanked Norman for his thoughtfulness as he slid into the front beside his brother.

The ride through Yerevan was fast, there being almost no others cars at this hour. The streets were slick from the accumulating ice, as there wasn't enough traffic to disturb the freezing nighttime temperature. Streetlights were infrequent and dim. We sped by rows of featureless gray structures as Goga drove deftly, avoiding potholes. He drove without lights for the most part, which made me nervous. He was conserving. Tanya was unconcerned and chattered incessantly, gripping and patting my hands. I asked if they had been waiting in the terminal the whole time, considering that the plane was so late. She assured me they hadn't, and had waited at her apartment, having phoned ahead to the airport for the arrival time. Norman was sitting sideways and I tried to bring him into the conversation, but he only smiled, watching me and responding meagerly, allowing us these moments to let our initial excitement subside.

We arrived at Tanya's block of apartments, more featureless gray buildings set back from the road in a small grove of scrawny, naked trees. Tanya led the way to her third-floor apartment through a crumbling entryway and up chipped stone steps, between walls which were gouged with gaping expanses and from which the fallen cement lay scattered along the stairs. There was one dim bulb hanging suspended at each landing, which were the storage places for toilets and bathtubs that must have been perched there since God knows when, awaiting some mythical future installation. *Third world!* How recognizable its characteristics are; whether they're met up with across the planet or in our own inner cities. The men were somewhere below us, speaking to each other softly as they maneuvered my heavy bags. Tanya unlocked her thick new door...it had just been hung, replacing the one that had been broken into only weeks before. She stepped through and held the door wide for me to enter. I walked into the warmth of her home. She had left on both the heat and a small welcoming light. For her, an extravagant gesture. I would have known the apartment was hers. Of course. Cozy, colorful, lots of Chinese ornaments and wall hangings. Simple but comfortable furniture, television, the sound system she'd had so much trouble procuring in China and transporting home, a piano against one wall, a large round dining table near another wall, and a grouping of chairs about a smaller table laden with the settings for tea. A glass-enclosed loggia was separated from the living area by curtained windows, and the curtains were pulled back with attractive ties.

"Tanya, it is lovely."

"Oh, my miserable, poor little apartment. Nothing like ours in China. This is so small. There is no bedroom. I'm afraid you'll have only the loggia to sleep in and it is so narrow, the bed is barely more than a cot."

"Don't apologize, my sister. I'm here with you. That's what's important." And we hugged again.

The men arrived with the luggage and there was commotion as Tanya instructed them where to put everything. As they followed her orders, she hurried into the kitchen to heat up the kettle of water and returned with a magnificent, large round torte and placed it with pride on the table already crowded with small dishes of various canned fruits from her own pantry. We stood, admiring the display. Norman took a pastry knife and carefully, meticulously, cut a circle in the center. I wondered why he was cutting in such an odd manner. Radiating out from the circle, he then sliced the torte into manageable pieces. Oh, how clever. Why had I never thought of it when cutting an unwieldy cake? I'd learned something new. We sat as Tanya poured the tea. Norman began serving me from this dish and that, wanting to make sure I sampled everything, in a way that was almost...fatherly.

He questioned me about the trip and the conversation picked up. I told them everything that had transpired, and Tanya and I reminisced about our time in China, sharing with them the more humorous aspects of our adventures. As we spoke, translations were given in Russian to Goga and he was able to participate in the celebration. Norman replaced each of my disappearing tidbits without missing a syllable. I found his vocabulary and accent amusing, and kept him talking just so that I could listen. He spoke English, no doubt! His vocabulary was extensive, but from literature and textbooks. I couldn't help but chuckle at some of his word selections. Vagabond? Intrepid? It was wonderful to my ear. I loved it. As the time passed it was clear that he was not only well read, but also had unique discernment that showed itself when he interjected some salient comment. I found myself relaxing into his nearness. There was something special about this man that was reassuring and comforting. I already knew from Tanya that he was a man of traditions, of European breeding, an old-world gentleman. As I sat beside him I could sense that he was, indeed, a cultured, gentle man. He seemed to be in the eye of a corona of...safety. Substance. That was the only word I could define him with. My first impression of him: a man of substance.

By the time Norman bent to kiss my hand goodbye, the sky had begun to lighten. After they left Tanya asked me what I thought. I hugged her and said he was very handsome and his company was enjoyable. I didn't say more, but went to the loggia, exhausted. I could hear her as she rummaged around in the kitchen, putting away the last of the dishes and running what sounded like a torrent of water. As I snuggled down into my tiny bed and pulled the covers up to my chin, I smiled to myself, calmly admitting a truth already discerned. *Yes, I think she's right. I think she's found him.*

It was midday when I awoke. Through the sheers at the tall windows overlooking the courtyard I could see that a heavy fog had consumed the scrawny trees, and the gray mantle obliterated whatever was beyond. The loggia was cold and there were meandering rivulets on the panes of glass. I felt, then thumped the tiny radiator to see if it was working. It was cold. I tried to pull on my clothes without getting out of bed into the chilled air, and was relatively successful. I heard Tanya in the kitchen and moved briskly in that direction. The door to that room was closed and I sidetracked into the small bathroom for the morning ritual. There was no hot water; no water at all. Two buckets stood in the bathtub, with a washcloth draped over the side of one. I made use of that water for washing up and brushing my teeth while wondering to myself if all the utilities had gone off during the storm earlier that morning.

I pushed open the door to the kitchen and its welcoming heat and homey aromas. Tanya gestured to close the door quickly. The kitchen was small, but with another marvelous, tall double window that overlooked the naked grove of trees. On the ledge were brightly colored plants, and the vivid red curtains were drawn back with lacy white ties. Placed in front of the window was a small table with a red and white checkered cloth on which was a teacup and a breakfast of fruits and bread. I sat and watched Tanya busying herself at the bubbling pots on the gas stove. It was the heat from the stove that had warmed the room.

"Good morning, Tanya, has all the power gone off?"

She poured my tea and came to embrace me again, saying how she couldn't believe I was really there. Then her tone changed, her cheerful countenance drew into concern. "I'm sorry, Adair, perhaps I should have told you before you came. Yes, the electricity and water are turned off regularly. I'm luckier than most. This apartment is a part of the science complex for the university and we have power more than nearly anywhere else in the city. Sometimes the gas is turned off, too, but not this morning, thank God. We have water and electricity during most hours of every day, and usually we have gas to cook with. There are thousands of others who aren't so fortunate. I hope you won't be too uncomfortable. I won't say that we get used to it, but we manage."

"Why is the power so erratic?"

"It's this damnable situation with Azerbaijan. They control all the pipelines and they are punishing us, trying to break us."

"Why 'break' you? How long has this been going on?"

"The blockade was in force even before that disastrous earthquake in 1988; do you remember about that? They are trying to get some border land back which the Armenians have been living on for generations. It's terrible, terrible. It makes our lives impossible. That is why all Armenian women prepare so many jars of food during the summer, so that we can eat during the winter months." And she pulled aside a curtain to reveal shelves loaded with jars of food.

"They control the food supplies, too?"

"Yes. We've always imported a lot of our food, but now the railroads are also blockaded by Azerbaijan, and it's difficult to get the food supplies to Armenia. They are devils! They're going to starve us." (I would hear other explanations later, but her rationale was shared by thousands of her fellow countrymen.)

I was trying to eat the canned fruits she had put before me, but they all tasted alike. I couldn't distinguish one from the other; each syrupy sweet. I didn't much care for them, but wouldn't allow her to suspect. I'd noticed it last night, but thought that it was only a product of my fatigue. Tanya was sitting across from me in her dressing gown, running her fingers through her hair. She was distressed.

"I should have told you all this before, but when we first talked it wasn't quite so bad. It's gotten worse over the months. Nowadays, each family has to select one person whose only job it is to go out into the city early in the morning and find a store that is open so he can get enough food for the day. Pascha usually does that for us, but often he is in school and I have to do it before I go to give my lectures at the university. Oh, Adair, I want so much to move to the United States, but it is impossible, I know that, but I want it so much. Can you help me to go to America?" Tears were forming in her eyes.

I sat staring at her, uncomprehending such a plight. The fact that I'd forgotten to even ask about Pascha and his whereabouts only darted through my mind and was gone. I was aghast at what she was telling me, couldn't think of which direction to take because my thoughts immediately shifted away from the impact on the Armenians and onto myself. How was I going to "manage"? I had no intention of staying with her for an extended period, only until I could move into the apartment the foreign language institute had promised to provide for me. But under the circumstances, how would I—a stranger to the city—be able to locate stores, maneuver the streets of an unknown metropolis, use public transportation without the language, let alone endure the freezing temperatures without heat or electricity? *Damn it, Tanya! What have you done to me?* It wasn't the time to ask, so I tried to refocus my concern and another question formed. I ignored the part about going to America. I'd heard it from her and discussed it with her too many times in the past. It had become almost a time-filler. No, I couldn't help her get to America, could hardly help myself in America, and had told her so repeatedly. I was aggravated, even frightened, but tried not to show it just yet.

"What about money? When you do find a store open, are the prices high?"

"Yes, and getting higher every day. As with anywhere else, there are corrupt ones among us who take advantage of the shortages. Not all, of course. There are many good and caring Armenians. But the others. We hate those people."

I got up from the table. "Just a minute, Tanya, I have something for you," I said, and went to fetch my wallet. I pulled out a hundred-dollar bill and handed it to her.

"What are you doing? I'd never take money from you! You've insulted me. You are my guest, my sister. I will take care of you."

"Tanya, I have no intention of letting you 'take care of' me. I am not a child; I'm a professional and I've come here to work, not to just spend some holidays with you. I brought money with me to take care of my own expenses. I won't allow you to be burdened with additional expenses for me. Now take it!" My voice was insistent.

She stood quickly and turned back to the stove. I slipped the bill under the edge of a small bowl, left it there, and thought the subject must be changed at once.

"What are you cooking?"

"Lunch for Pascha, he'll be here any moment. Adair, you haven't even asked about him."

"I realize that and I apologize. There has just been too much, too fast. Tell me, is he still studying music?"

She filled me in on his life and soon we heard his key in the lock. Her son came in and I was surprised at how tall and thin he was. I don't know what I'd expected, but not what I saw. We greeted each other and he spoke to his mother in Russian. Within moments their voices were raised and they seemed to be arguing. He turned abruptly and left the apartment. It would have been an intrusion to ask what was wrong, but what else could I do?

"Is there a problem with Pascha?"

"No, no. Not at all. It's just something at school. What would you like to do this afternoon? Do you just want to rest? Perhaps you should just rest. I'm sure Norman will be calling you this evening, probably he'll come over. Tell me now what your impressions of him are. Do you like him?"

She'd changed the subject too fast, but I let it pass. I told her the same about Norman as I had previously. "It's really too early to form an opinion. I'm glad I've met him and hope we become good friends," was all I was willing to say. I agreed with her that rest was what I really needed. I'd brought a few books and would read that afternoon, and nap, if she didn't mind.

By evening both the heat and electricity were back on, and we watched the videotape we'd made in China and chatted about people we'd left behind. Norman did not call.

The second morning the sun had broken through the cloud cover. When I went in for my tea I saw that the hundred-dollar bill had been removed, and was relieved that it would not become confrontational. It was not mentioned. I suggested we go into the city so that I could start to get some idea of the environment in which I would be living for the next several months. She advised me to hide my money under my mattress, which I did, then dressed in several layers of my warmest clothes and we went to get transportation into the city.

The boulevard was awhirl with traffic, the small Russian-made Ladas jousting as arm-waving pedestrians tried to flag them to a stop. Tanya signaled me to move onto the sidewalk while she nimbly angled her way to the front lines to catch some driver's attention. On the inside lane, buses already loaded with riders hanging precariously from the doorways whipped by. Autos that could be identified as regular taxis carried passengers who appeared to be sitting on each other's laps. The drivers of others, private cars called "gypsy cabs," were competing with one another to make extra money to support themselves and their families. Tanya was trying to flag down a gypsy cab.

Within minutes I was stamping my feet on the cement to keep the circulation moving, as were others milling about me. It was nearly a half hour before a car responded to her hail and Tanya bent to speak to the driver, raised her hand to me, and whispered as I approached, "Don't speak. If he hears English the price will go up."

The gray block buildings I'd noticed on our ride in from the airport didn't look much different in the daylight; indistinguishable one from the other. We reached what I later learned was the main square of the city and Tanya indicated where we were to get out, slipping the driver some folded money. She linked her arm through mine and held me close to her, warning me again not to speak loud enough to be heard by others. The English language! As we walked side by side along the sidewalks, the reality of her descriptions struck me. The few citizens of Yerevan who needed to be on the streets ignored their fellows, clutched their coats about them and hurried through the cold on their way to their personal destinations, passing begrimed storefront windows which stared vacantly back at a disinterested populace. Display shelves dusty from long disuse housed random stacks of unidentifiable cartons. The occasional partially dismantled mannequin stood or leaned awkwardly, immune to the humiliation of her nudity. Doors to shops were barred with heavy chains and outsized iron locks hung, protecting the empty interiors from vandals. Intermittent street vendors made no attempt to attract possible customers, but sat ruminating and drinking tea with one another while their poor merchandise went unattended. After passing by several such individual enterprises, it was apparent they were all offering the same selections—a few packets of cigarettes and gum, maybe a comb or two and the like. I held fast to Tanya. To this newcomer there was something almost sinister lurking.

"Are there no stores open?"

"Yes, there are a few international shops in the next block. I'll take you."

International shops. I knew not to expect the boutiques of America or the bustling open-air flea markets of China, but the label held a remote promise. The promise quickly faded. An iron railing jutted out from the side of another featureless building and opened onto a short flight of ice-encrusted steps leading down into a basement. Tanya navigated the way, guiding me so I wouldn't slip on the pockets of packed ice. She pushed open the door, displacing a crowd of would-be buyers. Inside, the room was brightly lit, but was scarcely more than the size of a single-car garage. A counter loaded with an ill assortment of unrelated items was staffed by three or four young girls. Over their heads and hanging from the walls and ceiling were wire clotheslines sagging under the weight of jackets and coats and miscellaneous shirts and blouses. The room was claustrophobic, packed with people struggling with each other as they inspected the offerings. There was an odor of wet wool permeating the crowd. The scene and the quality of the goods reminded me of some secondhand store back home. We had made our way to the back wall, but I felt the crush and wanted to leave at once, pulling on Tanya's sleeve. We disentangled ourselves from the mob and inched our way back out to the sidewalk. We were trying to decide what to do next when Tanya's face registered dismay.

"Adair, look at your purse. Look what's happened. Oh, I am so sorry."

I swung my shoulder bag around to look. There was a slit in the leather the full length of the material, obviously made by a thin razor. I pulled the slit apart. Whoever had done it had not realized that inside the leather was another lining. The slash had not been given enough thrust to go through to the contents of the purse. How could it have happened so deftly? The shoulder bag had been scrunched between Tanya and me the entire time. *Welcome to Yerevan, Adair.* It didn't matter whether I spoke in English or not. I might as well have been draped in the American flag.

"Let's go home," I sighed, and she nodded in agreement.

Over dinner that evening, Tanya told me she had made arrangements with her dear friend, who lived in an apartment across the complex, to visit her on nights when Norman would come to see me. Tanya wanted us to have privacy. As the after-dinner hours passed, she became increasingly nervous.

"Why hasn't he telephoned? What is he doing, playing some kind of game? He said he was ready to love again! Why hasn't he called?"

"Give him time, Tanya. There is undoubtedly a great difference to him between imagining a friendship from afar, a relationship with an independent American woman, and the reality which he has experienced. He'll need time to think about it, to adjust to it. Maybe he will decide that a liberated American female is not what he wants in his life. Give him time, I'm in no hurry. Good grief, Tanya, why didn't you just bring a priest with you to the airport?" I quipped, and she laughed.

We talked and Pascha came by. He was staying with a friend while I used his place on the loggia. With Tanya translating, I thanked him and said I hoped he was not too inconvenienced. All was well between them again and there was none of the previous tension. As they went into a lengthy conversation, I began to weary and excused myself to go to bed.

Through my drowsiness, I heard the telephone ring and then Tanya's voice, "Oh, Norair." The conversation became hushed and switched to Russian. Tanya's tone was low, intense, and sounded argumentative. I couldn't fully rouse into wakefulness, but did glance over at the clock. It was nearly midnight.

We had an appointment to visit the foreign language institute where I would be teaching. While having breakfast I questioned her about the late-night phone call, asking if Norman had telephoned, wanting to know why she had sounded angered. She said no, he hadn't called. I looked up sharply, but she was turned toward the stove. *She's lying. Lying? Why?* But I said nothing.

The institute was another building like all others, and bitterly cold. We located the office of the dean who had sent the invitation to come and teach. She was all smiles, but had little English. We were seated and tea was brought in. Tanya and the dean spoke together quickly. Tanya was becoming questioning, insistent. She turned to me.

"Classes have been discontinued on any regular basis due to the lack of heat in the building. The English language staff is eager to have you give them some lectures in methodology, but some arrangements will have to be made as to when and where those lectures can be held."

She again conversed in Russian with the other woman. Tanya was trying to smile, but her lips didn't respond quite appropriately. It was becoming obvious that something else was seriously wrong. She again spoke to me.

"The dean has informed me that there is no money in their budget to pay for an apartment for you. She is very sorry, but hopes that you will understand. They cannot provide you with any living accommodations, but she hopes that you will be able to find a place for yourself and stay to teach some classes."

I kept my expression blank as the women babbled on; a control I'd learned well in China. But my discomfort and disgust had been building since the flight and rumbling around inside me, growing, compounding with each inconvenience, my aversion to lack, and now this, no classes, no promised housing...everything collided at once. And underlying this latest...Norman's initial warmth toward me; was he a *European gentleman* whose natural bent was to make a woman feel special? And I? Was I a desperate middle-aged woman willing to cling to...anything? Maybe I'd misjudged him, misjudged myself. What was true? Why had Tanya been annoyed with him on the telephone and then lied about his having called? *What was he hiding?* My insecurities and this latest affront imploded. I felt the total fool. I was sitting there in a frigid room with the dull drone of verbiage I couldn't understand buzzing around outside of my head, upsetting my equilibrium and sense of control, and I was trying to keep the rug from being pulled totally out from under me. The two women went on talking while my thoughts rattled my self-esteem. *Rich American! You've been had, Adair. You're being used. Fuck this.*

Tanya hasn't got a lick of sense. What has she done to me? What am I allowing her to do to me? I can't manage this, any of this. I hate this fucking country. I'm getting out of here. Today. Tomorrow at the latest.

The interview was finally over. All the documents had been shuffled across the desk more than once in the appearance of professionalism. I was not impressed. The ritual handshakes and smiles accompanied the ritual good-byes, with the ritual promise to meet again. By the time we'd left the building my anger had detached, dulled; no reason to make it any worse. I'd just leave...chalk it up... I'd go back to America as soon as I could arrange passage. I was quiet. I had pushed down feelings of being confrontational. I don't do well in an argument. I can never think of the right things to say. I didn't want to discuss this with Tanya until I could do so with some grace. It was not her fault. Well, yes it was, in one sense. She had neglected to tell me about the living situation in Yerevan, and...why had she lied to me about Norman's telephone call? *Let it go, Adair. It's all history now. Just chalk it up and go home.*

"I'm so sorry. She had promised me an apartment for you. How could I know? I hope you don't blame me for this. Please don't blame me. I didn't know. Something will work out. Let's stop by the American University in Armenia. It's on our way home and maybe somebody there can help us." She clung to my arm as we made our way down the slippery hill toward the boulevard. I didn't want to go to the American University, and if I heard "I'm sorry" one more time, I was going to hit someone. I said nothing.

AUA, an affiliate of the University of California at Los Angeles (UCLA), was housed in an architecturally impressive building, quite a change from all those others I'd seen. Tanya explained that it had been a government headquarters up until three months before, when the Soviet system had collapsed and Armenia became an independent republic. The corridors were labyrinthine, running off in arbitrary directions from broad, winding marble staircases. We wandered. No classes were in session. The building was nearly deserted. She found some offices open and we were directed somewhere else. She didn't even know who she was looking for, just someone who looked like he or she might have some sense and tell her what she should do. We were lost and came back around to the top of yet another stairway. I looked down at the sound of an American accent. At the bottom of the steps stood an enormous man with a great shock of blond hair, and a smile and a voice to match his size. He was talking to what must have been a student. I felt a surge of relief at the sight and sound of the familiar, liked him the moment I saw him, felt unreasonably rescued by his presence even from that distance. I nudged Tanya and went flying down the stairs. He saw me coming and stuck out his hand to me while still talking to his student.

"I'm Jimmy Harris," he said, reminding me of some magnificent polar bear. I gripped his hand, gave him my name and introduced Tanya. He was carrying on two conversations at the same time. He introduced his "prize" student and the young man smiled some greeting, excused himself, and left.

"What are you doing in Armenia?" he asked.

The words gushed out, and within moments I'd given him a detailed outline of everything that had happened and what I was facing, and confessed what I was feeling. He slid his arm around my shoulders, giving me a half hug, and laughed.

"Sounds familiar. This place is the shits. But you'll make it, and you'll be glad you stayed. Give it more time. The Armenians are fantastic people living under impossible conditions. They are warm and hospitable and will make you feel truly welcome. When they say they're sorry, they really mean it. They'll want to give you the world, and are humiliated that they can't do it. But they'll compensate. They'll go without to give you everything they have—lovingly.

"You're here to teach methodology? Great! I want to pick you brain. I teach methodology, too, and we can work together. I'll come to your classes to co-teach with you, and you come to mine. When can we get together to discuss everything we know?"

I looked over at Tanya, my breath quite taken away, then back at Jimmy Harris. "Anytime."

Tanya gave him the phone number and directions to her apartment. We shook hands and he promised to telephone, adding that if he couldn't get through due to the bad service, for me to try to call him, and he scratched his number on a slip of paper from his pocket.

We rode home in a taxi and I decided...what the hell? I'd give it another day or two. Jimmy Harris had definitely rescued me...for the moment.

Dinner and the early hours of the evening passed without event. I went to bed, resigning myself to the notion that whatever Tanya and Norman had talked about the night before had in some way been related to his having decided I was not the woman for him. He didn't want me. When I'd told myself she'd found the man for me, I had been talking to my own...desire for a husband? Again, I was questioning who I was and what the truth about me was. I was more than glad that I hadn't mentioned it to her. I hadn't mentioned anything about Norman and all of that to Jimmy Harris, of course. I felt disappointment and embarrassment. I didn't know what I was going to do, but I'd wait a little longer before making a final decision. Maybe Jimmy could in some way help me with finding rooms of my own. Maybe I could buy some kind of heater. Maybe I could find a restaurant so that I could eat, at least once in a while. Maybe I could help the teachers a bit, for a few weeks, until my money ran out. That was the reason I'd come, I told myself, before dropping off to sleep.

My slumber must have been light because I was disturbed by the clicking sound of the telephone being dialed, followed by the hushed tones of Tanya's voice. I heard her moving toward me and she peeked into the loggia.

"Adair, are you awake? It's Norman on the phone. Norman has called you."

I was awake at once. I knew she had lied again. The phone hadn't rung, I'd heard her dialing. I let it go, and accepted the receiver.

"Well, good evening, Norman. How are you?" I put a lilt in my voice and we began to chat. He asked what I'd been doing and I related the events of the past two days. He was "sorry" my purse had been slashed, and "sorry" about the news from the institute. I lowered my voice and asked him if he'd called the night before. He admitted he had, but that Tanya had scolded him for calling so late. He was "sorry," but he'd only at that hour returned from an orchestra rehearsal, and had just returned from that evening's rehearsal when his telephone was ringing with this call from Tanya. We talked for nearly two hours. He said he'd come over that night, as he had no rehearsal, and we said our good-byes. I tried not to disturb her as I tiptoed to return the receiver to its cradle, but I didn't understand why she had lied about so innocuous a happenstance and wanted to ask her about it. I was happy when I crawled back under the blankets. Maybe I was who I thought I was and not such a fool after all.

Tanya spent the day shopping for precisely what she wanted me to serve that evening, setting the small table attractively and preparing a tasty tea to have ready when he arrived. She was more nervous and excited than I. When the time neared, she called me to come from the bathroom so she could see if I met her standards for a date before she left for her friend's apartment. She looked at me, horror-stricken.

"You're going to receive your future husband in *THAT!*"

I had put on light blue, form-fitting jeans and an oversized matching light blue turtleneck sweater which gave only a soft hint of my breasts. Just right, in my opinion. I was wearing bright red slipper socks to add accent, knowing that red is a stimulant. I'd chosen the outfit with care to give the impression of "casual relaxation" with a touch of sexuality. I thought I looked wonderful.

"Go right in and change. This is not acceptable. He'll think you don't care about your appearance."

"Tanya, this is what I want to wear. Don't worry. I know what I'm doing. I know my style."

"It's wrong, all wrong. And I've gone to so much trouble to prepare for your first evening along together. You just don't care about anything." She lifted her coat from the hall peg with a flamboyant gesture, and left.

His face was red from having dashed from the bus stop through the falling snow to the apartment complex and up the three flights of stairs. He removed his coat, scarf, and beret with one hand, holding mine in his other and stooping to kiss it.

"It's always so cozy in Tanya's apartment. She is very lucky. Mine has no heat or electricity." He was rubbing his hands briskly as he led the way to the living room. I noticed how at home he was in the apartment, but let it pass.

"Can I offer you some tea? Tanya has made special treats for us," I said, but he interrupted me.

"I'll do it. Tanya doesn't make tea to my liking." He escorted me to a chair. "You just sit here and be comfortable. I'll serve you." And he was away to the kitchen. I was somewhat startled, but relaxed into the chair as his humming and soft whistling issued from the other room. He returned with two glasses of tea. "One never drinks tea from a cup. It doesn't taste right, and it's not appropriate." He placed a glass before me and again began serving me bites from the plates left for us. As before, I found the food too syrupy sweet for my palate, but Norman ate it all with enjoyment.

"What do you intend to do about an apartment?"

"I have no idea. Perhaps you could help me, or the American, Jimmy Harris, whom I met at AUA."

The discussions led one into another with ease. He told a couple of bad jokes about "Big Joe" Stalin, about the KGB, and laughed with gusto. I've forgotten the first, but will tell you the second. Soviet humor!

> Soviet archaeologists joined world-known specialists to travel to Egypt to determine the identity and authenticity of a recently found mummy. All tried hard, but failed. The Soviet team said that there were specialists within the KGB and they should be invited to the site. They came and only had to be in the tomb for an hour or so. When they came out, they told the waiting scientists that the mummy's name was Hoetek. "How do you know?" the scientists exclaimed in wonder. (When telling it, Norman stood and placed his hand across his breast, dramatically adopting a look of innocence as he said the punch line.) "He told us, *VOLUNTARILY*." Ah, the ability to laugh about the KGB!

Norman took our glasses to make more hot tea. I followed and questioned him about his life as a musician. While waiting for the water to boil he spoke about his studies at the conservatory and his experiences with symphony orchestras. I watched as he went through an elaborate ritual of preparing the steaming drink.

"Did you ever want to become a violin soloist? To travel the world as a performing artist?"

Glasses in hand, we returned to the living room and he brushed the idea aside. "That would have been an unrealistic dream. An impossibility. Such thoughts were not encouraged by the system. There were very few who could elevate themselves in such a way. Can you name even one?"

"Sorry. No, I can't."

"It is better not to have such dreams."

Well, where have I heard words such as THOSE spoken before?

"It is difficult for people outside the system to understand it," he said, and spoke of repressions like those I'd heard about, too often, in China. He asked for comparisons with a capitalistic system, which I explained. And he wondered at the concept of freedom, at options, at making personal choices.

We'd finished our food and Norman stood to stretch. He walked to the loggia entrance and peered into my space. He didn't enter, but reached around and picked up a book I'd been reading which lay on my cot.

"Do you read in metaphysics?"

"Yes. I am a Buddhist. And you?"

He walked back and sat down, leafing through the pages. "I have no religious or spiritual beliefs. That was never a part of my upbringing in the Soviet system. Tell me what this is."

This sudden switch to such a weighty subject surprised me on a "first date," and I was momentarily at a loss, but he had asked. I wanted to avoid any in-depth discussion; however, to make light of it would be out of place and could be insulting. So, without him having any background in religious thought, I decided to move from metaphysics to commonalities with basic physics. I was unsure and asked about his studies. He said that his education had included a few courses and he'd done some reading on his own. It was of interest to him. I admitted that my own studies were also limited, but they had given me some interesting parallels with Yoga...which is the foundation of Buddhism.

I spoke about Einstein telling us that there is no such thing as a solid, but that what appears to the senses to be substantial is, in fact, mostly space, with atoms zipping about bonding into the appearance of solidity by their own energies...how Eastern philosophy teaches the same kind of thing, but takes it another step. Yoga adds that it is the power of our *belief* in the appearance of solidity that prevents us from overcoming material constraints, boundaries, and so forth...in other words, that it's our *belief system* that binds us to the material world, but that the material world is actually an illusion. He nodded, and I added that it seems that quantum physics is teetering on saying the same thing. Yoga teaches that once we have enough understanding, *belief*, we will demonstrate the truth about delusion. That's how Jesus walked on water and appeared to do so many miracles. He tried to explain this by saying that anything he could do, we could also do...that they were not miracles, but only the illusion of miracles because of our lack of understanding, our lack of *belief*. "If you had the faith of a mustard seed you would say to this mountain, be gone,"...or some such.

"I know nothing of Jesus, please go on."

"OK, another way to put this is to think about barriers. When the time comes that we *believe* that we have the power over an obstacle, have enough conviction concerning what we want, then we can command the barrier. For example, we would be able to say to this wall 'you have no power over me' and the wall would cease to exist as a barrier...and we would walk right on through it." I thumped the wall behind us. "This is to say, walls or doubt and fear."

Those deep soulful eyes were watching my face intently. "You mean like the Berlin Wall?"

That started me. Simultaneously, as I'd been speaking, he had gleaned the meaning and translated it into a reality with which he could identify. I had never thought of the dismantling of the Berlin Wall in those terms, but the parallel was surely there. There are a multitude of political and economic explanations, but it was recognizing failure and facing fear and doubt that ultimately opened mental doors to a new reality.

"That's a good one! Yes, truly, you are right, like the Berlin Wall." I traced his reasoning aloud to clarify it for myself. "Their conviction had replaced their cowering ways and they stood up to *ALL* those mighty barriers which had kept them enslaved for a couple of generations; which for so long they had believed, accepted, as their birthright through fear of reprisals. When that *belief system* crumbled, then the Wall could no longer stand because it was, after all, only a symbol of that old *belief.* Of course, most people would not think of it in those terms, would have more pragmatic reasons, but that would be the metaphysical explanation. Yes, thanks for such a practical application of an esoteric concept. You're kinda fantastic!" I reached over and hugged him as I stood to clear the table.

He only chuckled softly.

As I took the remnants of our tea to the kitchen he went to the piano. Soon I heard the melodic strains of familiar songs intertwined with interesting jazz rhythms, and went back to sit near him.

"I had no idea you also played the piano. I thought only the violin."

He smiled at me, a cigarette gripped between his teeth, a look of sexuality on his face. He segued into "The Man I Love," creating an intricate variation in chording and keys. I smiled at the choice and he nodded a smile in return. He brought it to a close with a series of arpeggios returning to the original key, then closed the cover to the keyboard, snuffed out his cigarette, and walked over to Tanya's sound system. He opened a cabinet and withdrew several cassette tapes, selected one and put it in; a romantic piece from the big-band era began to play. I walked over to him.

"Do you also dance?" I asked, and slipped my hand into his. He took me in his arms and we stood quietly for a moment. He drew me closer to him and we began to move to the beat. He nuzzled his face into my neck and caught my earlobe between his lips. We were dancing in this position when a key sounded in the door. We hardly acknowledged the intrusion when Pascha walked in. Then Norman spun us around so that he was facing Tanya's son, and spoke to him a greeting in Russian. Pascha answered, Norman laughed, and we continued to dance, the music filling the apartment. Pascha went to the kitchen, returned to the hallway, spoke again to Norman and left quickly.

We knew it was nearing the time Tanya would return. We let the music continue, but stopped moving. Norman held me closer and kissed me on the neck. I brought his face to mine and kissed him in return. We stood embracing lightly, nibbling and chuckling, then he pulled away saying he must leave. Standing in the doorway, he stroked my hair.

"You are such a natural woman." And he left.

I could hear his greeting to Tanya, whom he met on the lower stairs, and I held the door open awaiting her. When she came in, her face was tense and her smile forced. She asked me about the evening, but something was certainly disturbing her. I didn't want to hear what it was, so I babbled some bland comments, made my excuses and prepared for bed. Whatever problems she was having with her neighbor, or Pascha, would have to wait until morning. Nothing was going to spoil my rest that night.

I could tell by the rigid way she stood at the stove preparing breakfast that whatever had bothered her the night before had not subsided. As she brought my tea to the table, her eyes and voice were strained and her smile was not sincere.

"Tanya, is something the matter?"

"Yes, Adair, something is the matter. Pascha came to see me last night while Norman was here." She sat opposite me, vigorously stirring her tea. She didn't look at me. "Pascha told me that when he came to his home you and Norman were dancing and Norman was kissing you. He asked me why such old people were doing such a nasty thing, that it was disgusting."

"He said *WHAT*? Tanya, where did he get such an outlook? Is that what you taught him? What would make him have such an attitude? That's sick!"

"My son is not sick. How dare you say such a thing! Perhaps in your American society such things are acceptable. They certainly are not here. And I must ask you to keep in mind that this is Pascha's home, it is not yours, in America. When Pascha is here, I must ask you to be more discrete with Norman. Pascha doesn't need to see the two of you kissing." Her eyes were glazed with anger. I'd never seen her in this state before. Distressed, yes. But always soft and in need of emotional support. Not like this. I didn't know how to react. Couldn't think of anything to say. I was completely off balance.

"Yes, of course. This is Pascha's and your home. I've certainly been reminded of that now. I will respect your wishes concerning Pascha." I was regaining my equilibrium. "But Tanya, whatever is in his mind regarding sexuality must have been put there by you. That attitude is why he never allows you to speak to a man on the telephone, let alone have one over to dinner. Why have you done this to him, to yourself?"

"What do you mean, that he never allows me to have a man over?"

She had forgotten all that she had told me about this subject while we were in China.

"Yes, well, that's true. But I don't always bow to his wishes. I had a man over for dinner just recently and Pascha came home while he was here, and then stormed out after a terrible scene. That was why we had an argument that first morning you were here. But that is my concern, not yours. I will be accountable for my own behavior. You are my friend from America and he must not think badly of you." Her tone had modified significantly, and suddenly.

The incident was not mentioned again. We went shopping to find a bakery open. It took nearly the rest of the day to collect groceries for the evening meal, which she then prepared. She wouldn't allow me to assist her in any way, objecting to my offers because I was a guest and her beloved sister. I was beginning to feel a tinge uncomfortable with this arrangement. A guest and beloved sister? More like a helpless child, to my mind. An apartment of my own was becoming a pressing issue to me.

We fell into a routine. Norman came each evening that he was free from his duties with the symphony and Tanya went to her friend's apartment. The evenings were filled with good conversation, music, drinking tea, and watching videos. We snuggled and embraced, but always maintained a low-key control. He'd only smiled and shaken his head at her request for propriety. No problem.

I learned later that on the few nights when he left especially late, he'd had to walk all the way home, as public transportation had ended and he was unable to flag down a car. It was a distance of several miles through the bitter cold and ice. He never mentioned this to me; I discovered it by accident.

During the days, Tanya and I tried to connect with the foreign language institute, but always with the same effect. Either the phone lines were out of order, or no scheduling could be arranged due to the lack of an appropriate facility. On the couple of nights when Norman was unable to come over, Tanya took me to visit her family and friends.

It was into the second week after my arrival that Jimmy Harris and I were able to connect. I invited him for the evening. Again Tanya prepared a snack for us, then after greeting him went to her friend. Jimmy explained to me much about the Armenian difficulties and the courage of these people to survive their adversities. We spoke of educational methodologies and how we might combine our experience to bring student-centered teaching to a system rooted in rote learning. He told me of the shortages of books and resource materials and we considered ways to supplement their meager supplies. We laughed that although we were filled with good ideas and enthusiasm, the greatest obstacle we had to overcome was that there were no classes in which we could demonstrate our ideas. Tanya returned, but chose to sit in the kitchen while we were chatting, not wanting to interfere. Shortly after, Jimmy said it was time for him to leave, and he needed to ask Tanya for directions to get back to his apartment. His student had driven him to visit me and he didn't know that area of the city. Tanya walked him to the boulevard and assisted him in getting transportation home. The evening could not have been more innocent.

The following night Norman returned. It had been only a couple of days, but I'd missed the camaraderie, the joy of his presence, too much. Even before he had his coat off, my arms went about him, clutching him to me. He responded and intimacy was budding when the electricity went off. No doubt, the same thought came into both our minds, but he moved away, hung up his coat, and in the darkness led me to the kitchen and searched out the candles.

We sat, talking by candlelight in hushed tones. The intimacy which had begun was transferred to speaking more confidentially about ourselves. We spoke of our pasts and revealed to each other our problems with sustaining long-term relationships. He told me he had been married not once but twice, and I admitted the same. Both of his marriages had been brief, less than a year each, and both had produced one child—although he rarely saw either of them. One of mine was also brief, when I was a teenager, the other dragging on for several years after I knew it was over, staying married "for the children." We spoke of any possible future for ourselves and I confessed that I didn't want to marry, but felt that he and I could have a rich relationship without a legal entanglement. His only response to that was a smile. I asked him if it didn't bother him that between us we had four divorces. He shook his head no, held my hands and laughed.

The power came back on just before it was time for him to leave. We walked together into the entry hall. He held me in an embrace, stroking my hair, pressing me to him, caressing me, his hands moving to explore my breasts. I unbuttoned his shirt and ran my fingers over his bared skin, playfully counting the hairs on his chest. It excited him. His kisses were becoming deeper and more impassioned when Tanya quietly walked in. We broke apart and he quickly buttoned his shirt, saying something to her in Russian, laughing at our being "caught." She responded to him with a smile and what may have been a witticism, I didn't know. After his departure, her attitude toward me was distant, strained. I didn't know how to react to her mood swings and excused myself for bed, feeling uncomfortable, guilty, and imprisoned in her apartment.

The next morning I went early to the kitchen, put the tea kettle on to heat and picked up the phone to call Norman. Before I could complete dialing, Tanya came in. She looked as though she hadn't slept. Her eyes were lowered, her hands trembling. She went to the stove without speaking. She was undecided about something. I held my breath, not knowing what to expect from her, then cautiously returned the receiver to its cradle, for some reason not wanting to make any noise. I stood to leave the room when she spun around to confront me. Her voice was quivering with anger.

"You fool! Don't you know what he's doing? You are such a child. You are more of a child than Pascha. Why must I tell you everything? Haven't you got Norair figured out yet?" She spit his name as though it were something vile in her mouth. "You are a fool. You're standing kissing him and playing with him and he's using you for his own ends. Why do you think he's never taken you to meet his family and friends? And he never will. He's ashamed of you. You're older than he is, and you're not pretty enough for him. He's used to beautiful young women. You couldn't possibly interest him in any way except to get him to America. He'll say and do anything so you'll take him to America. He's no different from any other Armenian man. He's an opportunist. I've known it for years. He's using you and you're a damn fool not to know it. I've known it from the first. He's not to be trusted."

I sat abruptly, stunned. Felt the color draining from my face. Picked up a cigarette and lit it, then crushed it out. Tanya had turned back to the breakfast preparations, but was moving without direction. I stared at her back, swallowed hard, and tried to control my voice.

"Tanya, if what you say is true, if he is an opportunist and you've known it for years, why did you send the telegram? Why have you gone to all this trouble to encourage me to come to Yerevan?"

She didn't answer and stood fumbling, noisily rattling the cups and saucers.

I picked up the telephone and walked out of the kitchen, closing the door behind me, and went to the loggia to dial Norman. His sleepy voice answered on the first ring.

"Norman, something has just happened...between Tanya and me. I need to talk to you, to see you as soon as possible. I have to get out of here. Can you come and get me?"

His voice was low and controlled. "I'll call Goga right away and we'll come in the car. Get ready." And he hung up.

The next hour dragged. Tanya didn't come out of the kitchen; I bathed and dressed in a hurry and then sat on my cot, waiting. The knock on the door brought Tanya and she passed me in the entry, with a flurry of her dressing gown. She opened the door to admit the two men. They spoke civil greetings and Norman asked if I was ready. We left.

I sat in the front with Goga and Norman eased into the backseat behind me. We drove in silence. Norman leaned forward and reached across my shoulder, taking my hand in his, holding and caressing it with his fingers. Goga wound through the streets and down an ice-packed road, coming to a stop by a small river. He walked away to give us privacy and to gather sticks for fuel for his heater at home. Norman and I went to the river's edge and stood looking at the scene. The leafless trees were bent under their burden of winter's bounty and the stream gurgled over rocks, breaking up the chunks of ice that floated down and broke into yet smaller sections as they crashed against the larger stones. Except for the sounds of nature, the surroundings were quiet and isolated. It was the first beautiful place I'd seen in Yerevan. No one else was on our side of the river, but we could see others across, also gathering sticks of wood. Norman took both of my hands in his.

"Tell me what happened."

And I told him everything she had said. He listened without reacting, waiting for me to finish. He took me in his arms and pressed me to him. He tilted my face and kissed me lightly.

"She is wrong, Adair. None of it is true. My family is preparing a great feast for New Year's Eve to introduce you to each one properly and to all of our friends. Mother and Goga's wife are already shopping for the party. There will be many people there. It is our biggest occasion of the year, and you will be the guest of honor. Everyone is looking forward to it. It was supposed to be a surprise for you, but...

"And she is wrong about my being just like every other Armenian man. What she says about Armenian men is also wrong, it is only what she thinks. But you see, I am Armenian only by blood. I was born in Russia, by accident, because my parents were on holiday there, and I've lived most of my life in Tbilisi, Georgia. All of my family has lived in Georgia for generations. So, by culture, I am Georgian, which is different from being Armenian.

"And Adair, I could have gone to America on several occasions. When I was in Paris I had the opportunity to... to go to America. And there have been other times when I could have left here. I wasn't ready to sell myself for an airplane ticket. That would not be my way. I am not using you."

"Why would she say such things to me, Norman? What is the matter with her? She switches too rapidly from one mood to another. She is unpredictable, unstable...I don't know. I thought I knew her so well—in China. But I don't know her at all. Why is she doing this, now?"

He only held me, comforted me. "It is always difficult to understand another's character. Perhaps in time it will all come clear. But for now, we must find you a place of your own. I have been checking some hotels to find one where you would at least have electricity and water and heat. It is not so easy, but Goga and I are looking."

We walked along the river and met up with his brother who was coming toward us, all smiles, arms loaded with sticks. He spoke his few words of English. "Are you feeling better? You look better." Then he switched to Russian and they discussed the wood he'd found.

It was late afternoon, after they had completed various chores in the city, when they returned me to the apartment. I entered with apprehension. Whatever her mood I would have to face it. An assortment of words that I could use to rebut another confrontation had gone through my mind. But cheerful female voices were coming from the kitchen. One of Tanya's students was seated, working over some papers. We were introduced. Tanya was smiling, once again the friend I'd always known. She explained that the young woman was preparing a thesis to be submitted to an American university. Her major was agriculture and she hoped to pursue an advanced degree at the university in the United States where her father taught. We squeezed another chair into the small room. I sat with them and took a few of the pages to scan, interested in perusing the subject; even more interested in evaluating the level of the woman's English language proficiency. To enter graduate school, a foreign student must have near fluency. My responsibilities at the University of California had been to assist below-level students to meet that criterion. I suspected I was going to be asked to give an opinion. I wasn't wrong. Her spoken English was excellent; her written document needed work. I mentioned that there were problems in spelling and usage and indicated a couple of examples. Before I could continue, Tanya asked if I would step into the living room so she could speak to me privately, for just a moment. We excused ourselves. I couldn't imagine that she would interrupt this session to begin on Norman. What did she want now? I followed her to the couch.

"Adair, this is my best student and my dear friend. I want to ask you if you will help. You see, she is quite gifted, but she faces a terrible problem. Marta has lupus disease. She was diagnosed only two years ago. She was already married, and even after the diagnosis they decided to go ahead and have a child. Her baby is only six months old. She wants to live whatever life she has left, to do all the things she wants to do, to crowd it all into what time she has left. Her father will help her to go to the States with her husband and baby and study in his university. But the department must accept her first. Will you please help her?"

Tanya's words were sincere. I believed her. At the same time, my suspicion was that her altered attitude was related to the fact that she wanted my help; wanted to use me. What was more important? I delayed only a moment. The girl should not be punished because of the discord between the two of us. I agreed, but didn't like what was being done. The transition was too rapid. I spent the evening editing the paper and analyzing each correction for the young woman. There would be a few more such evenings to follow.

Christmas Eve morning came and there was a light snow falling. Tanya brought my tea to the table and bent over to give me a small embrace. "I'm sorry about the other day. Sometimes I say things I don't even mean. I just get started and can't stop. Please, Adair, you are my dear sister and I love you...want only what is the best for you. All sisters have disagreements. Will you forgive me and put it all in the past?"

I patted her hand, wanted to make the best of however many days I would still have to remain in her home. This was her home. Hers and Pascha's. I'd usurped his room, her space. That reality was inescapable; I had to move out of there. What's the old saying, "fish and company stink in three days"? And it had taken about three days for our friendship to start smelling.

"I have much shopping to do today. Will you be able to fill your time without me for a while?"

"No problem. I'll try again to connect with the foreign language institute. I want to go to work as soon as possible. Jimmy and I have some ideas we want to incorporate as co-teachers." I described for her what we had planned, not so much to share the information, but to keep the conversation going on a neutral subject.

Shortly after noon Norman called to say that he and Goga had found a hotel that was a possibility for me, and they would come with the car to pick me up so I could inspect it for myself.

The hotel was in the central part of the city just off the main square where Tanya and I had strolled that earlier day. We walked in and I cringed, took a deep breath and followed the men to the front desk, trying not to let my disgust show. The hotel was old and dirty and cold. They spoke to the attendant, were given a key and directed to the elevator. As we went up, Norman explained that although the hotel didn't provide heat or electricity for most of the floors, they did set aside one for internationals and that I would be given a room on that floor. We exited on the seventh floor and walked down a long, dingy hall. Norman turned the key in the lock and we went in. The room was small, with a single bed, a couch, a small table, a couple of chairs, a wardrobe, and a desk with a television set. A double glass door led to a tiny balcony. The view from the door looked out across the city. There was a private bath. They had negotiated a long-term price with the hotel manager, who had agreed because I was to teach at the foreign language institute and the school had been unable to provide my promised housing. I loathed it, but my desperation was stronger than my loathing. I nodded and we returned to the manager's office, where a handshake sealed the agreement. I was to move in on the twenty-ninth of December. *Only five days to go!* We went for lunch in the restaurant just off the reception area. At least I would be able to eat when I lived in the hotel! I would make it.

On Christmas morning I lay in bed wondering what I was doing. I'd been in Yerevan for less than three weeks—it seemed like three months. I wanted to take Norman and go home to my family. That was impossible. Armenia was miserable. The frigid temperatures, the gray days, the lack of proper food. I was losing weight, which I could ill afford. My energies were sagging and I tired easily. The tensions with Tanya, although diminished, were still hanging in the apartment. All communication had become surface. Why was I staying in Armenia? Did I really think it was because of Norman? What did I want from him? He from me? Was what I felt for him love? Or something else? It was safety. Yes, I felt safe with him. What did that mean? At my age I was supposed to know all these answers. But I didn't. The qualities I was finding in him reminded me of my father. My father! Norman was eight years younger than I. How could he be a father figure? Absurd, Adair. But my father had always been the role model against whom I'd measured every man. That was unfair and I knew it, but it was real. And there were character traits in Norman which matched those of my father. Substance and safety. Yes, I was staying because of Norman. Was I going to marry him? No, I would never marry anyone. Yes, of course I was. I recited my ritual morning chant to calm myself, repeating it in a low drone.

"Merry Christmas, Adair. Come...Pascha's here to have breakfast with us and to wish you a Merry Christmas."

Tanya had prepared a sumptuous meal including eggs and some kind of meat. She must have spent hours the previous day locating such rare items. I ate with enjoyment and tried to communicate with Pascha. I apologized for having replaced him in the apartment, but he waved it off. As she was clearing away the dishes, Tanya dropped her bombshell for the day. She had arranged for a grand Christmas celebration in my honor. All her family and friends would be coming. There would be many presents for me and she'd been able to secure enough food for a true party. She'd even managed to find a small Christmas tree and a few little decorations. She rattled on with excitement and then lowered her tone, confidentially.

"Please, Adair, I'm afraid I must ask you to call Norman and tell him you'll not be available to see him tonight. My sister and her husband and children will all be here and they are very proper and conservative people. They simply would not understand your relationship with Norman. It would be unacceptable to them, and I want them to think only the very best of you, and of all American women. I'm sure you understand."

My mind recoiled. I'd had enough of being boxed in. Enough of her attempts at guilt. Tanya and her insipid, hypocritical proprieties. Damn! I was not her fucking child! But what was I to do? I looked at her with my practiced, controlled, blank expression, delayed an answer. I looked at everything she had purchased for the evening—things which were still in bags and boxes piled on the counter and floor. Thought about the amount of time and money she'd spent, the invitations already extended.

"Tanya, I expect to be judged for who and what I am. I am not afraid of that, ever...and I do not represent all American women...anyway, I think you probably underestimate the sophistication of your own family. But this is your home and I am still your guest. I'm sure Norman will understand." I walked from the room and went back to my bed, slammed my fist into the pillow and cursed being dependent. I picked up a book and tried to read, but couldn't.

The party was exceptional. She decorated the living room with every conceivable piece of artwork she could locate and candles flickered on every surface. The tree was tiny and stood on the small table. Guests arrived carrying gifts. She had cooked all day and plates heaped with food were beautifully displayed. The cassette player was going and the well-wishers danced and laughed and sang along. It could have been wonderful except for the jabbing inside me. Norman wasn't there. This was not right; he wouldn't have done this to me. Guilt!

It was well after midnight when the last good-byes were being said. The small entry hall was crowded with each trying to retrieve a wrap and don a heavy coat. Tanya's brother-in-law stepped up to bid me a last Merry Christmas. He closed in to kiss me on either cheek, simultaneously running his hand up the side of my thigh and torso in a slow, massaging, sensuous gesture. His motion was hidden from his family members who were standing nearby, talking and laughing together at the commotion, ignoring him.

When the last guest had passed through the door I turned back to the living room and burst our laughing, tumbling onto the couch. *My family is so conservative and proper...such behavior would be unacceptable to them...they must think the best of you...etc., etc., etc. Oh, Tanya, you and your stupid hypocritical pretenses, or are you so naïve and blind...*

"What are you laughing at?"

"Nothing. Oh, nothing."

I had to tell her I was moving. The following morning I stood at my loggia windows watching the whirls of snow pummel the panes. Trapped by the weather. Caged in unfamiliar territory. Exasperated at being subjected to her mood swings. I pushed my mounting anger down and went to the kitchen, stalling to cloak my irritation. Trying to sound casual, I chose the moment and told her that accommodations had been found, and gave her the name of the hotel where I would be living. She objected.

"That is such an old hotel. You won't be comfortable there. You must stay here until we can find you a better place. I won't allow you to make such a move."

Won't "allow" me? Allow me? YOU will make the decision? Oh, no, you won't. Why did she insist on keeping me here? I'd had enough, more than enough. I chose my words carefully, but they were edged. Vicious and vindictive, I couldn't control my tone.

"Very well. I'll stay. But I will no longer pretend. I am not your child and I refuse to be treated as such any longer. Norman and I have respected your wishes and have not gone beyond casual embraces. But we both have waited long enough. I am a passionate woman and Norman is a passionate man. We've made our decision. We want to make love. There's no point in waiting. We're both too old to wait any longer. We'll use Pascha's bed to make love."

At my words, her body went rigid. Eyes went to pinpoints. Facial muscles flexed with instant rage. The veins in her neck were throbbing. "Never! Never! You will never have sex with that man in my house. I won't have him wiping his filthy penis on my towels. You are a whore! A common whore. Like all American women...a whore. You have no decency, no culture. You have no sense of friendship. You have never cared about me, or helped me. You have never had any interest in me. You didn't care about my love for the dean in China. You didn't care that he'd been taken away. You shrugged it off. I did everything I could to help you with Alexander, but you didn't even care that my friend might be dead, or how I suffered. You've never wanted to help me get to America. You'll do anything to get Norman to America and he is only using you. I have been your friend, but you have never been mine. You don't know what friendship is. You aren't interested in anyone but yourself. You've never been interested in helping me. You care nothing about my family, you care nothing about Pascha. You are an embarrassment to me. I'm always having to apologize for you, make excuses for you. I have done everything for you and this is the way you repay me. Repay me? Hah!" She broke off her tirade to grab a small bowl. She jerked out the hundred-dollar bill and slammed it onto the table. "Take your money. You owe me more than you can ever repay. But you won't repay because you're a common whore!"

How dense I'd been! Of course. Controlled, my eyes narrowed and I smiled, saying the vicious words softly. "Tanya, you were in love with Norman, weren't you? You wanted him for yourself. He rejected you, didn't he?"

She swung around close to me, her hysteria gone beyond any attempt at control. "Yes! Yes! Now you've guessed it. Yes, I loved Norair, wanted him. Yes! But he never cared for me. I did everything to make him love me. I prepared so many meals for him, made everything so perfect. But he only came and ate my food. Played my piano. Nothing more. I would have done anything, tried to do everything. But he never cared for me. And I wanted him to marry me, to be a father to Pascha, so much."

"Then you were never lovers with Norman?"

"Never! I'm not such a whore as you are. Never! I have my pride. My pride is still mine. I am still pure."

She was shrieking, face dead white, crazed with jealousy, arms crossed, holding her shaking body to keep from exploding, fingers gouging into her own flesh. Leaning toward me. Frightening me. I backed away, slowly. She was capable of anything at that moment. I was frightened by her.

"Pack your things and get out of my home." Her voice had dropped to a low, guttural growl.

Again, I inched away from her, slowly, facing her, afraid to turn around. When I reached the corner of the living room I hurried to the loggia and pulled my luggage from beneath the table. Panic was rising within me. My hands shook. Delayed reaction. My breath began to come in short gasps. Still three days to go. What was I going to do? Where could I go? Moments later I heard the front door slam. Tanya was gone.

As soon as the door closed I went to the telephone. Norman. Norman will get Goga and he'll bring the car. With any luck I'll be out of here before she returns. I grabbed the receiver and began to dial before it had reached my ear and waited for the ring. Nothing. I jammed the on-off bar and started to dial again. Dead. The line was fucking dead. The line could be out for minutes, or hours, or days. I dropped the receiver onto the cradle and turned back to the loggia. Taxi. I'd get a taxi and go...where? The extent of my isolation bombarded me at once. I only knew the English translation of the name of the hotel and I didn't know the directions to get there. I didn't know where Norman lived. I didn't know where Goga lived. I didn't know where Jimmy lived or how to get to his university—anyway, the university would be closed. Could I find a taxi driver who spoke enough English to make him understand the name of the hotel? I was standing in front of the loggia windows. The wind was driving the falling snow in gusts, the scrawny trees bent, flailing at the panes of glass. What would it mean to go for a taxi? If I could even get one in this weather...no, I probably couldn't. I'd have to flag down a private car like Tanya had done that morning. Either way, with my English language I would be a target for any unscrupulous driver. Where might he take me? Even if I took only enough money to pay, he could drive me anywhere, take the money and leave me stranded in this storm. Then what? A police station? Where? Would I even recognize one if I saw one? The prospect was dangerous. Marooned. I was fucking well marooned.

I dropped onto the side of the cot. Impotent, marooned; impotent, imprisoned. I wrapped my arms around myself and was rocking back and forth. I dropped my head onto my knees and clung to myself. What was I going to do? What could I do? I had to think.

OK, Adair, calm down, pull it together. How are you going to handle this? Do you have options? What are they? I forced my breathing to slow down. I straightened my backbone, stood and went again to check the phone line. Nothing. A futile gesture. *OK. Come on now. Think. Don't waste time. Time.* Then the other hit me. Tanya had gone out in the storm in only her robe and possibly a coat. I checked the coat rack. Yes. Her heavy coat was missing. But she was in her robe. She'd only gone over to her friend's apartment in the next building. She'd have to come back soon. I had to be prepared.

I closed my opened suitcases and slid them back under the table, pulled on my clothes and folded my nightwear under the pillow. I made up the cot and put the little room in order. Then I sat. She'd be talking to her friend, telling her God knows what. Her friend would react. But how? I didn't know the lady well enough to even guess. Would she calm Tanya? Or conspire with her? I didn't know. There was nothing to do but wait.

It was getting cold in the apartment. I curled up on the bed and pulled the covers over me. Initial panic expended, the words of the confrontation began to come back to me; I permitted myself to relive those moments. To think about what she had really said. A whore. A whore? That nearly drew a smile. It had been eight years since Jamaica, since I'd been with a man, and how many years before that? How long had it been for her? No. Those words had erupted out of her jealousy. Or was that the way she truly saw me? No. I didn't think so. But, maybe. Maybe she thought that because I could accept a loving relationship without marriage, that made me immoral, a whore. But she had been in sexual encounters without marriage. What did that make her...in her own eyes? No. They were just words, just lashing out. I didn't care about what had happened to the dean in China? I thought back, recalled that moment. Yes, maybe she had interpreted my cold nod as just that. Perhaps she had not been attuned to what that nod had meant to me...to accepting the inevitable... not to any disinterest in her. Helping her get to America? How many times had we discussed it? How often had I explained to her that I didn't have the money to qualify as a sponsor? That I couldn't help her. Couldn't even help myself. She hadn't believed me. Rich American. I'd arrived in Yerevan with two thousand dollars. That looked like a fortune to her. A fortune? To Tanya, who'd never seen a hundred-dollar bill until I showed her one in China, yes, two thousand dollars was a fortune. There was no way to make her understand it was nothing in American terms. I worked at one of America's greatest universities. Why couldn't I get her an invitation to come and teach there, too? She would never believe that I didn't have that kind of power. No power at all. I didn't care about her family, about Pascha? I had forgotten to ask about him when I arrived. Pascha was the center of her life and I'd forgotten him. It was true. Did I appear to be a self-centered, self-serving, uncaring bitch? Maybe. Maybe I did. Maybe people in this culture took care of each other in ways that we no longer did. Maybe there was more than jealousy in her hysteria. Maybe there was also something cultural. Perhaps there was a different code for friendship. Different expectations. I didn't know.

Jealousy. But why had she done this? Why had she gone to all this trouble to bring Norman and me together? What had she expected her reaction to be when she saw us together? Why had she done this? Nothing made sense.

The tensions had drained my energies. I was exhausted. I didn't know the answers. I watched the freezing snow pelting against the window. Its rhythm lulled me and I chose my only escape, falling into a dreamless sleep.

"Adair. Adair?" Tanya's voice awakened me.

"Adair, I realize that you have nowhere to go. You may stay here until it's time to move into the hotel." She turned and went to perform her daily household chores.

Late in the afternoon the weather had eased and the telephone lines were once again functioning. I called Norman and asked him not to come to the apartment until it was time to move me. That I would explain everything later. He accepted my request.

The next days were spent in silence. Meals were served and eaten in silence. I had become a non-person. Jimmy Harris called during this time and I told him where and when I would be moving. He said he'd meet Norman and me at the hotel.

When Norman and Goga arrived I was ready, had been ready for hours. Tanya's greeting to them was strained. Her smile was insincere and her lips barely skimmed her teeth as she spoke. She chose English.

"Well, Norair, I now turn Adair over to you to take care of. And you'll have to take total care of her. She is as helpless as a baby. You will have to do everything for her. I've done my duty and now she is yours."

"Thank you, Tanya. It will be my great pleasure to take care of Adair. You needn't concern yourself, or worry yourself. I am happy to take care of her."

That was all. The men picked up my luggage and I followed them to the door. Tanya was standing in the entry hall, silent. I stopped in the doorway, and then turned back to her.

"Yes, Tanya. You are right. I do owe you for bringing Norman and me together. And someday I will repay you. It's a promise." The words came with a gentle kindness. I followed the men down the stairs.

The hotel had made a mistake. The room they had promised on the seventh floor was not available. They'd not made a notation of my reservation and had rented it to someone else. The seventh floor was filled. They'd have to put me on the fourth—and it was not a heated floor. They regretted the mistake, but it would be rectified as soon as someone on seven moved out. No, they didn't know when that would be. There were some terse exchanges in Russian, Norman picked up the key and we went up to my room. It was colder in the room that it was outside. The two brothers set my luggage down and we went back to the lobby. Jimmy Harris was waiting and we said good-bye to Goga.

"Come on. I'm taking you to the countryside, to the home of my student's aunt. She's prepared a feast for us. I'm taking a couple of my other students, too. The car is small, but we'll manage."

Small? Jimmy's prize student was driving and the two female students were sitting in the back, one on the lap of the other. I squeezed into the middle and Norman could hardly close the door after he scrunched himself in. The sardine cliché was appropriate. We were off. The young man drove like a zigzagging bullet through the undisciplined traffic. Clearly, no driver's license was required in Armenia! Raucous jokes and laughter pyramided, everyone trying to top the other. I came to life. The hotel would be taken care of—later. I roared at Jimmy's ridiculous jokes. We told ribald stories and sang the old songs. We stopped near some fields and climbed around in the rocks, throwing snowballs and ducking the flying missiles. We created a circle of angels in the fluffy whiteness to leave as our winter legacy before climbing back in the car and on to our rendezvous.

The country house was simple and small and newly built, with remnants of the construction still strewn about. We were welcomed enthusiastically and the table was ready to receive us. The late lunch went on for hours. The hospitality of our hostess was gracious and her larder must have been well stocked. The food was varied and delicious. Finally, the after-dinner Turkish coffee was served. Our young man reached over to take an emptied coffee glass from his classmate. He turned it upside down on a small dish and twirled it about, redistributing the remaining grounds. He peered into the glass and began telling her future. He immediately had everyone's attention. Again there was much laughter and bad jokes to accompany the preposterous fortune he was predicting. He handed her glass back and there were cries of, "Read mine! Read mine!"

"I can't read coffee grounds. It's only a joke. But if you're really interested, we have an old woman in the village that is quite famous around here for fortune-telling. I'll take you all to her, if you want."

"Yes! Yes!" And we hurried back out to the car, cramming ourselves in it.

The tiny house was set back from the roadway of the little village. The six of us huddled around the vine-bordered doorway as our host tapped on the door. A man answered, and after their brief exchange we were told that the woman was not seeing anyone today. We exclaimed our disappointment and the man retreated into the house. He returned to say that because an American was there, the woman would read for us.

She was well into her seventies, I guessed, and just what one might expect of a village peasant woman. She held an unlit candle and led the way around the corner of the house, through a narrow arbor and down a couple of steps to an ancient stone building. She unlocked the door and stood aside as we entered. It was one room, without windows or electricity. Two short rows of aged theater-type wooden chairs faced each other against opposite walls. A battered card table leaned against a third wall. A faded picture of Jesus and a crucifix hung on the wall. The woman made her way through the crowded cubicle and lit the candle, placed it on the table and took her own chair.

We women didn't want the men in the room and shooed them out. When they had closed the door behind them, the aged woman turned to look at me and spoke in Armenian. One of the young university girls was fluent in both languages and would act as translator.

"How old are you?" she asked me.

"I'm sorry. I don't tell my age even to my own children," I joked.

She smiled and went on. "You are going to die at the age of ____." And provided that information without emotion.

Swell! That was exactly what I wanted to hear! My first time with a fortune-teller and the first words were about my demise. Oh, well. It was only for fun, anyway.

She picked up a tattered deck of cards and had me shuffle them. I handed them back to her and she distributed them on the card table, but didn't look at them again, except most indifferently. Rather, she stared at me and began to talk. As I've said repeatedly, I'd mastered the blank face while in China, and, although this was only to be an amusing adventure, I was leery because of the past debunking of charlatans which I'd always heard and believed. I'd adopted an expressionless face before she even began. But I couldn't believe what was coming out of her mouth. She quickly ran through my life, speaking about my two marriages; the number, gender, and approximate ages of my children; my career...how could she possible know? She was 100 percent accurate. She was not hesitant at any point, except to wait for the translation, and spoke rapidly. She mentioned the men in my life, the problems I had encountered with them, and described them sufficiently so that I knew precisely which one she was referring to as she went from man to man. She said that I'd recently had a falling-out with a woman I had considered to be a close friend...that I should be careful about this woman because of her jealousy. She had established her credentials, no doubt about it. She continued without pause making four specific prophecies.

"There have been several men in your life, other than your two husbands, who loved you, but you were not ready to be loved. The last one was some time ago, several years ago, maybe five to ten years ago. There is now a new man in your life that you've only known a very short time, but he is already in love with you. You are going to marry this man. There are going to be serious problems before you get married. These problems are going to take a long time to overcome. But you will solve them and then you will spend many years together. You will be happy with this man, and he will be happy with you.

"You must be very careful. You are going to have a serious accident on a street corner.

"There is something wrong with your health, with your stomach. You are going to be sick; very, very sick.

"Something most extraordinary is going to happen to you when you are sixty-two years old. Something un-expected, very extraordinary. It will come at a time when you are confused and unhappy. But it will be a great op-portunity. The most important opportunity that has ever come to you in your life. I don't understand what it is, but you will be traveling great distances, and often.

"That is all I see."

I thanked her and left the room so she could read for the two girls.

Norman and I went back to wait in the car. I told him everything she'd said—well, most of what she'd said, those things that related to him and to our future. He held me close and kissed me.

"She's right, you know."

"Right about what?"

"What she said about the way I feel." And he kissed me again.

It was late at night when we returned to the hotel. We went to the fourth floor and Norman opened the door. The temperature in the room must have been close to zero, but it was our first time together, alone. We were anxious to make love. Without taking off my coat I pulled back the covers on the bed. The sheets were stiff from the cold. No. That wouldn't work. We looked at each other and shuddered. I pulled him down on top of me, but we both still had all our clothes, boots, coats and scarves on. It was tangled mess. I tried to unbutton and slide my trousers down, but I could get only one side of my underpants to move and that side was binding my thigh and I couldn't raise myself high enough from under his weight to release the other. It refused to move. My clothes had gotten twisted up with his. Somehow, I had pulled his scarf down inside my pants. He was trying to help and we were both pulling, yanking, adjusting; eager, fumbling fingers getting in the way of other eager fumbling fingers. The tumbled bedspread and blanket had bunched up beneath us and he tried to smooth them by reaching under me. The tail of his shirt had come loose from under his bulky sweater and got caught in my pants zipper and we couldn't get it disconnected. Our legs were scissoring around trying to find some position, some leverage, so as to release ourselves from the blankets which had wound around one of my legs and one of his, shackling us together. We were kicking each other with our boots. My scarf was caught on his jacket button. Between us, we seemed to have six hands, all pulling in different directions. I reached to unfasten his pants, but he had on three pair; briefs, long johns, and trousers. I pulled my other arm between us to help myself locate his penis, but my thumb was caught in the hem of my coat and I dragged my coat into his open fly. He rose up on one knee trying to get into position to pull the edge of my coat out of his pants, but only succeeded in twisting my jacket around under my chin, nearly choking me, and kicking me at the same time.

And then the giggles started. We clutched each other and rolled from side to side, and the laughter came in great spontaneous explosions at the absurdity of our position.

"We have a lifetime to do this. I think we'd better wait for a more opportune moment," he said, and began to disentangle us.

Tears from laughter were rolling down my face. "Please check and see if there is any hot water in the shower. I really need to bathe and warm up."

He turned on the faucet and, miracle of miracles, the water ran steaming hot. As he was going out the door, I braved the temperature and ripped off my clothes, wrapping the blanket around myself at the same time. I tripped over it, then caught the ends under my feet and scooted into the bathroom, dropped the blanket onto the floor and plunged into the tub. There is nothing greater in this world than hot water! They had provided no soap and my own was in the unpacked luggage. That was OK. There was no shower curtain and the water was spraying all over the bathroom. That was OK, too. The force would wash away my surface dirt and get my blood circulating.

The water was still running when I heard the knocking—pounding—on the door. I stepped out of the tub and wrapped the now soaking-wet blanket around me, sure that it would freeze tight to my wet body before I could do anything about it. I opened the door a crack; it was Norman.

"Come on. Get dressed. They've moved someone out of a seventh-floor room and you can have it."

Only minutes later we were in my originally assigned room, which was cozy and warm. We looked at each other, deciding whether or not to try again to make love. We both shook our heads and said, "Let it go. Later." He kissed me once more and left me to my new home.

"What is this thing?"
"I don't know the name in English."
"Do you expect me to put this in my mouth?"
"Just taste it. Try it."
"It looks like a little dead mouse."
A great guffaw. "Taste it!"
There were no other pedestrians and no cars, but we had paused on the corner anyway, waiting for the light to change, and he was dangling a string of sugarcoated fruits near the tip of my nose. They were brownish and wrin-

kled, and looked repulsive. I made a face and bit my lips between my teeth. He jabbed with his finger and tried to pry my mouth open. "Taste it!" I tipped my head back, grimaced and opened wide, as if awaiting a doctor's tongue depressor. He slowly lowered one and I took a nibble. I don't know to this day what kind of fruit it was—dried persimmon, maybe. They were delicious.

We snuggled close as we walked the streets near the hotel. The sun was almost visible on this last morning of the year and the snow had stopped falling sometime during the night, leaving the trees decorated and the pavement crunchy. It was early, and the normal inhabitants of Yerevan had the good sense to still be hunkered down in their blankets. Not us, though. The city park around the corner had beckoned. I imagined that the row of fountains had been lovely in previous times and he told me that gushing water created interlocking umbrellas of spray on hot summer days. Now they looked rather...singular, standing apart, disconnected. Disconnected. The symbolism went through my mind and I mentioned it. He hugged me closer. Norman and I were no longer disconnected individuals, but had found each other and clung together, bonding, creating our own umbrella of intimacy.

I broke away and stepped up onto the low stone wall, pretending I was a gymnast on the balance beam, bowing to a nonexistent audience, then skipped along awkwardly in my heavy boots. He held my hand and ran beside me; reached up, grabbed me around the waist, swung me back down and folded me into an embrace; kissing my face quickly seven times—chuckling and counting between each kiss. "Seven, for good luck."

We walked the park, holding hands, coming toward some cluster of empty stone flowerpots, moving apart with extended arms to pass on either side, never letting go of one another. We laughed, chatted, one or the other stepping in front and walking backward—then reversing. He fed me as we wandered, his fingers placing some hidden tidbit from his bottomless pockets into my mouth. Nurturing. A parent bird feeding its offspring.

He led me along empty streets with deserted storefronts, down alleyways, across boulevards. Pressed me into some doorway for a tender embrace, swearing that his feet were incapable of further movement until he had a kiss, and then pulled me back out to find another avenue to explore. The morning passed and the sun hid itself completely as a light snow began to fall. We turned back to the hotel, hoping to find the restaurant open for lunch. It wasn't. We went to my room, where I used my electric coil to make instant coffee and we finished off the last of the reservoir of fruits and nuts from his pockets.

By late afternoon I was happy and fulfilled and ready to sleep. Before letting himself out the door, he bent over me once more, carefully rearranging the blankets and adjusting my pillow, stroking my face and kissing me while whispering that he'd pick me up around ten; to get some rest, as the New Year's Eve party would no doubt continue until three or four in the morning.

"Now, tell me again the names of the people I'm going to meet. I have trouble with names, can't remember my own without checking my wallet."

"Mama is Arfinia, Goga's wife is Tammy, our good friend is George," and he went through a roster that I would never remember.

"I'm nervous."

"Why?" His eyebrows shot up.

"I feel like a young girl being taken home by her boyfriend to meet his parents, to be checked out, to gain their approval. Do I look all right? What do your family and friends think about me, about us? Do they approve?"

"Approve? What do you mean 'approve'? Who do you think my family and friends are?" Surprised. "You look wonderful. You have nothing to be nervous about. They are the ones who are anxious. They've been preparing for many days to meet you."

Looked wonderful? Yes, I knew that. Only needed to hear it.

The walk from the hotel to Goga's apartment was about fifteen minutes and led through back alleys and across a small public square, along a busy boulevard and onto a narrow, elevated pathway bordered by overhanging tree limbs which tried to slap at passersby...and through a parking lot which was a maze of unrecognizable cars of indeterminate age, haphazardly snuggled together for protection from the swirling ice crystals. I held tight to his arm as we maneuvered the icy trek. Slipped more than once, was steadied by his experienced arm, and thought I might as well be nude for all the good my layers of clothing did.

We entered the apartment building by edging between cars parked inconveniently close to the doorway. The stairs to the third floor were wood, uneven, and worn from years of treading feet. The hand railing was unstable.

Norman tapped the family code and the door was opened by a woman I thought was his sister-in-law. I took both of her hands in my own and spoke a New Year's greeting. I was wrong. It was a serving woman who had come to help. Embarrassed. Nervous. *Slow down, Adair. Wait for introductions.* Thank God, I didn't kiss her! Norman didn't let on that I'd made a mistake. He guided me into a small, elegant entry hall of gleaming ancient woods where Goga and his wife were waiting to receive us.

"Ah, our dear Adair," Goga said as he came to me, his smile beaming, arms extended to enfold me for the traditional kiss on both cheeks.

"Adair, this is my sister-in-law, Tammy." She had already bypassed introductions, taken both my hands, and was giving me a welcoming embrace.

"Welcome to our home. Happy New Year. Forgive me, I have no English," she said, and her classic, finely chiseled face both frowned and laughed at her efforts to remember the phrases Norman had given her.

I was sharing her greeting when I glanced over her shoulder to see a woman I immediately recognized as Norman's mother, standing quietly and waiting at the end of the entry hall. Diminutive, with wonderfully soft, white, curling hair framing a beautiful face strengthened by the long years of endurance. She stood, gracious and self-assured, with that same erect, regal bearing which had set Norman apart from the crowd that first night at the airport.

Easing me away from Goga and Tammy, Norman took me to meet his mother. She smiled up at me and took my hands in hers, patting them gently, and we exchanged greetings. She looked at her younger son and nodded her smile of acknowledgement. Norman kissed her, speaking in Russian and stroking her hair. Although the gesture had been exchanged countless thousands of times before, there was something beyond ritual in the demonstration. Courtesy. No. More than that. Honor. And she received that honor as her natural right of motherhood. And it was all conveyed in the simplest of gestures in a fleeting moment.

The brothers both turned back to me. "Your coat. Permit me." They assisted me and hung my wrap on the hall rack, but I was not comfortable within myself. I was pushing down a lifetime of feelings of social inadequacy, of being...superfluous. I needed a moment to orient myself.

A large hallway mirror set in an intricately carved frame dominated the entry, and I turned to it on the pretense of adjusting my hair and clothing as Tanya's words in her earlier letter flooded my mind. "Noble. They are a noble family." I'd already made one faux pas, would I make a fool of myself? Intimidation. The feeling was mine. They had in no way initiated it. On the contrary, I had been assured I was welcome. I was their beloved son's, brother's, friend—more than friend. They had been preparing for me for days. I was the guest of honor. Yet, I stalled. I had been in their home for only a few minutes, but because of my insecurities I wanted to leave, escape.

"Come. The others are waiting to meet you." Norman's murmur was soft and the safety of his arm encircled my shoulders as he urged me on.

Goga opened the door to the living room and I walked into their world. There were seven more friends and relatives who interrupted their own conversations and turned, en masse, to greet me; moving toward me, smiles and laughter and extended hands. The room came alive with vitality as people moved away from tables that had been placed together and which were laden with dishes heaped with food.

"So, you are an American! I want to have a discussion with you about a critical political problem between our countries." Those were the first words from *best friend* George. He shook my hand vigorously, but there was no smile. I couldn't even imagine such an opening. Was I immediately going to be put on the defensive? I hadn't anticipated any political tension, couldn't imagine what was coming next, and needed to couch my response carefully.

"I'll do my best to answer."

"I will want more than an answer! I want action." I waited as he furrowed his brow and squinted his eyes. "I want you, personally, to give Alaska back to Russia!"

That broke the ice! I burst out laughing at the calculated absurdity, matched his squinted eyes and openly evaluated him. Rubbing my fingertips together, I asked, "How much are you willing to pay?" He grabbed me in a great bear-hug and patted me on the back.

The serving woman came in, and it wasn't long before the vodka was flowing, the wine glasses were tipped, the emptying food platters were refilled, and the conversation accelerated with each lengthy, verbose toast—in Russian, usually—to the health and happiness of the American. The feast progressed, and the more frequently the vodka glasses were raised and refilled, the more fluent became the English language.

We all kissed in the New Year while the tables were cleared for Turkish coffee and chocolates, bottles of an extraordinarily fine Armenian brandy, and carafes of cold water. A cassette of music from the swing era was put on and Norman pulled me to my feet to lead off with the dancing.

It was indeed four o'clock before we staggered out into the frozen morning to find Goga's car. He would drive all those home who were too inebriated to walk. If we had been sober, we'd have known that he was equally drunk—but we weren't, and he did.

The next days were spent rearranging the furniture in my room, creating as homey an atmosphere as possible, and trying—in vain—to connect by telephone with the senior teacher at the foreign language institute. My time was filled with reading and playing solitaire, eating the tangerines, nuts, and "little dead mice" which Norman was so conscientious about providing. I ventured out to take walks on my own, but often soon returned due to the frigid temperatures or stormy weather. He and I began to establish a routine which would be livable.

Because of the lack of heat and electricity in the apartment normally shared by Norman and his mother, she had been moved into Goga and Tammy's for the winter, the utilities being turned on somewhat more regularly in that section of the city. His family had discussed my needs, the food situation, and the lack of reliable restaurant dining; the one in the hotel was closed most of the time. They were each concerned about my health and well-being, and devised a schedule wherein Norman picked me up after his afternoon orchestra rehearsals (which were continued, although performances were canceled due to the lack of heat in the concert hall), and we walked over to Goga's home for dinners and to spend the evenings. Norman returned me to the hotel late each night and took the metro back to his apartment. We all adjusted and were functioning happily.

Dinners and evenings at Goga and Tammy's apartment were an experience in accommodation. The apartment itself consisted of the living room, which doubled as a dining area—and later as a sleeping area for Mama—one large bedroom, one bath, the entry hall, and a kitchen. A glass-enclosed loggia opened off the kitchen and was used primarily for storage. The living room was not large, but was paneled with extraordinarily dark woods which reflected the glow of candlelight. There were the traditional ten-foot ceilings, encircled with wide carved moldings, and two double French doors led onto a narrow balcony. On the floor of the living room was a moderately thick, hand-woven Persian carpet of deep, luxuriant colors, which was too large for the room and was folded under on the far side. (I learned about the history of the carpet and other excellent pieces when I questioned Norman much later.) Ensconced in the wall separating the living room from the bedroom was what I can only describe as a flattened, elongated stove which was stoked with wood for heat. That fixture blended into the overall design of the wall and was not, at first glance, noticeable. The brothers called it a fireplace, but it was not, in the ordinary sense of that word. Most unusual. The furniture in the apartment was an incongruous mix of expensive antiques and worthless castoffs. However, the women had arranged their living environment so that the overall effect was one of a cozy elegance.

The entry hall was always cold when we arrived and door to the living room closed. Once inside that room, though, it was warm and cheery. They would light the wall stove just shortly before our arrival, for my comfort. There wasn't enough wood available to burn for more than a couple of hours, and that wood had to be collected by Goga on daily searches to various locales. As gasoline for the car was both scarce and expensive, his trips to locate wood had to be calculated with care. Trips to search for food were made on foot or by public transportation, when available.

We arrived before seven each evening, by which time a narrow, multipurpose table was readied in the living room for the family meal. It would be best to say that we never *ate*. We always *dined*. No matter how simple and repetitious the fare, it was presented with a quiet dignity and style. Soup bowls, salad plates, fish plates, and entrée plates were served and removed in order, resting on larger, matching serving dishes, with silverware lined up appropriately on either side or water goblets spaced exactly. Most of the service pieces were quite ordinary, but there were a few of the finest china, and some classic antique silver and deep-cut crystal graced the table. Vodka was an ever-present tradition and was poured from an exquisite crystal bottle into tiny glasses designed for that purpose. Fine Georgian wine, when available, was served in stemware from an earlier era. I whispered to Norman one evening and asked if their family meals had always been so graciously presented; if this was the way he had been raised. He had looked rather surprised and had answered, "Yes, certainly."

Courses were brought to the table in sequence by Tammy and we would commence with a soup served from a beautiful tureen. Most often the lid of the tureen would be raised to reveal a steaming soup that was little more than a watery thin broth, but occasionally—marketing permitting—there were bits of vegetables, and once in a while even a taste of unrecognizable meat. Stuffed grape leaves were routine, served with a yogurt sauce, and cabbage was the staple of every meal. Periodically we could enjoy a grated carrot or a grated radish salad. On one evening a ragout of mutton was offered, with special ceremony and much ooh-ing and ah-ing, and consumed by them slowly, savoring each bite with delight and laughter at their great good fortune. Trays of lavash, a flatbread, were frequently, but not always, on the table. To end each evening, dessert, a compote of syrupy sweet fruits which were served by the single, individual piece, and tea—ceremoniously prepared by Norman, and which he presented in tall glasses fitted into silver filigree holders—completed the meal, but was not served until shortly before our departure time.

My frustration and guilt were at their maximum. This family was spending hours every day going from shop to shop in the worst possible weather and under the harshest possible circumstances. Whatever food could be found was often enough for only two, maybe three people, and they were going without sufficient sustenance for themselves to provide for me...provide for me lovingly and with special care and preparation. But the truth is that, although my eating habits are fairly simple and easy to satisfy, there are three foods I cannot tolerate, cabbage and mutton being two of those. Both make me nauseous. There were times when I thought I'd have to excuse myself from the table. I didn't. It never came to that. On the night the ragout was served, I nibbled a few bites and exclaimed with the others, then turned to feed forkfuls to Norman, as he so often did to me. The family thought my antics funny and chuckled as they watched my exaggerated, theatrical maneuver. But later, what little mutton I had consumed was resting so heavily on my stomach that I vomited it up. The best I could do at any meal was to take a few bites of this and that and push the food around on my dish. Norman questioned my behavior, but always ended up clearing my plate. My only excuse was that I had a small appetite—which was not true. The result was that very soon I began to lose an alarming amount of weight. To compound this, leftovers—when there were any—were reheated day after day. Within a few weeks I began to develop intestinal problems, which I never mentioned. I didn't know what to do about the situation. The people of Armenia were surviving on a near-starvation diet, and I couldn't eat the food this family was going without in order to share with me.

When the meals were completed and the dishes were cleared away, we sat each evening looking through their extensive collection of volumes on the master painters, analyzing and comparing pictures and styles. And, with Norman translating, we discussed a range of subjects: economics and politics being the most frequent. Most evenings there was electricity and they would watch the news on television. The family expounded on what Armenians had expected from independence: the freedom to determine their own destinies, to put behind them the constraints of the Soviet system, and to build a prosperous new republic of their own design, created by their own strong-willed, hardworking people. But those expectations had been dashed, with the controls only shifting from Moscow to Azerbaijan. To stay alive from one day to the next left no energies for belief in some nebulous future. An even more insidious reality was that both fear and generations of dependence on outside decisions had been so inculcated that there existed a mighty chasm between imagining liberation and utilizing it. Realistic goal setting, planning, and decision making are learned behaviors requiring years of practice. Normalization of life was still only a dream. Perhaps the grandchildren...We spoke of many subjects, of renowned philosophers and authors, of subjects large and small.

They explained the most mundane of their daily activities and asked about life in America. Although I was initially uncomfortable about doing so, I did begin to tell them. The women wanted to know about kitchens and shopping and the men wanted to know about cars and television. Their eyes would fill with wonder over the simplest things we take so completely for granted. A disposal unit in the kitchen sink. What an amazing idea! How did it work?

A microwave oven. Astounding! What a wonderful way to save money and food and time for busy Americans. Houses with yards and power mowers. The swimming pool in my daughter's condominium complex. Swimming pool? Was she wealthy? No, not at all. It was standard in many California complexes. Heads shook slowly with astonishment. Condominium? What was that? Pictures were shared. An apartment complex with trees, shrubs, and flowers, and secluded individual parking spaces. Awed. Supermarkets! No. It was too much to believe. They each began to live vicariously, through me. Would they ever be able to see these things for themselves? Would they ever be able to visit this *other planet*? I promised they would. No. It was impossible to ever leave Armenia. Passports were an impossible dream. And the expense...well...but just tell us. We'll create America in our minds. My heart was breaking for them. When conversations drew to a close Norman would indicate to me with a nod of his head to accompany him.

Kitchens: the nuclei for sustaining human life—be they a fire set in a ring of stones, or a food preparation center of technological sophistication. This one was simplicity itself. The room was long and narrow. Against one wall stood a heavy, aged wooden table upon which were jars containing smidgens of herbs, racks for cutlery, and under which nestled basins of assorted sizes and purposes. Next to the table stood the small gas stove, and opposite it a sink without hot water. Facing the table across the room stood a glass-fronted dish cabinet which had served more than one generation of cooks, and a tall refrigerator that could be used only for storage, as there was rarely enough electricity for its intended purpose. Foods which had to be kept cold were packaged and stacked in the adjacent back loggia. A small wooden chair had been placed between the table and the door, for my convenience. This room was the focal point of familial solidarity, and the years of love with which nourishment had been provided permeated the very walls. This unpretentious kitchen was to become the scene of one of the most meaningful moments of my life and the rock upon which I would be able to build the future. Each evening, I would take my place on the small chair as those scenes of his lengthy and ritualistic tea preparation became the seeds of my most poignant memories. I watched as he filled the kettle and lit the gas burner with the wooden matchstick, then systematically prepared his work space and placed the tea glasses. While he waited for the water to boil, my beloved stood beside my chair gently stroking my hair as I leaned against the comfort and security of his presence. One or another of the family would wander in, chat with us, bring order out of the clutter of dishes, then wander out. And we would remain thus until the rising steam and whistling kettle took him from my side. When the tea was to perfection, we returned to share the beverage and the closing moments with the family. Each ceremony was a culmination, and a beginning. My hotel room was awaiting us.

December's emotional turmoil had already faded away when my complacency received a jolt. The knock on my hotel room door was made by Tanya.

"Good morning, Adair." Face and voice both strained, trying for cordiality. Long pause.

"Good morning, Tanya." Formal.

"Happy New Year. The dean of the foreign language institute has connected with me. The teachers want to meet with you for some classes."

"Please come on in." I opened the door wider and gestured to a chair. "Let me take your coat. Can I offer you some coffee? I only have instant coffee, I'm afraid. Would you rather have tea?"

"Thank you, nothing. I can only stay a moment." She sat on the edge of the chair, without removing her coat.

"The dean didn't know you had moved. Why hadn't you called her? It doesn't matter. If you're still interested in teaching them, they will come to the institute for an hour or so in the afternoons. There is still no heat in the building, but a small electric heater has been found and— if the electricity is on—at least you won't be too cold. I know you don't know how to get there, so I'll come and fetch you for the first trip; then, when you've met them all, one or another of the teachers will come to pick you up each day that you meet. None of us wants you to take public transportation alone, or even a taxi. It would not be safe—or convenient for you. I hope you will do this, Adair, because I've gone to a lot of trouble arranging for your lectures for them and it will reflect badly on me, and on you, and on America, if you don't at least give them some of you time."

"I've tried several times to call," I said, "but haven't been able to get through. Anyway, she wouldn't have been able to telephone me on this line, as you can only call my room from inside the hotel. It doesn't seem to connect with outside lines, which you would have known if you'd tried to call rather than making the trip to town. It doesn't matter. Yes, of course, I'll be happy to meet with them. Just tell me when." My tone and attitude were duplicates of hers.

"Tomorrow afternoon at two, if that is convenient for you."

"Tomorrow at two will be fine." Long pause. Neither moving.

"We have a tradition. To celebrate the New Year, we face any problems we've had during the past year and try to reconcile differences. You and I have a history of being friends; we've been through a lot of difficult times together. It is my hope that we, too, can reconcile our differences." She stood. So did I.

"Reconciliation is a healing process and takes some time, Tanya. Words sometimes leave deeper scars than do actions. Human nature will take its own course. Let's allow that to happen. So, I'll expect you tomorrow about one thirty. Right?"

"Yes." She was at the door. "I'll leave you now to prepare for tomorrow's lecture," she said, and was gone.

During the interchange I'd been sitting primly on the edge of the small bed, facing her. My choice of seat was...deliberate. What is amusing to me is not only that I'd done such a thing, but that during the conversation she had so controlled her line of vision that she never allowed her eyes to stray from my face. She had not acknowledged that I'd made my shabby environment as attractive and homey as possible, or that there was a bed in the room. Women are territorial. No doubt!

For the duration of my stay in Yerevan, classes of some ten to twelve teachers were held either at the institute or in private homes (over a sumptuous—if repetitive— lunch), as often as the functioning of utilities and the weather allowed. The Armenian teachers were, as have been other teachers across the developing world, dedicated professionals—always forging ahead, plying their profession against odds that would defeat lesser souls. How do they keep going when they must face the daily lack of everything necessary to perform their duties? Virtually no materials, no books, no paper, no electricity, and—all too often—little to no salary. Nothing but commitment to their students with smiling faces, like the American teachers of frontier days. This is the stuff of heroism.

Jimmy Harris had found a small bistro that was sometimes open, and on those special days he came to take me to lunch. They served one and the same meal each time. He invited Norman and me to his apartment for dinner, on those rare occasions when the gods smiled and everything worked at once. On one such evening Jimmy was telling about the years he'd spent in Asia, especially in Thailand, and the plan he'd help devise and implement for refugees. He'd been working for the Office of the United Nations High Commissioner for Refugees during the late 1970s and early 1980s, and the success of the project had gained world attention. He was rewarded by sharing the Nobel Peace Prize for 1981. He asked, casually, if we would like to see it. To me, that prize is the highest honor humankind can bestow, and I held the document in my hands as though it were a holy relic, even touching his name. I was awed by the humbleness of this man.

Norman's concern for my mental as well as physical well-being was making a profound impact. There was never the slightest suggestion of jealousy over the attentions from Jimmy; he only raised his eyebrows in surprise when I asked him, and responded that he encouraged whatever respite from boredom my friend could provide. When not in rehearsal Norman took me on social outings, visits to museums and art galleries, a trip to a fourth-century cathedral, dinners with longtime friends—whatever he could create in a fragmented world.

The cathedral was of particular interest. Armenia was the first nation to declare Christianity as its official religion and the cathedral was dedicated in approximately 304. The psychology of the status of priest to congregation was carved in stone a meter or more thick. There were never any seats; congregants stood for the lengthy services. The pulpit was elevated to such a height than congregants had to look up to see the priests and attendants. There was no visible entry to the pulpit on either side, or if one was available, it must have been concealed behind a screen or other partition. The architecture of the cathedral conveyed to early Christian mentality from the onset that the authority of the priests was supreme over all, and whatever reward or punishment came from them had the unquestionable power of a hierarchy wherein the individual worshiper was clinging to the bottom rung of the ladder. One could never bridge between being a miserable sinner and being the anointed of God, except through renunciation. The Armenians did not have a written alphabet until 405, when it was developed by the monk Mesrop Mashtots, at which time the Bible was translated from the Greek.

The inception of writing in about the fifth century BCE produced readers only among the elitist few in all countries, over several centuries. The control of the written text gave "divine" power to the clergy in the Christian world. Their daily messages of the abiding love found in the New Testament lived under the shadow of the vengeful God of the Old Testament; fear and guilt, and the demand for total conformity under threat of eternal damnation dominated the life of the illiterate. Clearly, this agenda for ultimate control had been well established by the forefathers during the developmental years of Christianity in order to sustain for eternity their position of power. That pillar of domination had been planted deep in the theology, and the architects of this first cathedral had the concept well in mind. They designed Echmiadzin so that the wretched supplicants stood for hours on cold stone floors, looking upward toward a priest that held total dominion over how to live their lives in order to avoid the unquenchable fires of damnation and to be welcomed with love into the Eternal Kingdom.

I've pondered for years where all this came from; about those early bishops' conferences held in the formative days of the Christian church, and puzzled over how they established the canon of authentic texts. Where did they get the authority to decide this is in and that is out? Have the centuries granted them greater divine inspiration than, say, today's biblical scholars who so diligently parse the manuscripts found in the twentieth century? The early bishops had the magic power of reading, but divinely inspired? I don't think so. Too many conflicts were going on. Too many impassioned, divergent opinions divided too many bishoprics representing too many communities into warring factions. Was Jesus of one nature, or two? Well, which concept would give the priesthood greater power? It was probably more like any good ol' boys club; they prayed devoutly for guidance and then argued from the point of view of advantages for themselves and their heirs—rather like our Congress?—until finally those bishops still standing claimed the grace of divine intervention, thereby negating any challenges. Challenges would be short-lived, in any case. The threat of excommunication would be an effective sword of Damocles. For many theologians, then as now, the finalizing of the canon closed and locked the doors for eternity against the coming millennia, protecting the canon, barricading it against any disorder that future discoveries, insights, and inspirations might bring; relegating the totality of humankind's future queries to the circular thinking contained within the confines of second-, third-, and fourth-century mentality. It rather reminds one of facing a medical condition by having one's physician turn for the cure to second-, third-, and fourth-century medical papyri.

But I digress. Whatever the agenda of the bishops, it was blessed by the early Armenian supplicants with what financial resources they had, as the riches of the relics on display in the cathedral museum demonstrated. I couldn't help but wonder; for whom was this historic Echmiadzin sanctuary and all other cathedrals built? How different from my open-air Buddhist temple on a hilltop across the world. Where would an itinerant young rabbi have been more comfortable? Tsk, tsk. Sacrilege, right? Well, all of that matters not one whit because to counter that argument, there is a greater truth that makes all my rhetoric just so much babble. Geographically, we all know Mount Ararat very well. That mountain is clearly visible from Yerevan and was originally within the domain of Armenia, although it is inside Turkish borders at this time. Armenia during biblical times was a territory many times larger than today's map shows and was mentioned by name in the Bible as a crossroads and an area much coveted by her adversaries. Their economy and status rose and fell depending on the strength of their kings and military. The Armenians' faith in their belief system, which became Christianity so early on, has protected them from their enemies and near total annihilation on more than one occasion over thousands of years, and even to the current time. They are a people who have an indomitable spirit and a tenacity born of an unwavering faith in themselves, and in God—when permitted, and even when not permitted! (What was it that itinerant young rabbi said about faith and a grain of mustard seed?) In the past hundred years, they've survived the genocide in 1915 by Turkey of one and a half million Armenian people, the repressions and atrocities of the former Soviet Union, and today's struggles against this newest degradation being foisted on them from outside.

As the weeks passed I began to marvel at Norman's consistency and devotion. The dimensions of his love seemed inexhaustible. The tenderness and passion. The quiet moments and the laughter and play. The serious discussions and the naughtiness. The caring. Caring and sacrifice. How many nights did he leave the hotel too late to catch transportation home? How many nights did he walk the miles back to his apartment in the freezing weather, the whirling snowstorms? He never complained, neither did he watch the hands of the clock. All was for me. My growing love for his man carried a depth and respect that brought pathos on those nights when I watched him pull his ancient greatcoat about him, secure his wool cap down over his ears, and close my door behind him to begin his long trek home through the black and frigid streets of Yerevan. *Oh, stay with me, Norman. Stay the night. Don't go out in this.* But he couldn't do that. The hotel knew the whereabouts of each visitor and overnight guests were not allowed. But neither would Norman's own value system allow it. His moral standards were...unique. Make love with me, yes. Stay overnight, no. That, to him, carried a different meaning. One could have a lover, but to stay the night implied that we were living together—without matrimony. It would reduce my status. It would minimize the marriage which he wanted. My suggestion in Tanya's apartment that we could have a loving relationship, could live together without a legal document, was unacceptable. An incomparable man.

Meetings with the teachers were sporadic, but our routine with Norman's family was steady. Life had taken on a shape; one that required flexibility and was molded by the caprices of weather and the vacillating whims of the Azerbaijani authorities. (We joked that whether or not the valves controlling Armenian utilities were turned on, and the frequency of the rolling of trucks of food, were all determined by the quality and quantity of the Azerbaijani officials' sex lives.) That shape was also beginning to be influenced by the onset of the medical crisis that would force me back to the United States. Too much weight loss. Intestinal distress. Diminishing reserves of strength. Everyone was giving me everything they had in order to keep me healthy, but everything was not enough. I was fading. The fortune-teller's prediction was beginning to come to pass: "There is something wrong with your health, with your stomach. You are going to be sick; very, very sick."

Norman went to pay another round of hotel expenses. He was told that the cost of my room had been recalculated. He came up to get me. We went to the manager's office. He spoke excellent English.

"Armenia is now entering a market economy, and, as an American, you understand, I'm sure, that our hotel rates must keep pace with those of the international community. We've done our research and found that the rate of one hundred dollars per night is the market value being charged. We must, therefore, adjust our charges to meet those of the market." Conciliatory smile.

Bullshit, buddy. This is a zero-star hotel. Gouging is the word! "Yes indeed, I do know about market value, only too well. So, if you're going to charge me international rates, then you will, of course, provide me with the same international services and standards that I would find in any international hotel. Do we understand each other?"

"Yes. It is unfortunate that we must, therefore, ask you to find other accommodations." Smile never wavered.

"Most certainly. And I'm sure that you will have no trouble finding international travelers who will pay those rates for this hotel. Perhaps you could charge even more, as the guest will have the companionship of the mouse that lives under my bathtub." Laughter. Handshakes.

Norman and I had spoken before about the possibility of my moving into his apartment. He'd been reluctant because of the lack of utilities and the discomfort it would cause me. And it would compromise his moral standards. Now there was no choice.

"Please don't be startled by the appearance of the entryway. There was a fire some time ago and the damage has not been repaired." Norman opened the door to his apartment building and I walked into a vestibule that was charred a shocking black from floor to ceiling.

"How long ago was the fire?"

"Three years."

"I see. Did the fire reach your apartment?"

"No, no. Only the entry."

His flat was twice the size of Goga's and the ambiance was the same. Mama was scurrying about with a dust cloth in hand, putting all in readiness for me. She'd had them bring her the previous day and had taken charge of cleaning up and having them rearrange furniture, moving her own antique sleigh bed from her room into Norman's bookshelf-lined music studio; an area that opened off both the apartment-wide loggia and the living room, therefore giving it more light and making it cozier.

She embraced me warmly, chattering in Russian, directing her sons to attend to my luggage and to put this here and that there. When all was to her satisfaction, she looped her arm through mine and guided me to a deep armoire, talking constantly. I wish I could tell you what she was saying, but of course I had no idea. It doesn't matter. Her tone and the lilt of her voice carried all meaning. She took a small key from her pocket and unlocked the storage cabinet to reveal stacks of wrapped belongings from the past, then withdrew several items, handing them with care to her sons. Clearly, they were precious and had not been used for a very long time. They laid the items on the bed and she unwrapped each with a meticulous guardianship. There were exquisite bed linens and gigantic European pillows, which she quickly encased in matching embroidered cases, and several smaller pillows which she slid into their complementary lace coverings. From the largest package she unwrapped a goose-down comforter which I swear must have been six or eight inches thick! From the last she took a deep emerald green satin cover into which she deftly slipped the down comforter.

As I watched her agile fingers move so expertly I pondered what was happening. That these treasures were of an expense that I had only admired in magazines and could never have afforded was apparent to me. That she handled them with gentility yet total familiarity also spoke volumes. There was still another statement, though, that was being made. Not one of trying to impress me, but one of...inclusion. At the same time, I wondered, with a mild jealousy I must admit, if she had provided these bed linens for Norman's previous wives, and then tried to put that jealousy aside as a part of his past.

"Tell me about Mama." We stood on the loggia that evening looking out over the rooftops of Yerevan to historic Mount Ararat, which seemed to be rising from his backyard.

"Mama? What do you want to know?"

"About her life. Everything. She is a marvelous woman. But a contradiction. Like earlier today. She was a queen—holding a dust cloth. Explain her to me...please, I really want to understand."

A look of sorrow and love crossed his face. His brow creased. "My family, my grandparents, and back beyond them, were very wealthy...what is the word? Vintners? Yes, vintners. No, maybe wine merchants. I'm not sure how to explain. They made and sold the finest wine in all of the Republic of Georgia. They also had their own wine shop, in Tbilisi. Mama was born and lived in a great mansion in that city. Her home was in what was like a park and it was a great distance from the back of the house down to the river. The house had three floors and many, many rooms.

"You know the carpet in Goga's apartment, on the living room floor, the one that is folded under on one end? That carpet is five meters long and three meters wide and was on the third-floor...what do you say? Balcony? No, not balcony. Landing? Yes, landing. The third-floor landing. That will give you an idea of how big that house was. That carpet is more than a hundred years old and was made by hand for my family, in Persia. We have another like it— here, in that storage closet—that was on the second-floor landing." He indicated one in a row of storage bins along a wall of the loggia.

"Have you been in that house?"

"Oh, yes, I've lived in it."

"Lived in it? How is that possible? I thought that when the Communists took over, everything was lost."

"Yes. They came and told my grandparents that they were bourgeois capitalists. They stole everything connected with their wine business and told them they didn't need such a big house. Mama and her grandparents were given one room in the back of the house to live in. In the servants' quarters. They collected everything from the house that they could fit into that one room. Like the carpets. They were on the floor in the winter and rolled up and stored against a wall in warmer weather. And some of the furniture and other things you have seen. The rest, everything else, was taken away from them. Things that had been in our family for generations. Things that had been bought with money, hard-earned money, from years of tending their wine business. Decades after decades of hard work, caring for it all. Providing work for so many employees

"Later, Mama and my father were allowed to live in that one room also, and that is where I was brought up. Mama and my father and Goga and me. In one room. In her own home. Just one long, narrow, dark room." The sadness and the resignation to the injustice were deep inside of him.

"But even so, Mama and my father always raised us as though we were still the same family that had been, before the Communists. She raised us as she had been raised. When there was so little to eat, and life was so difficult, she never wavered. She couldn't waver. That was who she was. She adapted to poverty, but she maintained her standards.

"Mama's great dream is that someday she will get her house back. But it is only a dream. It will never happen."

"And the bed linens that she took from the armoire for me?"

"I can't remember when she last took those out. There are more like them, I think in one of those chests, but I'm not sure where. We never used them. They were always stored. I think she keeps things hidden away because of her dream."

Mama had left some bread and cheese for us, and Norman made tea when the electricity finally came on, briefly, for that evening. After eating, we bundled into our coats and went again to the loggia to watch the soft snow falling...to watch Mount Ararat hiding beyond that shifting white veil. And he told me about an earlier night, a night more than a year before when he had looked out at the mountain and wondered if there would ever be a woman in his life. A woman he could truly love. He held me close to him and kissed my hair and my neck.

It was late when he finally helped me unpack my suitcases, and then he told me to go to bed, as he would have to wait up for the water to come on at midnight.

"Will you come to me, then? Will you stay the night beside me, here on this bed?"

He smiled and tucked me in, adjusting the pillows and bed coverings, stroking my head, nurturing me.

I didn't know how much later it was when I opened my eyes to the flicker of a small candle. Norman was standing beside the bed, looking down at me. The room was bitterly cold, and he had on his greatcoat over his long johns and a wool nightcap was pulled low over his head and ears.

I thought that standing thus, holding that candle, he was the funniest, most precious sight I'd ever seen. I slid the covers back a bit to welcome him to my bed. He stood for a few moments longer just looking at me, as if in wonder.

"Come to me, Norman. Come and let me warm you."

He pinched out the candle, slid off his coat and cuddled in beside me, and in our little nest of warmth, we made love.

"Where are you going? What are you doing?"

"I'm going to my own bed now."

"Why are you doing that? Why don't you stay here beside me? I want to sleep beside you. I want to feel you here in my bed when I reach out. I want you here in the morning when I wake."

He bent and kissed my cheek. "No. It is not time." He went into the adjoining room to his sofa, and I could hear the crinkling sound of the cardboard as he eased himself between the cold blankets and pulled his greatcoat over the top of his bedcovers.

Dark gray morning...and stomach cramps. Damn the stomach cramps...hurrying to the bathroom, tiptoeing past my sleeping beloved. It was happening too often. Would have to tell Norman. How embarrassing.

Hanging on the bathroom wall was a large electric coil. I took it and went to the kitchen where the buckets of water were lined up along one wall. *Be on! Get lucky, Adair,* and I flipped the switch. A burst of light! Some guy over yonder must've gotten lucky last night, too, bless him...or her. I tapped an opening in the ice and secured the coil in a bucket of water. A small hot pot was on the drain board beside my jar of instant coffee, and a cup. A small heater waited on a chair. *Ah. All the comforts...he's so thoughtful.* I plugged both in and tiptoed back into the studio to get a book.

The hot pot was gurgling away as I checked the Celsius thermometer on the wall. *Minus ten degrees. How much is that Fahrenheit? Zero? Five? Ten? Don't know, will have to calculate, but...what a mighty little heater this is. We're having a heat wave!*

Surprisingly, it only took a few minutes for the bubbles on the surface of the water bucket to bounce around announcing its readiness. *Hallelujah! Saints be praised. I can wash my face, and some clothes.* I tiptoed back to get my stash of laundry. I found a plastic basin in the bathtub and carried it back to the kitchen, dipped some water and washed myself. I couldn't find anything that looked like laundry detergent, so I used my face soap—and the same water—to scrub my underwear, then turned a chair toward the bitsy heater and hung them to dry over the back. Appraised my handiwork. *I sure ain't no helpless child, Tanya. I'm a real pioneering woman...good ol' American peasant stock. You just don't know what I can do—when I'm happy.* Made a second cup of coffee and picked up my book to read.

"Domesticity. I see you've found everything." He slid his arm around my shoulders and I nestled my head against his stomach.

"Good morning. Everything except laundry detergent. But it's OK. I improvised. Want some coffee?"

"I'll do it, and there's some bread and cheese left in the fridge. Even a few eggs to boil, I think. You'll need to get dressed. It's too cold to sit around in your robe. You'll need to dress completely each morning—first thing. It helps."

"Norman, are you going to sleep in your own bed every night?"

"Yes."

"You know, you are really quirky. Very quirky, Gasparian."

"What's 'quirky'?"

"It's what *YOU* are. Strange. Weird. Somehow...wonderful."

"Wonderful? Do you think so?"

"Absolutely," I replied, and hugged him to me.

"Well, if you think so, then...I must be." He pushed me away, indicating the door and waggling his fingers for me to leave. "Go. Put your clothes on."

He was right. Dressed in my woollies, I went back to the table. The radio was playing some classical music, softly. "What's on for the day? What are we going to do? I need to buy a few things, if that's possible. Some detergent and stuff like that. What time do you go to rehearsal?"

"I won't be going. I've told the conductor that I won't be coming to rehearsal for a while." He placed my breakfast before me. "You needn't be left alone. Not here. There's nothing for you to do but sit and wait for me. That wouldn't be right."

"But won't you lose your salary if you don't go?"

"No. I get paid whether we play or not. It's the way they do things here."

"Norman, how much do you make with the symphony?"

He laughed. "Let's see, it would be about...four dollars a month, U.S."

"Four dollars!"

"It's enough. I can even save a bit. We'll go to try and find whatever you want to buy, but it may not be available, whatever that is you said you want. We'll try. First, though, I will practice. Then we'll go. And then to Goga's for dinner. We'll go by metro, but it's a longer walk from the metro station to Goga's than it was from the hotel. Eat some more. We may not eat again until tonight. You must think of your health and your energies and plan ahead. Must be prepared."

It was mid-afternoon before he put his violin aside. I had been reading, off and on, and listening to him. "Tell me about your violin," I said. He was placing it carefully in its case and folding a cloth over the strings.

"My father bought it for me when I was still a very young student. I knew from the time I was seven that I wanted to play the violin. Before that, I had taught myself to play the piano that was in our room." He lifted the violin back out of the case and showed it to me with pride. "It is about two hundred years old. See. If you look carefully inside, right here, you can see the name of the man in Germany who made it, and the date, see...1792."

I looked. "How much is this violin worth?"

"I'm not sure, exactly. But I've been told it is well over twenty thousand dollars."

"How could your father ever afford to buy it?"

"He used some money he had saved. He bought it from another student, an older student. You see, in those days, each country was like a small circle and everything in the circle just rotated around. People didn't know the true value of things and my father was able to buy it for a small price."

"Your father must have believed in you very much. Must have loved you very much. Did he do the same for Goga?"

"He would have, if Goga had been interested. But he was more interested in sports." He replaced the violin. "I'm sorry, but this is the one thing I must ask you never to touch." He lifted it onto a high shelf.

"Don't worry. I wouldn't! Was your father also from a wealthy family?"

"Yes. Perhaps not so much as Mama. But he was an educated and cultured man. Education was the most important thing to both of them. It was because of him that I learned to speak English."

We had gone back to his studio so he could stow his violin. "Yes, I was going to ask you about that." I was sitting on the edge of the bed. He sat beside me, and then we leaned back while talking. We postponed our departure and snuggled onto the pillows, and he cuddled me against his shoulder as he spoke.

"He knew about the outside world. He was a quiet man of deep thought. He knew that neither he nor Mama would ever leave the Soviet Union, and that if either Brother or I were ever going to escape from the Soviets, it would be through education. But specifically, he believed that it would be through learning English. So, that is why he hired a tutor."

"How could he afford to do all of this?"

"He always worked two jobs. You see, he was like an orphan. My father's father had died very young and when his wife remarried, the stepfather wouldn't accept his children. So, each of the four children was sent to others to raise. They couldn't decide what to do with my father. Some American church people had come to adopt orphans and take them to the United States, and there was some question about sending my father. But instead, he was sent to live with an uncle. That uncle was a renowned tailor with a great certificate; an award for a competition, from Paris, which hung on the wall of his house. I remember that certificate well. And that uncle taught my father to be a tailor, also.

"Then later, when he got his education, he was a brilliant student and was sent to study in a university. Later he was sent to Leningrad to the great university there, to get his specialization. He was an engineer. His specialty was the building of railway tunnels and so forth. He earned what you would call a Ph.D. He wrote his dissertation in Leningrad. And when we were growing up, he was a professor in his specialization at the Railroad Institute in Tbilisi."

(I didn't learn until much later that both Norman and Goga also hold the equivalent of advanced degrees in their respective fields. Goga has a Ph.D. in engineering and Norman is a graduate of both a university and a conservatory of music. Neither their upbringing nor natural modesty would ever allow them self-aggrandizement.)

"How did he die?"

"He had a heart attack. He was fifty-four. He had a heart attack." He averted his face.

Change the subject. "So, tell me about the English tutor."

"From the time he was a small child, and knew about those American people from the church group, Father knew that America was where a person could live and make a good life. He wanted that for my brother and me. But Goga was not so interested in learning another language. So, Father hired an old woman who spoke English to tutor me. She was the daughter of a great Armenian family of wealth and influence in Tbilisi, in the earlier days, and she had traveled. Father was not satisfied with the poor English that was taught in my school, so he wanted me to learn from someone who really knew English. I was eleven years old. She lived just across the street from us and I went every day to her rooms. She taught me."

"You were...eleven? How many languages did you already speak when you started English?"

"Let's see. We spoke Russian, mainly. But I also knew Georgian and some Armenian."

"English was your fourth language? At eleven?"

"Yes, I guess so. I never thought about it."

"I'm so glad he chose English rather than some other language, like French, for example. If he hadn't chosen English, we wouldn't be here together."

"Yes, I've thought about that. Do you think it was... destiny?" And we giggled over the thought.

We had pulled the quilt over us and cuddled to stay warm. Fingers stroking. We didn't go shopping that afternoon. It had gotten too late. We loved and dozed. I wondered about the conversations of these past twenty-four hours and thought about our waiting until we were in his space before discussing his family. Of course. That was the way it had to be. His space.

It was the following afternoon that we readied ourselves to go to the stores.

"Norman, where have you put my money? I want to get some dollars and change them so I can shop."

"The envelope is in the closet. I'll get it for you."

He handed me the packet and I withdrew the American currency, counting to see how much was left of my original two thousand. It was all there.

"Norman! I don't understand this. Why is there still all this money? Didn't you pay my hotel bills?"

"Of course I did. Why need you ask?"

"But...but...*NORMAN!* Did you pay for my hotel from your own money?"

"Yes."

"Why did you do that? This money is for my expenses. I had told you to change whatever was needed and to pay for my hotel! I expected you to do that."

"That would not be appropriate. That money is yours."

I held the dollars in my hand and stared at him, not believing, knowing that he had probably depleted most, if not all, of his savings to pay what was, for an American, a pittance—but for an Armenian, an exorbitant hotel bill.

"Come. Let us hurry along. We need to go now if we will shop before going to Goga's house." He pulled me to my feet. That conversation was, quite definitely, over.

I guess I must explain something of my physical condition. Writing about diarrhea, or dysentery, is not the most pleasant of subjects. My knowledge of anything medical is a peeled zero. I didn't know for sure what was causing my distress, but figured it was something either in the food or the water. It could have been because I was on a near-starvation diet, or because I'd picked up some particular bug that was foreign to my digestive system. But how could I bring myself to tell Norman that it was possible that the food he and his family were going without in order to provide for me was making me sicker and sicker? And if so, what could be done? Nothing.

The truth was that I was becoming increasingly weak. It had gotten to the point where our walks from the metro station to our destination on either end were so fatiguing that I'd have to cling to Norman for support to stay on my feet. I pretended that it was because I loved to hold on to him. He had questioned my extreme loss of weight and the fact that I looked pale, and asked why I had to excuse myself to use the bathroom so often. I told him that I just had not become adjusted to the food and environment yet. That I would be fine. But I don't think he really believed me.

It was near the end of my second week in his apartment that I finally couldn't get out of bed. The dean from the foreign language institute had called for me to give a lecture on that day. The institute was less than a ten-minute walk from his flat, but I didn't have the strength to even go to the kitchen. I had to tell him the truth. He would have to telephone the dean to cancel my class. And I needed a doctor, and needed one badly. I should have sought out one much earlier, but had been afraid of what the standards of hygiene were in Yerevan and hadn't wanted to insult Norman's country. So again, I delayed.

"Why are you still in bed? You don't look well. Are you sick?"

Little tears began to trickle down my face. "Yes, my love. I am sick. Very, very sick."

"Let me get a doctor for you. I can get someone to come here."

"No, Norman. I'm sorry, but I'm afraid of getting a doctor who isn't American. I'm so sorry, but—"

"It's OK. I understand that. I'll call Jimmy Harris. He'll know what to do for you."

"Yes, please call Jimmy."

"Why didn't you tell me? Couldn't you tell me the truth?"

"Please don't scold me. I'm so sorry. Just call Jimmy—and the dean, please."

"Yes, of course. Do you want me to bring you some coffee? Let me bring your coffee to you."

"Thank you. No, not coffee. Some tea, maybe...yes, some tea. I'm so sorry..."

The electricity was not on so he couldn't make the tea. I could hear him in the kitchen muttering something in Russian, and could tell he was cursing the system or swearing some terrible oath. The telephone was working. He made the calls and came back into the studio, telling me to try and sleep. He said that Jimmy was on the way, bringing with him medication of his own, from America. Norman was going out to try to find some neighboring apartment building where the power was on and see if he could get a thermos of hot water. He would be back as soon as possible. And he left, heading into a driving snow-storm.

"Adair...Adair. Wake up. I have some tea for you and some bread and cheese, and some tangerines. You must eat something."

He'd placed a small tray on the table beside the bed. He spooned the hot tea into my mouth. Although even the thought of more bread and cheese and tangerines nearly gagged me, I forced myself to swallow as he fed me.

There was a knock on the door. "Jimmy. It must be Jimmy. Eat more. Eat it all. I'll be just a moment."

Clad in a white down coat with snow still clinging to it, my friend looked more than ever like a great polar bear. A welcome sight.

"Oh, yes. This sounds familiar." The greeting was over. "I've brought a couple of things that helped me. It comes and goes. I don't have a lot of these left, but we'll share what there is." Jimmy handed me a couple of pills, putting a packet on the nightstand. "I told you this place was the 'shits.'"

"You're not funny, Harris!" He gave me a hug.

"When you're serious about a doctor, I know one. He was trained in the U.S. and has some kind of courier service that provides him with American supplies—medications and needles and so forth. Armenian-American doctors send them from time to time. When they can get them through by somebody who's trusted to deliver them. Mostly, medications that are sent by agencies are hijacked and sold on the black market, but he's got some kind of link that works...on occasion. He's OK."

"Thanks, Jimmy. Let me try your stuff for a few days and see how I feel. But I don't want to use all of yours."

"It's OK. I know a guy who's coming over and he'll bring more. I'll fax my doctor for a prescription and he can pick it up."

"Fax? Fax? You have a fax machine?"

"The school does, yes. We've also got an AT&T line, if you want to use it. They don't usually let anybody other than us use it, but I'll take you to the office. They'll let you, if I'm with you."

"God, Jimmy. That's welcome news. We've been trying to use the Armenian operators to call Barbara. We've gone to the international telephone office and waited for hours, but it hasn't worked. Even once."

"You should have said something. Or I should've. Get well, get on your feet, and I'll take you to use our line."

By early evening I was able to dress to go to Goga's for dinner. Along the way there was a tiny shop open for business. In the window were a few packages of Italian spaghetti. "Norman, look! It's food. Real food!" I pushed open the door. We bought all he had. That night, I boiled an enormous amount of the spaghetti and ate it, too much and too fast, without any sauce. I might as well have been in a five-star restaurant the way I savored that food. It was so good I cried. The tears were rolling down my face. I knew I must be hurting the family's feelings, but I couldn't stop. I couldn't care. I inhaled that God-given pasta with nothing on it except salt and hot water.

As I ate, Norman was talking rapidly to his family, in Russian. He told them everything, in detail. I had been completely mistaken. Their feelings were of deepest sympathy for my condition. They understood exactly what had happened and why I had done what I'd done. Their only concern was that I'd not been honest with them earlier, not that I had insulted them—or their country.

With the combination of Jimmy's medication and the spaghetti, I was once again functioning, but barely. Over the next week we were able to buy one large pumpkin and some popcorn. Not a nutritionist's ideal diet, I'm sure. But it kept me going.

I must relate the amusing purchase of that pumpkin. Goga, Norman, and I had gone by car to a marketing day in a nearby town. The way that happened was also interesting. Goga had heard where the gas tanker-truck would be parked on the following day, so I more or less insisted that we visit the open-air market. (The gas tanker-truck was the closest substitution available in lieu of gas stations, which had long since closed.)

We drove to a side street and there stood the huge, ugly black truck, and a line of waiting cars. The brothers went to negotiate a price, an agreement was reached, and the petrol was measured into a bucket. They brought the bucket to the car and funneled a thimbleful into the tank. I spoke out the window.

"Norman, did he fill it up?"

He came to the window to whisper. "No, it is much too expensive. Goga has calculated the distance and bought enough to get us to the market and home again."

"Just fill the gas tank, Norman," I said, and reached into my wallet and pulled out some dollars. He hesitated, but then took the money and they filled the tank. Goga had a look of disbelief on his face as he thanked me.

We continued on to the small town. It was drizzling a cool rain when we got out and strode into the market area to peruse the plentiful supply—where hundreds of people were buying the same foods available in Yerevan. There was one pumpkin standing as the lone item on an out-of-the-way counter. Goga had seen it first and called Norman over. They stood, just looking at it, talking and chuckling and gesticulating, marveling at its incredible size. I sidled up and whispered to Norman to buy it. He raised his eyebrows in surprise, then asked the price, and in muted tones discussed the cost with his brother. Their mumbled discussion went on and on.

What in the hell can they possibly be talking about? It's a simple enough matter. Just pay for it and let's get going. We're standing here in the friggin rain talking about pennies. This isn't the national debt you're paying. Come ON! Finally, he turned and murmured to me that it was too expensive— outrageously expensive. "For God's sake, Norman. *BUY THE GODDAMN PUMPKIN!*" I had spoken aloud, too loud. He looked at me, shocked; I giggled in embarrassment. Then he bought it. Goga lifted it from the counter and carried it to the car. I sloshed along behind watching the scene of those two brothers strutting across the square. Pushing pathos aside, I smiled with incredulity. One would have thought Goga was carrying the crown jewels. Perhaps he even drove more cautiously on the way home. When he placed it in his kitchen, Mama and Tammy just stood, staring in wonder at that gigantic pumpkin resting on their table. Mama reached out and touched it. Then she said "hmm" and picked up their great butcher's cleaver, and with one forceful slash whacked it open. She reminded me of myself.

There wasn't much medication left, and unfortunately it was no longer as successful in controlling my frequent trips to the bathroom. In addition, after days of nothing but spaghetti (and pumpkin), that menu was becoming too tedious to continue much longer. The decision had been in my head for days, buffeted by emotions trying to surface, not being granted their own space. I was tired; too, too tired, and weak, and sick, and cold—even though it was well into March. I was always cold. Any future here was too bleak to be considered. It was time to go home. But the words couldn't be mine. To Norman, America was another planet, an impossibly far place peopled by aliens who basked outside the realities of lack. He would think that I'd be so grateful to get back home that all memories of him would be enshrouded in negativism and I'd shudder them off. I had to consider what to do. It had to be in a roundabout manner. Norman had to be the one to say it was time for me to leave. But something had to be set in motion.

"Let's call Barb again. We need to start figuring out what to do about a visa for you to come with me to the United Sates. She can connect with immigration in Sacramento, and we'll call the American Embassy in Moscow."

"How will we know what number to call in Moscow?"

"No problem. I'll phone the embassy here and ask for it."

"You can do that? They'll just give it to you?"

"Of course."

The new American Embassy had opened a few weeks before in Yerevan and I had attended the grand opening with Jimmy. I'd asked at that time about consular services and was told it would be some time before they would be set up to handle those activities. Everything connected with visas had to be processed through the embassy in Moscow.

We returned to AUA, Jimmy's university, and placed the call to Barbara.

"Sure. I'll see what I can find out and fax you back. Are you going to marry that guy? Are you going to spend the rest of your life with him? Are you sure you know what you're doing?"

The pause was scarcely a microsecond. "Barb, how often have we talked about how unfair it is to make comparisons? You know...about Pappy?" I was cloaking my response, but wanted to convey volumes about the qualities we so admired in my father.

"Yeah...often. Why?" Slowly, hunting for the code.

"It's OK to compare."

"Oh, you're calling from an office and Norman's standing right there. Message received and understood, Mom. OK. Go for it! Can't wait to meet such a man. I'll fax you as soon as I know anything. Love ya the most."

"Love you, too, Barb," I said, and gave her the numbers before hanging up.

"Who's Pappy?"

"My dad."

"Oh." He asked nothing further.

The information from the Moscow Embassy and from Barbara's fax was the same. The process was going to be an endless round of notarized documentation. And Armenia's requirements for a passport to leave the country were as absurd as China's had been. A U.S.A./Armenian/ Russian interchange of documentation would be a near-impossibility. *Another f—ing inconvenience. Life is just one long, infinite con-f—ing -spiracy of roadblocks—so some damn fool can stamp a paper that's already been stamped thrice over by three other damn fools.*

The Ides of March; I was too sick...couldn't get out of bed again. It was midday when Norman brought my tea and some lunch. The March rains were washing down the sides of Mount Ararat, preparing a new canvas for whatever spring wanted to paint. We watched for a few moments. Silence. Symbolism. He sat on the side of the bed, looking with great compassion into my eyes. "I think we both know what has to be done."

I waited, the tears rising.

"You must go home, Adair."

"Yes."

He held me while I cried and clung to the safety of him. Afraid.

"I'm so sorry, Norman. I'm so sorry I'm such a wimp."

"I don't know 'wimp.' I do know you are a strong and courageous woman. I'm the one who is sorry. I've tried my best."

I pulled back from him. Reached to caress his face. "I know you have. You've tried so hard to create a mini-America for me, in so many...countless...ways. I know that.

But you aren't able to do that. You mustn't blame yourself for what's happened. It isn't your fault."

"I will miss you. I'm afraid, Adair...I'm afraid—"

"No, no. Don't speak that thought. You will come to me. I promise it. With every bit of my being...I swear my promise to you." I stopped his words with my fingertips.

He took my hands and pressed them to his chest. "Adair, I know you have tried to explain to me the problems you've had...in the past...with your husband...and I haven't understood. Not really understood. But I now also give you my most solemn oath. Whatever abuses you've suffered in the past...those abuses stop...right here," he said, and drew a great circle around himself with his hand.

I moved inside that circle and clutched him to me, hiding myself in the safety of his substance.

The following morning he moved me into Goga's apartment where I was given the small sofa near the stove to lie on. During that day he connected with a travel agent to arrange a flight. I didn't know how I'd make the trip, being much too weak. It crossed my mind that I'd have to be medevaced out of there. I tried to eat, but the food lay heavy on my stomach. He returned in the late afternoon and said that they could ticket me for only the Yerevan to Paris leg of the journey, but that a representative from Air France would meet me at the airport and give me the tickets to Los Angeles. They couldn't arrange anything into San Francisco.

That night, Tammy moved a cot in beside the sofa and brought candles and a flashlight...just in case. She would stay right beside me. Norman kissed me and went to catch the metro.

The next day I could do little more than sit up. Norman spent hours beside me, holding my hand, speaking softly. Late that afternoon he went back to the travel agent to finalize the arrangements. When he returned I was desperately ill. I mentioned to Norman that the prediction by the peasant woman in the village had certainly come to pass: "There is something wrong with your health. You are going to be sick; very, very sick." He shook his head in despair.

He left again and went to get Jimmy. How was I going to get home? Norman came back and said Jimmy had gone to get the doctor. I was nearly delirious. Mama gave instructions to the family and then went to heat up a kettle of water. Tammy brought a bucket and Mama brought a pitcher of the hot water and a glass. Norman held me upright, supporting me with one arm, and with the other forcing me to drink glass after glass of the water.

"Don't sip. Gulp. Gulp. Drink it."

I drank. The hot water gagged me.

"Drink it!" he demanded, and forced it down me.

I drank and the vomiting started. I threw up into the bucket that Tammy was holding.

"Yes, yes. Get rid of those poisons," Norman said, and held me as I vomited, puking up everything, retching again and again until I was emptied and spent.

Jimmy Harris and the doctor arrived. Jimmy stood aside as the doctor quickly unpacked his medical bag, showing me the sealed American needles and bags of saline solution, talking nonstop, explaining how he came by the American supplies. He attached the bags for the drip to a wall fixture and inserted a needle into each of my arms. "By the time these empty, you'll want to get up and dance. But I'd advise against it. Wait until tomorrow for dancing." He added a second syringe to each drip, the contents of which I have no idea.

He was right. Before the hour was up I felt, miraculously, relatively normal; weak, but functioning. Before he and Jimmy left, the doctor instructed Norman and Goga to bring me to the hospital the next morning and left specimen paraphernalia.

The specimen sample and blood tests told him nothing. He couldn't identify what was causing the dysentery. He did tell me during our hours-long stay at the hospital that dysentery was the number-one killer in Armenia. That came as no surprise to me.

Late that evening the travel agent came by Goga's apartment with my airline tickets. The brothers sat at the table, handling the tickets, pointing to this and that number, mumbling about the supposed meaning of the coded messages, discussing, looking only at each other. Their words camouflaged their shared sorrow. Mama took the chair beside me, hands folded in her lap. Tammy occupied her time with household chores, slowly, head down. Mama reached and took my hands into her lap, patting them gently. My departure was real. Unbearably real.

It was nearly midnight when I went to sit in the kitchen while Norman prepared the last tea which would be shared with me by the family. Talking was subdued as first one and then another wandered into and out of the kitchen. No one knowing what to do. Touching me. Everyone uneasy. Sad. I sat, silent, leaning my head against Norman's side as he stood close to me, stoking my hair, waiting for the water to boil. Consummate grief. When would I...would I...ever...ever again...I couldn't have spoken any words. I sat, watching the scene, imprinting every iota of those moments. Clinging to time.

Mama came to the doorway and beckoned to Norman. He walked over to her. She had something in her hands. She spoke to him quietly and handed the object to him, pressing her palms over his. His shoulders curved in a sudden emotional tremor, and then he straightened and inhaled deeply. Tammy and Goga, waiting quietly behind, both reacted to the moment with a quick intake of breath. Putting his arm about her shoulders, Norman and Mama came together to my chair and Mama reached out for my hands.

There were tears in Norman's eyes as he eased open the lid of the little box. Inside, lying in its velvet bed, was a gold wedding band. He lifted it out and took my right hand. He slipped the ring onto my finger.

"This is my father's wedding ring. Mama wants you to have it, to bind our family to you. Adair, Mama took this ring from my father's hand while he lay in his coffin. This box has not been opened for nearly thirty years."

I gripped them both to me, and then reached for Tammy and Goga as my tears flowed.

I boarded the flight from Yerevan at nine o'clock the next morning.

HOME AT LAST

Have you ever sat among new immigrants in an airplane, listening to the babble of the different languages? And when that first dim outline of the United States touches the horizon, have you ever heard the whispers of recognition spin through the cabin, and seen the hesitant fingers point, and then watched as those hulking men dropped their braggadocio and the women quieted their chatter as each turned a face to the windows? Have you felt that silence which descends when the reality of the coastline begins to take form? And have you noticed the minuscule trembling in each voice as it says, "America?"

America. California. Los Angeles. San Francisco. Gateways.

"My God, you're a skeleton! The most beautiful skeleton I've ever seen, but let's get you home and feed you. I'm never going to let you out of my sight again." It had been thirty hours since I'd left the Yerevan airport when Barb wrapped her arm about my shoulders and escorted me through the San Francisco terminal to find the car. "I'm not even going to let you stand on the curb and wait. You'll tip over. Come on. Move those scrawny legs." Family words of love.

"Stop at the first drive-in. I want a chocolate shake."
"You've got it!"

The Bay Bridge. The Berkeley Hills. The freeways. The spreading fields. The Woodland turnoff. The Covell turnoff. Davis. Home.

Recuperation. My physician identified the bacteria even before the blood tests and specimen were taken. Davis physicians are used to dealing with the university professors and researchers who travel abroad and bring back foreign representatives in their innards. His prescription worked its wonder in days. The mental and emotional healings were to take longer.

Reentry culture shock and separation. The stories were oft repeated; to Barbara, to my sons, and to Jennifer when we reconnected. It was good to have her back in my life. She lived just a few minutes away from me, in Sacramento. It was comforting. I told my stories to my adolescent grandchildren, who wrote school compositions on deprivation. Commiseration. Then, when the needle on the bathroom scale began its climb, evaluation.

"Are you sure, Adair?" Jennifer asked. "Are you sure Tanya's not right? Are you certain he's not looking for passage out, not an accomplished actor, that it wasn't a family conspiracy?" Her analytical attorney's mind was at work; probing deep into the wound, searching, suggesting alternative causative factors. "Look at it carefully, my friend. I want your happiness, but I want it long-term. Don't be duped. Take your time. Be sure, in your gut. Listen to the 'small voice'—is it sending the remotest of signals?"

The suggestion was excruciating. Visions of night after night of Norman trudging back to his home, greatcoat and scarf wrapped tight, cap pulled low, facing into the driving blizzards, without hesitation or comment. Constancy. My puking into that bucket. And never the backward step. Steadfast. Goga's kitchen. Mama. Norman's eyes. His father's ring. Family inclusion. The pain of her questions plunged deep. But her training, her experience, insisted on the questions—and they came out of love.

"I'm sure, Jennifer. I'm sure."

"Mom," Barb said, "can he support himself, the two of you, here in the United Sates? What are his chances of getting into a symphony orchestra? Or is he going to have to chuck all of his talent and a lifetime of training and experience and go to work at a fast-food chain? If they'd hire him. Probably part-time, or temporary...with no benefits. At his age there'd be nothing other than entry-level for him." Her thinking had been hovering in my head, cloaked by fear, hidden under bravado, from our earliest Yerevan meetings. Barbara's business managerial mind at work, searching in her area of expertise, insisting on voicing the questions—and they came out of love.

"I'm not sure, Barb. Not at all sure."

"You are going to have to do a hell of a lot of chanting, Mom."

"Yes, I know."

I picked up some classes at the university, and thought about it all as I taught English to the incoming internationals. Spoke to a few people, and knew. No. His chances for a chair in an American symphony were nil. Too many excellent, young, highly trained, unemployed American musicians. I'd have to look...elsewhere. Never mind. Start the documentation for his fiancé's visa, anyway. And I did.

Sandwiched in between my calls to Norman, I received one from Tanya. Surprise, then panic, then back to surprise as she explained herself.

"I've had a chat with Norair recently, and he tells me you're arranging for his visa to America. I'm wondering, Adair, if you could possibly do the same for me." Her tone was friendly, without a hint of any past difficulties.

Reconciliation? Oh, well, what the hell. That was another time, another place.

"Lordy, Tanya. I don't know if I could convince the United States government that I'm going to marry you." Laughter.

"No, no. But I've talked with some colleagues of mine and they've told me about someone who was able to get a visa to come as a visiting scholar to give lectures in an American university. I was hoping that you could speak to the Russian department at your university and arrange the same for me."

"I know no one in that department, Tanya, but I'll try."

I asked about Marta, her beloved student whose thesis I'd worked on. Marta had died.

It took several calls to finally connect with the head of the Russian Language Department. The conversation went more or less as anticipated as he responded to my query. "I've just returned from a trip to Moscow and can't begin to tell you how many Russian language teachers asked me the same question. I could staff every university in America with Russians. We won't hire any. Most universities won't. We've had experience with them. They come, teach a few weeks, and then disappear into the woodwork. Immigration comes back on us. Sorry."

I called Jennifer. She was teaching some classes in law at the community college in Sacramento and knew everybody.

"Adair, I don't want to do this."

"Neither do I, but I owe her."

"*YOU* owe her. I don't! OK. I'll ask around. But I don't have good feelings about this."

The community college was interested in having Tanya give some guest lectures and doing some tutoring, and agreed to provide the invitation for a visa, but that was all. The position would be unpaid. Immigration problems for the college would be avoided.

"So, Adair. Who's going to support her while she's here? Is she going to stay with you and Barb? Sleep on the floor?"

"Come on, Jennifer. Help me out on this. You're living all alone in a house big enough for three families."

"Bullshit! You ask too much. I didn't like her in China. I don't like what she did to you in Yerevan. I don't want her in my house. Why are you doing this? Forget it."

"Please?"

"No. I won't. Well, maybe I'll think about it. But I don't like it."

A week later Jennifer agreed and obtained the formal invitation from the college. I called Tanya. Together with the money she'd saved—and converted to dollars at my insistence and with my assistance during her two years in China—and the hundred dollars I'd left on her kitchen table, Tanya had just enough money for a round-trip ticket to San Francisco, with a few dollars to spare. She was ecstatic, and chattered with unreasonable optimism about everything she was going to be able to accomplish while in American for ninety days.

"Mom, why are you doing this?"

"I don't know, Barb. You guys, leave me alone. I owe her."

"Exactly how much, Mom? Think about it."

"Knock it off."

All the while my mind was churning. If Norman couldn't work in America, then where? Thought about it, investigated, and thought some more.

A couple of my students were from Guadalajara, Mexico. They joined me one afternoon while I was having a coffee at the dining commons. We'd already formed a compatible relationship and conversed easily. They spoke about their hometown, and when I mentioned to them that I probably would be looking for another foreign post, they enthused about Guadalajara. Yes. There was a fine symphony there, and a rich cultural life. The University of Guadalajara had an intensive English program. Besides, it would be the closest place to my family that I could move to and still be outside the U.S. Why didn't I check it out?

The Davis library provided a variety of books and travel guides which gave me practical information. The climate, cost of living, and good life provided an ideal retirement spot for many Americans. I mulled it over and then told my family and Jennifer that I was going to take a quick trip and investigate the possibilities on my own.

"Jesus Christ, Adair. You're going to go off to Mexico and leave me to take care of Tanya by myself?"

"Please, Jennifer. Try to understand. Tanya's ninety days will pass. I've got to find a place for Norman and me for a lifetime. Help me out." Desperate. "Barb'll be right here in Davis. She'll take her off your hands from time to time, won't you, Barb!" Pleading.

Long silence. "Yeah, Mom."

MEXICO

The taxi ride from the Guadalajara airport to the Hyatt Regency Hotel took me through sections of the old city, with its gracious, well-maintained Spanish architecture standing side by side with small, poorly maintained business structures. A city of contrasts. We drove in the brilliant, hot, late-afternoon sunlight, passed beneath a short underpass and entered an obviously wealthy district. The buildings were glisteningly clean, set amid trees and shrubs and flowers, the vivid colors and sizes reminding me of the landscapes of Jamaica. The ultra-modern Hyatt Regency Hotel might as well have been in San Francisco, or any international metropolis. Of course. What else would one expect? Broad escalators bordered a rising, miniature sculptured mountain of potted trees and plants. The foyer was enormous and comfortably furnished, with a glass-enclosed elevator separating the main area from the coffee shop and passageways leading to specialty shops. Those passageways overlooked an ice-skating rink on the floor below.

I was a bit intimidated by it all, but went to the reception desk and checked in. I wasn't sure how long I'd be there, but thanked the Lord for plastic. I'd put the expenses on a credit card and worry about paying for it all—later. How American I am! My room had every possible extravagance. Déjà vu, the Sheraton in Shanghai. I chuckled to myself, "Here I am, broke, looking for a job and staying in a palace—one hundred and eighty degrees from my hotel in Yerevan. Adair, you are such a creature of irrational extremes!"

It would take three days of being shuffled from one obscure office to another, from one building to another, from one district to another, to finally locate the university's Department of Intensive English that I was trying to find, the actual name of which I didn't know. I was interviewed by the young woman in charge and yes, the department would surely hire me, they needed my expertise badly, and when could I report to work? I explained that I had to return to California to finalize necessary arrangements and could be back in a couple of weeks. It was agreed and I signed a contract. My interviewer, Maria, gave me her card, wrote her home phone number on it, and told me to call her with the details of my arrival; she would arrange a less-expensive hotel to stay in until she could help me find more permanent housing. All was in order.

HOME AGAIN

The quick trip home was uneventful except for complaints from Jennifer and Barbara. Tanya was due to arrive in three weeks. Her arrival was looked forward to with... dread. I was threatened with excommunication from human contact and doomed to banishment beyond the River Styx.

I called Maria for the name and address of the hotel she had recommended and took the flight back to Mexico. Guilt-ridden, but driven by my highest priority.

MEXICO—SECOND TRIP

Less expensive for good reason. Stuck in the middle of the older section of Guadalajara, one could enter the hotel only after catching the attention of an attendant inside—who might, or might not, be within hearing distance—to come and unlock the door. I was expected and was shown to a small, filthy room off an aged cobblestone patio. I had no assistance with my excess of luggage, and had to make several trips to the entryway to get it all into my room while a couple of men sat a small table, chatting, laughing, and watching me struggle with my suitcases. I opened the door to my private bath. A toilet which probably had never been cleaned. A small basin with no table or counter space, and an open shower with no curtain. The water drained into a hole in the middle of the floor. This would never do.

I got a cab and reported at once to my university department to find Maria, but was cautious about explaining my reaction to her hotel recommendation. Perhaps to her mind such accommodations were not out of line. I was right. I suggested we look for more permanent housing in the district where the Hyatt Regency was, as that was near an expansive and modern mall, which would be convenient for shopping. Could we find rooms in that area that would be reasonable? It would be difficult and would necessitate a long bus ride to my teaching site, but she would try.

A couple of evenings later she took me to inspect a room in a home. The home was a one-story L-shaped structure with the individual doorways opening off a lovely brick patio. The landlady spoke excellent English.

She normally rented only to students and young American teachers, who shared not a room, but small two-bedroom, one-bath apartments. We went to the one she had available and it was beautiful, with one of the bedrooms being rented by a young American girl who was studying Spanish. Since she regularly rented the two-bedroom accommodations to four ladies, she would double the price for me to live alone in the second bedroom. I didn't ask if she was doing the same for the other renter, but did some quick mental math and agreed. I moved in that night.

My teaching schedule was set. It was an hour's bus ride from my home to the campus, including two transfers. Four classes of advanced English each day and an hour back home. I could handle that and began the following Monday.

The next weeks were spent getting acquainted with the one American girl who was residing in our apartment, acclimating myself to my students' needs, correlating those with the department requirements, and meeting my colleagues. Once my routine was established I would begin trying to connect with the conductor of the Guadalajara Symphony to see if I could interest him in Norman for his violin section.

Communicating with Norman became a...challenge. I couldn't use the landlady's telephone for such a long-distance call, but could use the public telephones at the Hyatt Regency. I calculated the time difference between Guadalajara and Yerevan, and each Saturday morning walked to the hotel to place my call. The challenge arose because the Mexican operators in the hotel didn't understand how to connect the lines. I did my best to give instructions, both verbal and written. To me, it was simple; I'd made the call so many times from California. Since the hotel used the same AT&T lines, it should have been equally simple for them. It wasn't. I couldn't make them understand that a busy signal might have three difference sources; one, that Norman's line was in use, which I knew it never would be since he would be sitting by the phone waiting for the call; or two, out of order, which was the more probable. The last was that the line she was using to access Armenia was in use, and to try another international line before telling me she couldn't connect. This was by far the most likely and was the idea I couldn't get across. The situation never changed. It normally took about two hours for the operator to place the call. I sat in the booth and waited...for a three-minute conversation with Norman. Oh, well...

I won't go into detail about the next several months. Suffice it to say, I realized early on that Mexico was not the place for us. The cost of living compared to salaries was not at all what my readings had promised. My salary did not cover my expenses. I would have had to move back into a hotel like the one on my arrival to stay within my budget. I did connect with the symphony conductor and he requested an audition tape from Norman, which was impossible given the problems of acquiring a blank tape and getting it recorded in Yerevan. The conductor could not, of course, offer Norman a contract without hearing him. I knew that, but hadn't calculated on the lack of a blank tape in Yerevan. I should have, but hadn't. My students were a joy, as all students around the world had proven to be. I was a training teacher and other teachers visited my classes regularly. I assisted the department in reevaluating its program and redesigning its testing procedures. Several of my colleagues became my good friends. The young woman with whom I was sharing my apartment was a delight. The human factors were more than satisfactory, but the financial burden would be too great.

The reason I am including this section at all really has nothing to do with Norman, or with Tanya and her trip to the United States, or with Mexico per se, but rather with the fortune-teller in that Armenian village so many months before.

It was a blistering hot Sunday noon when I boarded a loaded bus to meet one of my colleagues in a downtown restaurant for lunch. I had to wedge my way up onto the step, just inside the open doorway of the bus. The driver was careening around through the heavy traffic at excessive speed. He came to a side street and slammed on the brakes to avoid crashing into an oncoming car squirreling around the corner. The crowd of standing passengers lurched forward. I was instantly squeezed between two men, then thrust from the bus. I fell headlong out of the vehicle and into the street, my face jammed against the curb at the corner of the two crossroads. I passed out at once. The bus had driven on without concern. The next thing I knew, a woman's voice was speaking to me in Spanish and her hand was resting on my shoulder. I came around and was aware that my mouth was full of broken-off teeth; crowns, actually. I spit them into my hand. She spoke again. Through my semiconscious haze I looked up at her and murmured that I didn't speak Spanish. She switched to English and said, "That's OK. I'm originally from San Francisco. I live in this house right here on the corner and I saw your accident."

I couldn't stand, so she waved down a passing car and two men came to my sides. They lifted me to my feet, half carried me to her home and lay me down on her sofa. I was still far from fully conscious, but did notice that I was holding my crowns in my hand. I slipped them into the pocket of my blouse. I also knew I was in considerable pain. The woman brought a cloth and warm water and began cleaning the blood, dirt, and ground-in gravel from my face. She asked if there were someone she could call. I told her of my appointment and also where I lived. She tried to phone the restaurant, but couldn't get through. She called my landlady, who responded that she would come and get me as soon as her husband returned with their car. The woman came back to me. I was beginning to revive. She brought me a glass of brandy, which I sipped gratefully.

After a few swallows, the words of the fortune-teller came into my mind: "You must be very careful. You are going to have a serious accident on a street corner." I mentioned this to the woman who had rescued me. She laughed and said that it was quite a coincidence. I asked for a mirror, and she suggested that I might not want to see one right away. I insisted. My face was a hideous, bloody mess, with the skin scraped from most of it. My mouth was blood-coated and bits of gravel were clearly visible in the multitude of open cuts. All of my crowns were gone from my mouth, and the stubs on which the crowns had been cemented stared back at me like something out of a horror movie. I didn't recognize my reflection. I gasped and shuddered, agonizing over my appearance. My pain was eclipsed by what I was staring at. She took the mirror from me and began again to gently clean my face with the warm water, speaking to me with the softest possible words of encouragement and support. She worked tirelessly over me for the next hour or so. She didn't call a doctor because she said she trusted herself more than any doctor she knew. She told me I was more than lucky that she had been at home and witnessed the accident. If left to chance, I would probably have lain in the street for possibly hours before anyone would have assisted me. That was simply the way things worked in Guadalajara.

By the time my landlady arrived, the woman had removed all of the debris from my open wounds. I was taken home by my solicitous landlady; I remained in bed and was given her undivided attention for the next several days. She also was hesitant about calling in a doctor, but did call my university after a couple of days. Maria came later and insisted I see a physician. My face was still badly swollen and my blackened eyes were turning that wretched color of yellowish-green. The open wounds were beginning to scab over. When I regained enough strength, my landlady took me to the doctor Maria had recommended. He checked my face and commented that I had received good care. Everything was healing normally. Did I have insurance? No. Did I have the number of the bus? No.

As I had lain in bed those days I had made my decision. There may have been perfectly capable dentists in Mexico, but if the two women who were longtime residents of Guadalajara had been hesitant about sending me to a physician, how would I ever find a dentist? There was no way I was going to allow just anyone to start all the oral surgery that would be needed in my mouth, so I would go home as soon as possible. Anyway, this was not the place for Norman and me. I returned to California. It was late November.

HOME TO STAY

It was back to sleeping on Barbara's sofa in her living room. Back to stashing my belongings into her already overcrowded closets. Always made to feel welcome and needed, but damn, would I never have a home of my own? I telephoned Norman in Yerevan to tell him that I had returned to California, and why. He was deeply concerned over the accident. I assured him I was in good health and only needed a little dental work. I didn't want to burden him, worry him. What could he possibly do except fret? No need for that. He had problems enough processing the documentation for his visa and passport.

Back to my longtime, trusted dentist. When he examined my mouth and informed me of the extent of the work to be done—and the thousands of dollars that work would cost—I had to struggle not to cry right there in the dental chair. There was no possible way I could ever pay for it. Even working two full-time jobs, the price was prohibitive. As my mouth was not healed enough for him to commence, I told him I'd have to find financing and would come back when the healing was complete. I had no idea how to manage. How could I even look for work when my mouth was in that condition? I was repulsive to look at. I wouldn't be able to face a classroom full of students, let alone possible employers. And with this sudden added expense, how could I expect to bring Norman to America? I couldn't. My world had collapsed with the "serious accident on a street corner." I had come home to cry.

With my tears finally spent, there was nothing left but a dull depression. I decided that to fill time I would go through the mechanics of some mundane housework. First, unpack the rest of my suitcases which were still jammed under the stairwell. Near the bottom of the last one I pulled out the blood-stained blouse which I'd had on at the time of the accident and went to toss it into the washing machine. I felt something in the pocket and reached in. There were my crowns; I'd forgotten about putting them there! I clutched them in my hand. Didn't know if he could use them, but...maybe. There was a glimmer of hope. I slid them into an envelope.

Hiding from the world I waited for the days to pass, for the mending process to be completed. Returning to the dentist's office, he nodded that he could cement them back on, but that the solution would be only temporary, as oral surgery had to be done in order to save my natural teeth. But at least I could look for a job.

On the day when the work was finished, I was able to smile into a mirror, and I immediately connected with my department at the University of California. Not only did they not have an opening for me, but due to budget cuts, they had let go several of the teachers on staff. With fear rising I dashed back to the condo and called the office at the State of California through whom I'd taught the Mexican immigrants several years before. The project had been discontinued; lack of funding. Just one fucking thing after another. I paced, waiting for Barbara to return home from work.

"OK, Mom, let's take a look at options. How about substitute work in Davis or Sacramento? Then working your way into a full-time position for next September?"

"Can't do that, Barb. I don't have a California credential—only Nevada—and would have to take the licensing exam. I'll find out when it will be given again. I don't know. Anyway, how would I be able to accept substitute work in Sacramento, with no car and inconvenient bus service?" Considering substitute positions would be impossible without reliable transportation, considering that the need for substitutes changes from school to school, sometimes day to day.

We spoke of other possibilities—office work? No, my skills in that area were minimal and badly outdated. I had no experience outside of education that was marketable. My spirits were diving.

"Why don't we let this rest for a while and call Jennifer to come over for the evening? You've procrastinated long enough."

Because I'd been so distraught over my appearance, I had avoided everyone. I hadn't seen or telephoned my friend since returning from Mexico and felt guilty about that, and doubly guilty about having postponed what I feared could be a confrontation regarding Tanya. Barbara had already told me that she hadn't seen or spoken to Tanya; that the woman hadn't wanted to meet my daughter. It was a bad omen, and it was time to face Jennifer about Tanya's months in the U.S. I made the call and Jennifer came for dinner.

Greetings and hugs of forgiveness over, she queried me. "Tell me about Jimmy Harris," she said, and I filled her in on my good friend in Armenia.

"How good of friends were you?" She raised an eyebrow.

"Friends. Why do you ask?"

"Tanya told me about the first time he came to visit you. She said that she walked in unexpectedly and that you were climbing all over him. She said you were coming on to him and that he was trying his best to push you away."

Stunned! "Jennifer, there's not a word of truth in that. He and I spent a pleasant evening discussing our educational methodologies. She came home. He didn't know how to get transportation back to his flat and she walked him out to the boulevard. For God's sake, why would she say such a thing?"

"'Hell hath no fury'...Do you think she was trying to undermine the friendship between you and Jennifer?" Barbara asked.

"No idea. Sure, her jealousy was making her crazy. But why would she extend that to include Jennifer? It's beyond me. Let's talk about something else."

"Not so fast! I haven't told you what happened." Jennifer was holding a juicy tidbit of gossip and anxious to share it.

Her audience demanded at once, "What?"

"Tanya is married!"

"She's *WHAT*? Married? How is it possible? She only had a three-month visa. How did she snag someone so fast?"

"She got involved with a fundamentalist church group, asked them, begged them, to help her stay here, and they arranged for her to meet a man in their group who was looking for a wife. Get this! They were married in Reno the day before her visa expired!"

"Who is he? Did you meet him?"

"No. She kept him away. And Adair, I must tell you that she told me at least a hundred times that you were never a friend to her. She also told me that you were an embarrassment because she'd gone to so much trouble to get that invitation from the foreign language institute and that you never met with the teachers. She thinks that you owe her a great debt, but she doesn't expect you to ever repay."

"Never met with the teachers? I met with them as often as possible, sometimes at the institute and sometimes in their homes. And she knows that very well. Damn! And did you tell her that it was because of me, at least indirectly, that she was able to come to the United States? You know, the day I moved out of her apartment I promised her I'd repay her for all she'd done. I thought I'd done that."

"Sure! She knows that. But she can't accept—or doesn't want to accept—that connection. Basically, she doesn't want to believe it. Let it go. She has her own life here now. She's got a husband; she's doing some tutoring in Russian, and some translating. She's got what she wanted."

"You know, she talked so many times in China, and in Yerevan, about coming to the United States, but I never thought it was possible. But I was wrong; she's walked through her own personal Berlin Wall."

"Yes." Barbara understood.

"Berlin Wall?" Jennifer didn't.

"Oh, it's something Norman said once. I'll explain it later. Anyway, I guess I'm glad for her—she's here and married, and all. She spoke about reconciliation, once... but it wasn't, isn't, really possible. Too much pain and anger. Anyway, she's snubbed my daughter. I don't want to see her, or talk to her. And I'm sure she doesn't want to see or talk to me. How strange it's all been. The extremes. I'll never understand it."

"What's interesting is that she may have been really projecting onto Norman her own maneuverings to get to the U.S.," Barb said. "She is the one who would say or do anything to get here. To use you. Whether her jealousy was real, or contrived. Think about those mood swings. Maybe she figured, after an outburst, that she was killing any chance she might have of you helping her. So, she'd come back. And then she had the balls to call you here. And, Mom, you bought it."

"I wonder...how early on...how much of all this was for me, and how much for herself? What did she have in mind? And when? Or did the scenario just play out...one step at a time, unplanned? No. It was not so premeditated. She couldn't have planned it all. That jealousy was too real."

"Are you sure it was real? How do you know? She can be pretty theatrical," Jennifer added.

"True. But no. Real enough. Norman even told me that she'd been trying to get him interested in marrying her."

"He told you that?"

"Yes. Well, no, not at first. That day I called him to come and get me and we went to the river...remember?

I told you about that. Anyway, he only said that it takes time to know another person's character. That it would all come clear in the future. Later, though, when I asked him outright, he did tell me of the times she had invited him to dinner, over the years, and how she tried to maneuver him. But he was never interested in her. And when I'd asked him why he hadn't told me that from the beginning, he said that it wouldn't have been proper to do so."

"Proper?" Barb asked.

"Gossip. The family doesn't really encourage gossip. And it would have been, to him, gossiping."

Barb snorted, "A clear case of propriety getting in the way, I'd say."

Jennifer added, "Who knows the answers? Probably not even Tanya. Well, the 'green-eyed monster' and all that. It's history. And I just want to thank you for putting me in the position where I had to take care of her, then taking off for Mexico. What a 'friend' you are! Those three months were...difficult."

"Oh, God, Jennifer, I am so sorry. I'll make it up to you, I promise. I know. I'll arrange for you to go to Yerevan and stay in Tanya's apartment and teach law at the foreign language institute, when they get the heat and electricity back on. How's that?" And we all laughed.

We changed the subject and talked until late into the night about my failing career possibilities. She spoke about the cutbacks in personnel in all the local universities and community colleges. Other than suggesting I might think about going back to China to teach, she had no more idea than either Barbara or I as to how to solve the problem.

We all three rejected the idea of returning to China in one breath, and I voiced my sincerest promise:

"I swear—I will never again leave the United States. I can't cope with ever again moving to a foreign country. I am here to stay. That's all there is to that."

The winter months crept by and blended into a late spring. I rode my bicycle every morning and every evening along the miles of beautiful greenbelt that opened off Barbara's patio gate; mindlessly, automatically intoning my chant as I pedaled the meandering pathways. Wandering while wondering about possible futures; I thanked my foresight for having taken early retirement funds from my school district in Nevada. They were meager, but were sufficient to take care of my personal expenses while living with my daughter. I was worried, concerned, but the loveliness of this environment was therapeutic.

With Barbara at work and my grandchildren in school, I had the quiet time to ponder the spiritual aspects of my life. I thought about Judeo-Christian doctrines over the centuries and went back once again to my readings in Eastern philosophy and Yoga. And what of Buddhism? I had accepted initiation and the chanting was always a great comfort. But it didn't seem to be enough. As I pedaled along and immersed myself in the beauty that surrounded me, some stray thoughts began to formulate. Since childhood, things have had to make sense to me. We're supposed to have left polytheism behind us millennia ago, but have we? What of money and status? Are those not the demigods that we worship and adore, and for which we dedicate our lives? And pursuing this a bit further, the Romans and Greeks had their own brand of demigods, those who could transmute from divine to human and back again and intervene on behalf of the pitiful supplicant. This was still the dominant thinking in the first century CE. Is it not familiar to us today? Have not humans been transmuted into saints over the centuries; elevated from human to divine by a vote of church hierarchy, and are not they and the angels available to us for the same purpose as those of the Greeks and Romans; to intercede? Perhaps the pagan ritual of sacrifice is a practice of the past, but how many times do we, in our extreme moments, not make some promise to God that we will sacrifice some valued aspect of our being if He/She will only grant us this one last request. It's always the *last* time we'll plead—until the next time. How far have we actually evolved in these past two millennia? These are not new arguments. Yet, after thousands of years of attempted debunking by scholars and thinkers who are much brighter and better at it than I, religions still persist. There's got to be something there. Something that I can hold on to. Without becoming burdensome; I needed to connect the dots.

I questioned what I had always meant by Truth, questioned what I thought about God, and questioned what I meant when I referred to Divine Mind, phrases that fall easily from my mouth, almost as space fillers. What of the meanings of individual mind and the purpose of the brain? I sat alone on the patio for hours in the winter sun ruminating, mulling it over and over. I visited libraries and bookstores and picked up several volumes on the teachings of The Buddha. I thought it was all old material to me, but as I read I began to find that was not the case. A few sentences began to compete for my attention. Then more and more. I was finding connections with the sermons of Jesus. Why hadn't I noticed these before? What began to come to me was, and continues to be, that the similarities between these two great spiritual leaders—whose lives were separated by five hundred years—mean that they were both dipping from the One and Only Universal Truth; call it the Divine Mind, call it God. The three are synonymous. And they were both telling us that this same source is available to all; equally, in accordance with one's expression of his/her Personal Divinity. "The *Kingdom of God* is *within* you." Luke 17:21. (Italics mine. Here and elsewhere I've referenced the King James Version of the Bible). If one goes to that well with a thimble, a thimbleful will be the reward. If one goes with a bucket... and so forth.

Bear with me just a bit longer as I stretch mentally.

Yogis have been teaching the *stuff* of the universe for thousands of years. They describe it as *the intelligent totality of the cosmos*. (Where is the total knowledge about the discovery of anything *before* it enters the material domain? It is *somewhere, waiting; in place, but without space*. How often do we describe new discoveries and artistic creations as "inspirations"? But how much "perspiration" is sweated out before "inspiration" is achieved? Do we put that much effort into understanding our own spirituality?)

Everything that can be known is already available within the realm of Ultimate Potential, Ultimate Possibility, Universal Truth, Divine Mind, God; Consciousness. Choose a label. Humankind has pondered for millennia, and continues to ponder, how to avail ourselves, gain access to the Divine Mind. There have been teachers from time to time who tugged at the Truth. We are the most familiar with those who lived it: the Buddha from the fifth century BCE and later Jesus...both of whom knew and taught and demonstrated for us the power of that Truth and told us that we can also demonstrate the Divine Mind, according to our level of Belief.

Buddhahood and The Christ Consciousness are one and the same thing; the realization of Personal Divinity. Our Personal Divinity is without beginning or end and must, in the long run, be realized. (I'm sure it's been said often before that one needn't expect the physician to search for and find the soul because *each person is not a body with a soul, but a soul with a body.*)

Free Will exists only until we reach the point in our own Spiritual evolution when we realize there is no Free Will. The purpose of our creation ("Why was I ever born?") is to attain Buddhahood/The Christ Consciousness/Enlightenment. We are given an eternity in which to realize the goal. Hence, reincarnation and its corollary, karma; great gifts. Once karma is understood, one need never again ask, "How could a Merciful God allow such catastrophes to happen?" God doesn't. It's all karma. Accountability. Deathbed conversions just don't cut it! Sorry. Atonement is a must.

Individual mind is that personal reservoir of Universal Truth which we choose to express in any given lifetime, and the human brain is the conduit. My fifty-plus-year quest had reached the point where I no longer had to fight against established dogma. I knew I was a Christian-Buddhist. I finally recognized Jesus as my Beloved

Elder Brother and I have been walking beside him ever since; sometimes arguing, sometimes totally pissed off at him and demanding he keep his Promises, and sometimes hand-in-hand in loving gratitude. Jesus, the man, is not our Savior; he is our Guide to the Christ Consciousness— and that Consciousness is the Savior. Each one of us is responsible for our own "Saving" by *"Letting that mind* be in [us] as it is in Christ Jesus," as Paul wrote to that early community in Phillipi (italics mine). That is far too much responsibility for many people to accept, regrettably, so they label it self-aggrandizement.

I spent the days otherwise caring for the house, caring for my family, preparing meals, checking the classified ads; resisting the rise of smoldering depressions.

I longed for Norman, for the safety and security of his nearness. I needed him. Our weekly telephone calls were too brief, but I clung to them. They were the center of my being. I spoke of daily things, of family, of whatever would be of interest to him, but not of the financial matters that were plaguing me. From time to time he questioned my pretenses, my tone of voice, but I made light of it with some excuse.

Throughout the winter, he continued with his paperwork, giving me a weekly progress report. We already knew that his visa would have to be granted by the American Embassy in Moscow. The installation of the U.S. Embassy in Yerevan was still too new to handle consular activities. In early December he told me that he had spoken by phone with the embassy in Moscow. I had already sent all the documents, as I had been instructed, but they advised him that they still needed a notarized "invitation" from me before they could process a fiancé's visa. I sent the requested document by Federal Express and informed him that the last paper they needed was on the way. A few days later he took a plane to Moscow.

Arriving at the embassy, his turn at the counter was met with seeming confusion. The clerk checked her computer, then rifled through papers at her desk. She excused herself and went to an office behind a glass partition. Norman could see her talking to what appeared to be her supervisors, one of whom he suspected was the woman he'd spoken to on the telephone. They walked the clerk back and remained near the door. The clerk informed Norman that there was no record of him and no documentation had arrived concerning him. He knew at once that she was lying. But why? How was it possible? *They don't want me to enter the United States. They probably have destroyed my papers. I am unworthy. Armenians are not welcome.* It took him two weeks before he was able to arrange a return flight to Yerevan. I didn't hear from him until he arrived back home. He was distressed, fully believing that the United States government did not want him, personally, to go to America—for some reason he couldn't explain. I told him I'd see what I could do and he gave me the name of the woman he had spoken to on the telephone, but with whom he had not been able to connect with directly while in Moscow. Sensing I might need outside help, I telephoned the office of the House of Representatives member for Yolo County. I was able to speak to him directly and he said he didn't know how much help he could be, but took all the relevant information. I called the woman at the embassy a couple of days later. I truly do not know what happened between my call to the representative and my call to Moscow, but the woman was most sincerely apologetic, saying that the immigration desk had made a terrible mistake. Norman's documentation was indeed there, he was in the computer. I asked her the date of the entry. It was dated before he had made the trip.

When I explained to Norman that it had been a mistake, he was hesitant to believe it. He eventually accepted my assurances, but with some reservations. However, to make an immediate return sojourn to the Russian capital was not possible. He didn't have enough money for another round-trip airfare. He would have to work and accumulate more funds and borrow what he couldn't earn. It was to take more than two months for him to raise the money.

When that time had passed, I again phoned our embassy in Moscow, spoke with the same woman, and she set the date for his personal interview. He made the trip in mid-February and took the interview. He still needed to have a physical and an HIV test. The earliest date for the medical examination was mid-March. He would have to remain in Moscow, virtually without funds or any possible way to earn money. Fortunately, he had distant relatives living in that city and they helped him. Once the results of the examinations were in, he was given sufficient documentation to return to Yerevan. With his papers in hand, he went to the Department of Visas and Registration in the Armenian Ministry of the Interior. It would take another six weeks to have his passport ready. It was nearly the first of May when all was in order. He called me, his pride bursting through the telephone. There would be only one more step to complete before he could board a plane for the United States. He would have to return once again to Moscow so the United States could stamp his visa into his passport. The "red" tape became the butt of our jokes.

While all this was progressing on the other side of the world, I had investigated the local school district for substitute work and possibly a full contract for the next year. The district personnel office was most gracious, but it was clear that there would be no job because of my age. That was hardly a surprise. (The illegality of age discrimination is too often a joke, as many seniors will attest to.) Without laboring the point, I never failed to check the classified sections in the daily newspapers or to send out all feelers I had at my disposal, anything and everything to get work. Nothing materialized.

In my extremity, I told Barbara I wanted to borrow her car to go to Reno and ask my former supervisor for work. After a lengthy argument about the "insanity" of my even imagining I could return to Reno, she gave me the keys. I drove back, chanting nonstop, to the site of my former district and went directly to the office of my previous employer. She was greatly surprised to see me and welcomed me with an embrace. We had a long talk over coffee and I filled her in on all of my experiences, my coming marriage, and my need to work. She listened not only with interest, but expressed envy at the road my life had taken. When I asked her about employment, her response was immediate.

"Adair, you are welcome to come back here at any time. But I cannot advise strongly enough against it. With all you have accomplished, they would take you out of here in a body bag in less than three months. Please, my friend. Don't do it."

I knew she was right. I'd known it as soon as I had crested that last hill and the city had come into view. It was not for me. Regardless of my desperation, it was not my answer. I thanked her and bade her good-bye.

It was late spring when my problems compounded. The temporary dental work, which I had been told would have to be replaced eventually, began to cause me great distress. All the oral surgery had to be done. I postponed it. The damn toothaches. Stupid damn toothaches. Postponements.

The old saying about the ill wind doing somebody good was never truer. I'm almost ashamed to tell about a death that was my blessing. But, what happened, happened.

Through my son Gregory, I heard that my ex-husband's mother had just died. My ex-husband had been living in her palatial home on the oceanfront near San Diego since our divorce. (How often had that image come to mind while I was struggling to raise the children, and later, when I had to spend so many months homeless, sleeping on my daughter's couch, without sufficient funds for a place of my own?) The situation was that my ex-husband was an only child and his mother was a wealthy woman. During our marriage, she had been a loving mother-in-law and we'd shared many enjoyable vacations together. I'd often mused how such an admirable woman could have raised such an abusive son. With the divorce, she had turned her back on me and on her grandchildren. All communication between us had stopped.

In writing up my divorce papers, my attorney had stipulated that child support was to be paid until either the children graduated from college or turned twenty-one years of age. Neither my ex-husband nor I paid the necessary attention to that stipulation and he had stopped paying when each child turned eighteen. It was during one of my excessive cleaning sessions before leaving for the Peace Corps that I came across the divorce decree and read it—thoroughly. It took a few moments to grapple with the revelation. I was owed a large amount of money in back child support and phoned my attorney. He advised that I would have difficulty collecting due to the fact that at the time I instituted the claim I was living in Nevada and my ex-husband was living in California. In those days, collecting across state lines was not easy. My attorney suggested I wait until my ex inherited his mother's estate and then make my claim. As soon as Gregory notified me of my former mother-in-law's death, I called Jennifer. As an attorney, she would know what to do. She did. With the legal negotiations under way, I returned to the dentist. He was also Jennifer's dentist and had known us both for years. He had total confidence in her legal abilities; consequently, he agreed to initiate my dental work before the money was in. Through Jennifer's connections, she was able to freeze my ex-husband's accounts and start the proceedings. When he found his bank accounts inaccessible, he called me with his all-too-familiar opening words of endearment.

"You goddamned fucking bitch! What in the hell do you think you are doing? You'll never get away with this. Fuck you!"

"Please do not call me again. You may speak to me through my attorney," was my only response.

Although we were able to collect only about half of the actual amount owed, it was sufficient to cover all my dental expenses—but nothing more. My needs for a job, for money, were desperate.

May would soon be June and I kept my telephone calls to Norman centered mostly on his activities. He was gleeful, a giggling schoolboy again, the envy of his friends. He was filled with the anticipation of a new life and a new wife. He was in love and reborn.

I was the consummate actress, never letting on that there was the slightest problem, but guilt-ridden and fearful, focused on maintaining control. Too much tension led to migraine headaches and muscle spasms. What was I doing to myself? To him? This couldn't last forever. I had to face the truth. To tell him. Had to accept responsibility. Metaphysics is metaphysics, but I had to come to grips with reality. And what was that reality?

What had it all come down to? I had exhausted every possibility; there was no job for me at my age, I was virtually penniless, had been deserted by my cherished belief system, and had to face the miserable, ugly facts. I must telephone Norman and tell him that all our dreams had come to nothing. I would not be able to bring him to America. There would be no marriage. We probably would never see each other again. Norman had made those two difficult trips to Moscow and survived eighteen months of combating and overcoming a nearly insurmountable ordeal. He had his passport and was sharing his good fortune with family and friends in an ongoing round of celebrations. He was ready to come to the United States. I had to tell him. But I could not bring myself to do it. How could I tell him how totally I had failed? I'd overstepped my bounds. Procrastination compounded procrastination. I would have to eke out some kind of existence and would probably spend the rest of my life living with my children. That was to be my future. And what was his? I had to call... had to face it, for both of us. It was my responsibility. July was well under way. Sleep eluded me that Saturday night. I was so sick with grief that there were no tears.

I heard Barbara performing her Sunday morning ritual of preparing the coffee and leaving for the supermarket to buy pastries. That morning she also picked up a San Francisco newspaper. Thinking I was asleep, she had come back in quietly, picked up her cup of coffee and gone out to the patio to read. During my sleeplessness, a strength had been found, a resolve made. I got up from my sofa, strolled into the kitchen, poured my cup of rejuvenation, and returned to the living room to click on the television. This was the day I would call Norman, but would tell Barb later. I had to collect myself, get some words together. I sat, staring blankly at the babbling television set, unconsciously rotating Norman's father's wedding band on my finger, as I'd done so many hundreds of times before. The movement caught my attention. *Take off the ring. It'll make it easier to call.* I sat looking at it, staring at it, rotating it around and around. My memory became awash with the

clutter of dishes. The simmering water kettle. Goga's infectious smile. Tammy holding his hand. Norman's eyes.
Mama. No. I folded my hands. The ring remained where it
was. That's all there was to that. The momentary strength
had drained away and was gone. Alone. Afraid...and small.
Not today. Maybe tomorrow. I set my coffee cup on the floor
and lay back down, hugging my pillow.

"Mom, bring your coffee and come on out here," Barbara's voice intruded.

Obediently, I pushed myself up from the sofa, clicked
off the TV with the remote control, and moved toward
the open patio doors, coffee cup in hand, to see what she
wanted. She looked up at me.

"I want you to come and sit down." She had the paper
open to the classified section and elbowed another pile of
papers from a chair. I sat.

"Now, I know that you've sworn you'll never again
leave the United States, but I just want you to sit here
quietly and not say one word until I've finished. OK?" I
shrugged and nodded, and she read.

The Binational Fulbright Commission was looking
for eight highly qualified educators, preferably retired
teachers, with international experience and master's degrees in the Teaching of English to Speakers for Other
Languages to initiate a pilot project in the Egyptian educational system, at the invitation of the Egyptian Ministry
of Education, at the request of Egyptian President Hosni
Mubarak. The project would provide stateside salaries, a
housing allowance, and the full benefits package, including all airfares for both the educator and his/her spouse.

The project was funded by USAID. Those who were qualified and interested were requested to send a fax to the director in Cairo, Egypt, immediately, as the project was to commence on September first.

Suspended, dumbfounded. Fulbright and USAID combined. It had been ten years since I'd been coaxed to attend that afternoon social gathering of the Peace Corps volunteers in Jamaica; the result of which had been my decision to pursue the advanced degree. Cairo? The lost documents of six years before. And here it was. All of it.

We sat for an instant in silence, focusing on each other as her words registered. I felt...overwhelmed. I didn't know if it was real...what was happening. The transition was too swift. I sat there, numb. Afraid to believe. Barb reached out and took my hands, then pulled me close to her and began rocking me, stroking my head and shoulders, speaking steadily into my ear. "It's OK, Mom, it's OK. Let it out, let it all out. He's yours, Mom. He's yours. It's all yours." Nurturing. As she had been from her childhood, my ever-constant rock. I sank into her embrace and my breath began to come from deep within me as my tears flowed. She never stopped holding me, stroking my hair. "This gift is for you, Mom." The job was already mine and she knew it more clearly than I. We telephoned Jennifer to come and help with working out the details. I'd been through this many times before, but this metamorphosis held me in a grip of hesitation and disbelief. Fear. I needed support, and with them walking me through each item, I sent the fax.

I was interviewed in San Francisco on July 21, and was later told that I was the first one hired as soon as all interviews had been concluded. Perhaps they told that to everyone, I don't know, but it was good to hear. I had to report to Cairo in...less than six weeks. It was just as the Armenian fortune-teller had predicted: "Something most extraordinary is going to happen to you when you are sixty-two years old. Something unexpected, very extraordinary. It will come at a time when you are confused and unhappy. But it will be a great opportunity. The most important opportunity that has ever come to you in your life. I don't understand what it is, but you will be traveling great distances, and often." She couldn't have been more exact.

Norman arrived in the United States on August 7 after eighteen months of the most exasperating frustration possible in procuring his right to be with his intended wife. Again, it was as had been predicted that late afternoon in the village: "There is now a new man in your life that you've only known a very short time, but he is already in love with you. You are going to marry this man. There are going to be serious problems before you get married. These problems are going to take a long time to overcome. But you will solve them and then you will spend many years together. You will be happy with this man, and he will be happy with you."

We spent the next two weeks marveling at the glories of our lives. He did not make love to me upon his arrival or during that time. New world, new life, new beginnings. He spent long nighttime hours standing and looking out through the open windows at the beauty of our surroundings, inhaling the miracle of where he was. His days were consumed with getting acquainted with my family, with shopping, with American life—trying to figure it all out at once.

On August 22, we drove to Reno, Nevada, for our wedding. My family was in attendance—Barbara serving as matron of honor and Larry standing as Norman's best man. (Greg was out of the country at the time.) Of course, Jennifer was right there beside me, camera in hand. I'd called Angel to tell her all what was happening and she had come from San Francisco to celebrate with us. We all went together—as any giddy, nervous, joking wedding party would—to the courthouse to be married in a simple civil ceremony.

The small, pleasant room calmed our anticipation. We were introduced to a gracious woman of middle years who was to seal our commitment. As we took our places, Barbara whispered to her the briefest of explanations and told her that English was not Norman's native language. With an expression of warmth and admiration, she came forward and clasped our hands in hers. When all was in readiness, she stepped back and commenced the ceremony, holding the book but speaking directly to us, slowly and with care, from memory. The timeless words were said in a peaceful atmosphere permeated with the wonder of our love.

When the moment arrived for him to place the symbol on my finger, it was with deepest emotion that I extended my right hand so he could finally transfer the one I'd been wearing. But he paused, raising a hand in the gesture of patience, and with the slightest inclination of his head, Norman withdrew from his pocket a tiny envelope and handed it to Larry. My son's nervous fingers fumbled momentarily with the pasted ends, and then he tipped it, emptying its contents into his hand. Mama had sent her own wedding ring for me.

The room hushed in recognition. Our eyes met, and an ethereal presence, as of other persons, graced the chamber as I slid his father's ring from my finger and we exchanged the bands.

We departed for Cairo on August 29.

CAREER EXTRAORDINAIRE

CAIRO

I began writing these memoirs from my journals and diaries and from my Chinese postgraduate students' copybooks and many of their papers which they had graciously given to me. I wrote as I sat at my desk in our spacious, comfortable apartment on Zamalek, an island in the Nile River as it courses through Cairo. From my vantage point, I could look out over our broad balcony to our spectacular view of the river, and the minarets and rooftops of Cairo beyond, and listen to the cacophony of the five-times-a-day call to prayer, the ceaseless honking of car horns, and the cries of street vendors with their carts of steaming food in this chaotic, exotic city.

My seven American colleagues came to Cairo with their assortment of spouses and children and we formed a cohesive group, taking on a task welcomed by some Egyptian teachers, resisted by others. For the latter, nothing could be worse than change, when one has been rewarded for performing one's duties the same way for years in accordance with the way it was done by occupiers who had come and gone many generations earlier. The British system and aging texts were much in evidence and use when we arrived. They were not producing the results that President Mubarak wanted for his people; therefore, he made his request for the update and our arrival.

President Mubarak had spoken of his request during a television address. The chief administrator for the Binational Fulbright Commission had been watching and thought to herself...*we can do this.* She wrote a brief proposal and sent it off to the Minister of Education, expecting a reply within the next several months, as was the way of things at the time. The following day he had couriered over his response that they should speak together about her proposal. At the meeting, he suggested that she bring in a hundred teachers. She was able to agree to eight, with an increase as the program progressed. She had to come up with a definite plan, and with her usual or unusual) gifts, she put it together in days. The minister accepted her completed proposal as written and asked for it to begin the following September...giving her just the summer to put it into effect.

We were placed in "experimental schools"—which they were not, since they'd been in existence for many years and were working well. The difference between the experimental schools and public schools was primarily that the former were English- immersion schools for which parents paid a nominal tuition and for which the potential students had to be tested and interviewed before being admitted. They are a step between private and public schools. The school where I was assigned was a secondary school (high school) of some two hundred-plus students. My staff of teachers reflected varying degrees of resistance, but with many hours of tea drinking and discussions of our families in the staff office, their resistance was resolved and we all came to a working agreement. I co-taught with the English Language Department teachers in their classrooms. The students loved the change and took no time getting into the swing of our differing yet complementary teaching styles. They responded with enthusiasm to student participation in their own learning. Soon, we were all deep into animated discussions concerning the text materials that had to be the core of our lessons, but became only that—the core—from which we expanded our lessons to include a wide variety of "thought" questions and "possibility" answers; challenges eventually initiated by the students. Their language efficiency increased rapidly as they were allowed to think and question for themselves, a new experience for both students and staff. What was especially interesting about this was that the methods we were using had carryover effects, and students were applying their new thinking skills to their other classes and asking provocative questions; sometimes to the amusement and sometimes to the irritation of those teachers!

I would like to relate just one teaching incident: a first-year teacher brought her mother to visit our class. She introduced us. Her mother was a retired librarian and had received her degree in library science in the United States. The woman took a seat at the rear of the classroom and we went on with our lesson, which happened to be an analysis of one section of Charlotte Bronte's *Jane Eyre*, a required novel that may have literary value for these young Arabic speakers—who must struggle through the sometimes archaic English—but whose nineteenth-century British theme has little relevance to their lives as young Egyptians.

Their assigned reading had ended with the arrival at Mr. Rochester's party of the woman Jane believed he was planning to marry. The students' first activity was to do a five-minute, nonstop writing exercise...which activity is not graded, thereby allowing them to write freely without fear of the *red pencil*. Each girl was asked to take on the role of Jane and write a letter to Mr. Rochester telling him how she felt. Each boy was to take on the role of Mr. Rochester and write a letter to Jane telling her how he felt. At the end of the five minutes, volunteers read their letters aloud and discussion followed, including a hypothetical backstory—history—for Jane that could determine her reactions, and one for Mr. Rochester. How might they handle their feelings? My teaching point for the day was how to cope with jealousy, which is a common emotion among adolescents, and especially relevant in an Islamic society that allows plural marriages for men. When the word "jealousy" was mentioned, I directed the conversation to the lives of their teenage peers and to adults they knew, and asked how jealousy was handled...not requiring them to speak of themselves, only of "others." What are the downsides of such a strong emotion? Are there any upsides? Their teacher facilitated—and championed—the girls' participation; I facilitated—and championed—that of the boys.

To encourage participation during such activities, I do not require that students raise their hands to speak, only that they recognize and respect taking turns. The discussion became very animated, as I expected it would. Their whole range of concerns came up, including having their parents choose their spouses, and the role of wives in marriages where the husband chooses to have the four allowed by Islamic law. As the class period came to an end, one of the boys asked me what I thought about men having four wives. I replied, "I'm all in favor of it...so long as I can have four husbands." The girls tried to hide their giggles and snickers behind their hands. The boys did not even try to conceal their shock and disbelief at what I had just said. Finally, the whole class was laughing. To close the period I assigned the next several pages, to see how Bronte had resolved the problem of jealousy in the book. (At the conclusion of the novel we would watch the film version of *Jane Eyre*. The students would note the variances between book and film and discuss why the screenwriters might have chosen to make those changes.)

The next day I asked my young teacher why her mother had paid us the visit. She answered, "She wanted to meet the woman who teaches love." Such an idea had never crossed my mind and I was humbled at the thought. I wish to thank both of them and do so here.

The results my teachers achieved were...more than rewarding. The Egyptian education system, as with educational systems in many countries, used end-of-year final examinations to evaluate both the quality of its teachers and the learning of its students. It is a nightmare and one for which the teachers traditionally gear their lessons. Rote memorization to answer rote questions. It must be said that this model can produce some excellent and outstanding contributors to any country's reservoir of experts in this field and that. However, that reservoir is usually quite small, and the majority of test-takers memorize volumes of information in order to do well on the tests, and then promptly forget everything they've memorized since it is no longer relevant. That is not my, or most of today's educators' idea of education. That method provides the society with undereducated graduates easily influenced in their life choices. Utilizing what has become called student-centered learning, our students are involved in the materials and bring meaning from them—meaning that elicits their creative and analytical thinking skills. A new population of challengers to the status quo is produced. These were the results we got at my school. At the end of the first year, our students placed number one in all of Egypt on the final exams, a first for the school. At the end of year two, they also placed number one on the exams, a first in the history of recordkeeping for any one school to accomplish, according to the Ministry of Education. The minister sent his representative to the school to present a plaque to that effect during a student-body gathering in the courtyard. I was given a similar plaque in English, thanking me for my participation in this extraordinary event. Unfortunately, I cannot report what happened at the end of year three, as my schedule had been divided up between different schools to expand our paradigm, and by the time the test results were in, I was already out of the country and preparing for a new placement. It doesn't matter. The "new" methods were well established and functioning as a part of the learning process. My goal for the school had been achieved.

Our three years in Cairo were challenging and exciting and exhausting. It would not have been possible for me to complete this valuable work if it had not been for Norman's constant attention to our every need. Before meeting me, Norman's familiarity with the kitchen was limited to his expertise in tea-making. When it came time for him to be introduced to my style of American cooking, he rebelled. My response was simple; with all I was involved in he either would learn to enjoy my cooking or learn to cook. He opted for the latter and, in time, became quite accomplished in preparing our meals—a compromise between Armenian cuisine and American, with Egyptian mixed in for added "spice." Norman was also able to take on a temporary position as a violinist with the Cairo Symphony Orchestra.

Our summers were interspersed with vacations in Athens, London, Amsterdam, and Tallinn, Estonia, where we visited my son, Gregory, and his new love, Jana, who would eventually become his wife. They were able to come on vacation to visit us and we took in the museums and the Nile boat trip to see Abu Simbel, the Karnak Temple at Luxor, the Valley of the Kings, and Hatshepsut's Temple. Another great joy for us was the arrangements we were able to make for Mama and Goga to come and spend several weeks with us in Cairo. The trips out to the pyramids with camel rides and carriages pulled by decorated horses were family experiences that enriched the lives of each of us.

At the close of our contract in Cairo, I wanted to spend some quality time back home with my family and Norman wanted to visit Yerevan. When he returned to the U.S., it was with pride that he told me of all the modernization that was transpiring in Armenia, and that he had connected with the American University in Armenia, the overseas affiliate of UCLA that I knew from my months in Yerevan, and the administrators were interested in having me join their staff in the English Language Department. I was dubious about the conditions in Yerevan, but Norman assured me we could live quite well with the vast amount of upgrading that had gone on in the intervening years since my previous visit. With some hesitation, I agreed.

YEREVAN, ARMENIA

Great improvements had indeed taken place...but there was still ample room for more! AUA found an apartment for us that was very livable. Even on the stormiest days the view from our loggia gave us the historic sight of Mount Ararat and "little sister" at her side, as they hid behind the threatening cloud banks, stood unyielding as the blizzards beat upon them, and then eventually dressed their sloping sides with the verdure of the new seasons. I stood watching the awesome changes as had thousands of years of passersby before me.

As a side note: my most recent trip to Yerevan (2007) showed a city burgeoning with growth in vitality and creativity. The opera house/symphony hall is the center of the city from which the various downtown areas branch out, which gives one an idea of the role of music in the life of Armenians. During summer, the extensive area around this cultural center is bustling with outdoor coffeehouses, several with live bands; the expanse of the space allowing them to play their own individual genres without interfering with other bands. There are now downtown pedestrian malls between modern multi-story apartment buildings, and several five-star hotels for visitors from the widespread Armenian diaspora. The city welcomes guests with a new world-class airport and the comforts and conveniences found in any major metropolitan area. The historic sites are familiar from biblical times and are fascinating.

Returning to my story, Jimmy Harris had moved on to other challenges so all members of the staff were new to me. There were four of us representing UCLA and the rest were Armenians. We were a good group and did much worthwhile work.

We spent two years in Yerevan, during which time it was of interest to watch the city take major steps toward becoming the capital it wanted to be. A wide variety of food was readily available and the flow of electricity was normal. Water was still intermittent, but we—like most others living in Yerevan—had water-reservoir tanks installed by having them attached as a false ceiling over our bathtubs, thereby guaranteeing a full supply of water. Heat was still a problem, but Norman found a small heater for me which I could easily carry from room to room at home. The university building had no heat, so we were given extended vacations from the middle of December through February. We used that time for traveling.

Spring of 2000, and the new millennium had been born while I was on vacation in the U.S. Returning to Yerevan, though, there was still something nagging at me. I thought I could do more. Being a university professor has its rewards, but it is repetitive. I was ready to move on

to another assignment. I began networking via email with
my friends and colleagues around the world and someone—I'm not even remotely sure who—wrote back about
the Department of State's programs for placing senior fellows in their sites across the globe. I emailed the address
given and was contacted by telephone within days. Russia
was looking for specialists and my credentials filled all requirements. A contract was offered.

RUSSIA

The multilane thoroughfare from the Moscow airport into the city gives the first panorama of the vastness
that is Russia. As we began the long slope that gradually
flattens out onto the plane where the city lies, I could sense
the increasing energy level of that powerful metropolis.
The energies were something more than just the combined
activities of Muscovites. It was as a waft of power that I'd
not experienced before, even in our own nation's capital.
Power is still not the complete word, does not capture an
underlying melancholy...passion...tinged with negativity...
that I came to know as uniquely Russian. As we rode along
I was reminded of the music of Tchaikovsky, of Prokofiev,
of Rachmaninoff, and how it could stir the soul. I gripped
Norman's hand and he smiled at me. He had lived many
years in Moscow and knew the city, and much of the country, quite well. My thoughts skittered back to Victor and
his comments on that last night in Jamaica. "This island
is too small for your talents." Surely, this would be big
enough!

Through Norman's knowledge of the city we were
able to locate living accommodations that were excellent,

and within my budget. Moscow had, and still has, one of the highest cost-of-living standards in the world. Good luck was with us, and we were able to move into a furnished apartment on the ninth floor of a building, with a magnificent view of the Kremlin and St. Basil's Church from my studio windows; and from our loggia, out across the busy district in which we lived. The only problem was that there were times when the elevator stopped working for days, occasionally weeks at a time. Nine floors! Quite a climb, especially when toting a load of classroom materials or groceries. All our daily activities had to be organized so that we had to make only one trip out of the apartment. As always, Norman took full charge of our lives, doing all the shopping and cooking and caring for the fundamentals of life, allowing me time and energies to prepare for and present my classes, workshops, and conferences.

The four years we spent there cannot be readily encapsulated. A country struggling to regain its prominence on the globe, a people who are divided as though by a cleaver into two mind-sets; some ready and able for the mantle of individual freedom and all the responsibilities that incurs, and others equally ready for a return to former days, even to the days of the czar. There are those who want a father figure to tell them what to do, how to live, to do their thinking for them. Those people have not cast off the sinkholes of dependency that the seventy years of Communist repression and earlier years of Imperial Russia have left as legacies. After generations of being controlled in every aspect of their lives, the need for those controls has become entrenched in their genes. I got to know both mentalities through multiple trips from village to village and from city to city, from Kaliningrad on the west to Vladivostok on the east, and the schism was everywhere to be found. What was especially interesting was that the mental division was not necessarily related to age or gender, or even rural- and urban-based. I found many freethinking, freewheeling personalities in remote areas.

I was invited to give frequent presentations to large audiences of educators. One in particular I'd like to recap. This one was for a conference in St. Petersburg for the English language teachers in that area. I chose to speak about the Cultural Revolution that took place in the United States during the late sixties and early seventies. As I prepared my materials on the various movements that were dividing our country at the time, such as civil rights, women's liberation, gay rights, ending the Vietnam War, and others, I began to wonder if I was overstepping the boundaries of political correctness. I would, after all, be speaking about areas of conflict between the young protestors—of which I had been one—and the police and militia...I would be speaking about Kent State and about the University of California, Berkeley, about which I knew a great deal. As I selected the music of the Beatles that I intended to use, and made the slogans and signs that had been visible everywhere across the country, and that would be fronting my podium and chalkboards, I had misgivings. I would be speaking against the establishment and the government. We are often told that we serve as quasi-ambassadors when we teach abroad. Would I be in trouble with the embassy? I didn't stop, though. I loved the subject. I had a large and attentive audience. When the Beatles' music was playing, they sang along. They stopped me from time to time to ask probing questions. I answered forthrightly as much as I knew. They were involved with me and with the subject. Afterward, a group came up to me and the spokesperson said, "You are very lucky to be so proud of your country. We wish we could feel the same pride about ours, but we can't." I'd had no idea that *pride* was what was being conveyed. Their comment tells me that when the truth is spoken without an agenda, the message has power and that power is positive.

Vladivostok, the Russian Far East, is a land unto itself. There is a spirit very much alive in that area that I had not expected, quite unlike what I'd found in European Russia. It reminded me of the American Wild West for some reason I couldn't quite identify. The fact that Vladivostok is on the water and built on hills reminiscent of San Francisco may have contributed to the feeling, but there was something more. They are pioneering in their mentality. When I tried to introduce an Internet program that would have linked my Ph.D. candidates in Moscow with their counterparts in Vladivostok, those in my Moscow group was far too immersed in their own superiority to participate. Their Far East counterparts would have been eager to share, but with the thought that they could contribute to the academic expertise of their colleagues in Moscow. Very interesting. I brought up the subject with my coworker who was stationed in Vladivostok and he said that he was aware of that spirit also. He'd had the time and had earned the confidence of the people enough to discuss it with his Far East associates. They explained that during the Stalin purges, thousands of Russia's most educated and intellectual academic elite were dissidents who had been evacuated to the gulags of Siberia and the Far East. They had been confined there for decades, and many of those who survived opted to remain in that part of the world. They married each other and had their families. The children of those couples were raised in educated, intellectual environments that stressed the importance of individuality, a characteristic that is inherent in being a dissident. Hence, the current generations of the Far East are spirited people who feel themselves to be a part of their own nation and neither need nor want assistance from Moscow.

My role as a teacher-trainer/professor put me in close working relationships with educators across the country, and allowed me the opportunity to affect not *what* the teachers were teaching, but *how* they were teaching. What we fellows were bringing to them met the same types of acceptance and resistance as anywhere else in the world, including our own country. What we also found was that within Russia there were already groups of educators who were well aware of the techniques of analytical thinking skills and of student-centered methodologies, and were promoting modernized education within their domains. Since the collapse of the Soviet Union just over a decade before, the intelligentsia had been finding their voice, and that voice was dynamic. What was equally dynamic was the government's lack of funds, or lack of willingness to provide funds to these great minds so they could collect even minimum salaries. It was heart-wrenching to see congregations of physicists, chemists, and other prime academicians grouped on the grounds of the Russian "white house" in the depth of the freezing winter months, having to demean themselves by demonstrating for wages;

not a rise in salary, but to be paid salaries long past due. As that "white house" is just steps away from the United States Embassy in Moscow, it was commonplace for me to observe what was happening there as I went to regular meetings with my colleagues in the embassy.

My primary site was the prestigious Moscow State University, formerly one of the most respected and outstanding universities in the world. I was invited to work with several departments and found some interesting inconsistencies. Staff members were for the most part excellent representatives of their fields. However, in order to regain their international standing and to collect a larger portion of the educational budget, they needed to produce multiple Ph.D. recipients. In order to do that, it was clear that standards had been compromised in those disciplines I came in contact with. The several dissertations I scanned were at about our undergraduate level. Fortunately, I was not asked to critique, but only to read as an interested party.

During my fourth year in Moscow, President Vladimir Putin requested that a special department be established within the university, primarily for the well-qualified sons and daughters of Russia's leading industrialists and political leaders. Even they had to apply for and be invited into the department. It was his thinking that these young people would follow in their parents' influential footsteps, and as future leaders of the country he wanted them to maintain specific levels of expertise in specific subjects. He wanted them to meet the highest possible standards. I was invited to work with these outstanding young people in the area of the meaning and functioning of the United Nations. The UN very graciously provided me with a bounty of materials to take with me to those classes. The students got into the swing of it straightaway and had great fun as they took on the roles of various countries, researched that country's needs, and dialogued for that country's interests in a mock United Nations General Assembly format, and to participate in debating UN Resolutions as they might apply to that nation. I was flattered to have been invited for this special grouping and hope the results pleased President Putin and the administrators as much as they did us, the participants.

It was all drawing to a close. In the past twenty years I had gone from the miseries and confines of my life in Reno, where I'd been alone, unchallenged, and suffering waves of deep depression, to where I was at this time. A voyage of incredible, nearly unbelievable scope—from the warmth of rebirth in Jamaica, through the pains and heartache of China, the miracle of Norman, and the depth and expanse of experiences in these other exotic locales where I had been assigned since our marriage; a voyage that culminated in one more final accolade. For my last year in Moscow, the U.S. Embassy office had promoted me to regional coordinator for all of European Russia, a vast area from the border with Eastern Europe to the Ural Mountains. The journals of my childhood had been fulfilled.

My farewell address was scheduled: I was invited by my Russian counterparts to be a special presenter at the Far East International Conference in Vladivostok. This would be my second trip to that city, and was to be my last conference before retiring. It was very near to the date of my birthday. I wanted to go out in style. I booked my round-trip ticket first class. My driver let me off at the entrance set aside for the privileged passengers and I entered the terminal to cheerful greetings and immediate assistance with everything. I relished this attention and the elegance that comes with the meaning of first class. It was my first time in this section of the plane in all my hundreds of thousands of miles in the air, and I felt I'd earned it. It is a nine-hour flight from Moscow to Vladivostok. It was while we were flying over Siberia that I picked up my champagne flute and looked out my little window at the cloudless sky and to the vast expanse of land that stretched out so far below us. I thought about the multiple other times I'd done the same; looking out at other vistas as I had said farewell to Reno, to Jamaica, and more than once to China. On this day I saluted the distant horizon of the Russian Federation: "Happy Birthday to me. What can be better than this? Here I am...seventy-two years old, flying first class over Siberia, and sipping champagne on my way to this prestigious, multinational conference. And I am an honored guest speaker. It's good. It's all good."

RANDOM NOTES FROM THREE-QUARTERS OF A CENTURY OF LIVING IT ALL

Whatever the problem, whatever the challenge, search out some person, some group, some country that has met the challenge and is doing something *right...with success,* and adapt it.

On China
On National and Cultural Identities
The Four Forbidden Topics
The Best of the Best

I am supposed to be in retirement, now, but I'm not sure if the term includes or excludes the multiple activities I'm still involved in. Just this summer, I was invited as a "specialist" to go to Venezuela for seventeen days. Of course, I arrived right at the beginning of student demonstrations against President Hugo Chavez and the activities going on in the country. I did not get involved! I had come to present two lectures at the Venezuelan Teachers of English to Speakers of Other Languages Conference in Caracas. My subjects were today's teenagers, Generation Y, and their place in our changing world, and using children's literature in the elementary school classroom, to be followed by a series of workshops for teachers. After the presentation on teenagers, I was invited to give a synopsis of my program on Venezuelan television, which unfortunately I did not have time to do before traveling to my next assignment in Merida, Venezuela. The series of workshops resulted in the local teachers developing their own venue for continuing the work to which I had introduced them. The opportunities just keep on knocking.

When not gallivanting, I spend my time putting together these random thoughts to share with anyone who would like to ask questions of me. I've learned a couple of things that I have come to believe about this world we live in. They are here in no particular order.

ON CHINA

I firmly believe that the seminal reason why China has emerged as a major market competitor and world force is because of what those thousands, millions, of students did in Tiananmen Square and across the country in 1989. Their actions changed the direction within the government, and opened the eyes of the world to the situation in China and to the strength of will of the Chinese people. They brought their country into the limelight. The deaths of those massacred students were not in vain.

My last trip to that country was in 1989, but Jennifer made another several years later. She told me that when her taxi neared our university she didn't even recognize the area. What we had called the boulevard had become a divided highway lined with American-style department stores and markets. Gone were the water buffalo that were often herded down the street. Students who had been riding bicycles now had their own cars, private ownership of which had been forbidden when we were there. Young marrieds are earning significant salaries and now own their own apartments and condos, rather than living with the parents of one or the other. The wonderfully colorful alleys surrounding our apartment building which I so dearly loved to explore, are, for the most part, gone... replaced with streets that can accommodate motorized vehicles. Our city has lost much of its color, and looks and behaves much the same as any other major metropolitan area anywhere in the world. But it has gained modernization and the conveniences of a more lucrative lifestyle. Progress!

As for the punishment meted out to my postgraduates for their participation in the students' demonstrations, the last I heard was that they were forbidden by their home universities to advance within their departments. Others, less informed and less educated, were promoted to the higher chairs. Two of them, Kevin and Mike, were offered teaching posts in our university upon completion of their master's degrees. Their home universities told them the only way they would be released from their contracts would be for them to repay their universities for all the salaries they had earned in the several years they had been teaching before leaving their posts for their advanced degrees. Of course, that was, at that time, impossible for either of them.

I think of my Chinese students often, and still cry over the events when I relate them to new friends and acquaintances. I have never forgotten that older gentleman's admonition as we all stood together in the rain at the square the morning after the Massacre, and he told me never to let the world forget them and those days. I've done my best, sir. They are very much in my heart.

As an addendum to the repressive sufferings by both the Chinese and the peoples subsumed within the Soviet Union; if you consider Adolf Hitler to be the most evil man of the twentieth century, you might look again at the lives and deeds of Chairman Mao and of Joseph Stalin. The numbers tell quite a story.

ON NATIONAL AND CULTURAL IDENTITIES

Once, very many years ago, in one of my sociology classes, we were speaking of nationalism and the ranking of countries on the planet as they struggle for political and market clout. Our professor said that the way we think of the world is not correct. He used the analogy of a large cake. We divide up that cake by cutting it vertically into slices: this slice represents this country, and that slice represents that country, and so forth. That is in error. We need to cut the cake horizontally. Each layer represents a socio/economic/academic level of the world's population. Those people on each level have more in common with others across the world on their own level, than they do with other members of their own nation who are on levels either below or above them. I know from my experiences that this is absolutely true. Over the past twenty years, I have been living and working in seven countries on five continents. I find that I have no difficulty whatsoever relating, conversing, and maintaining friendships with others in all of these countries who share my interests. Theoretically, I could easily invite dozens of my colleagues from around the world to a gala dinner party, and the room would quickly fill with chatter and banter and laughter as these educators shared life experiences and conversed and discussed subjects of weight and importance, and non-importance, that had commonalties personally and globally. I could not possibly get the same camaraderie at a dinner party to which I invited a genuine cross-section of my own country. How often does one find university professors sitting in coffee shops having real discussions—lasting more than a few moments—with, say, perpetually homeless persons? Or, put it the other way around: how often does a homeless person invite working professionals to lunch? There is of course a financial barrier there. But eliminate that wall. What do they have in common to talk about after the initial opening jargon? Not much. They're not in the same comfort zone. The same is true within even narrower confines; for example, secretaries in a group of business executives. Gotta go for the cliché, here: water seeks its own level. Sorry about that; however, it does lead on to thinking about globalization from a broader perspective, a perspective of multiple dimensions; the evolutionary future of the world's populations.

By the way, I particularly like the word *comrade*. I wish it didn't have such negative political connotations.

THE FOUR FORBIDDEN TOPICS

There are four subjects we are requested not to discuss as educators in foreign countries: sex, religion, politics, and evolution. Requested not to, yes, but of course I always do allow the students to discuss them, as these are the topics of greatest common interest across the world; therefore, it gives them the most rewarding opportunity to use their new language. However, I have learned to skirt my own opinions. I've become adept at being evasive.

The first, sex: I'm in favor of it.

I certainly do not use the following in any way with students, but for you, for here and now, I am putting in something of what I've learned over the decades about making love—no...my Chinese students would not accept that label—about having great sex!

Not quite sure why we look to the twenty-something women as our models of sexuality, when they are still engrossed in thinking about themselves and have had so little experience with the meaning of what it is to be with a man over the years. Well, my daughters, listen attentively. Jokes are made about the penis...*he thinks with his dick.* Much of the male psyche is directly connected to that male appendage. That's history and that's real. So, why the joke...your embarrassment? Or your anger? Most of a man's thoughts and much of his decision making are penis-based, either consciously or subconsciously. That's neither good nor bad; it just *is.* How do we as women deal with this? First, it is essential that any lingering medieval repressions about purity and virginity are put where they belong. In a history book. *When* a girl decides to have sexual relationships and *with whom* she decides to have them are not the questions here. It's what to do once the initial out-of-control romps burn down and become more or less a thing of the past. Then what? How do we keep the excitement in the sex act? Well, many men name their penis. So, consider this: the penis is a third person in your bed. Its protector is this big guy who has long ago outgrown his mother's tender care that he had clung to so completely as an infant and toddler. But his penis has not outgrown the need for that care. Think of the penis as an infant cradled in his pillows. Adore him, fondle him, caress him. Play little fun, even naughty games with him. Talk to him in your little voice and teach him all the creative lessons he needs to know about you with gentleness, with patience, and with sincere care for his pleasure as well as your own. Admire his being there with you, extol his virtues, encourage him to parade himself before you with pride, and marvel at his performances the same as you would a child in a nursery-school play—always keeping in mind that regardless of the quality and quantity, he's doing the best he can. Consistency is not to be expected. Sometimes toddlers fall down. It's OK. They soon enough get back up again. This third person is to be appreciated, especially at unexpected times. Be loving, be naughty, be—or pretend to be—proud of this prized possession. Once you've learned to genuinely care for his penis, you'll be amazed and gratified at the results that infuse your day-to-day relationship with its protector. Enjoy, my daughters, enjoy!

Second, religion: I've already gone into considerable detail as to my spiritual/philosophical (religious) beliefs— beliefs that make sense to me. Incidentally, it is an interesting exercise to count the number of time Jesus states emphatically that the healings were the result of the sufferer's *faith* or *belief.* He also states quite clearly that heaven is not some place far away for some distant enjoyment, but that heaven is within us. It only follows, then, that if heaven is within, so is hell. Opposing states of consciousness.

Before leaving the subject *for good,* I would like to refer to the ancient papyrus documents found at Nag Hammadi (Egypt) in 1945, which Web link will be found with the other references at the end of this manuscript. Relative to Jesus' awareness of the teachings of Yoga, there are several citations in the *Thomas* document that are directly connected to yogic teachings. I include just three. Jesus (Y'shua) is quoted: verse 22—The likeness of what is below is that which is above; what is below is nothing but the *delusion of those who are without knowledge* (italics mine—delusion in this context is seminal to both Yoga and Buddhism); verse 42—Become transients (passersby) [nonattachment is both from Yoga and Buddhism]; and verse 90—Come unto me, for my yoga is natural and my lordship is gentle—and you shall find repose for yourselves. (*Matthew 11:28, 30—Come unto me, all ye that labour, and are heavy laden, and I will give you rest...For my yoke is easy and my burden is light.*) Yoga and yoke are synonyms meaning spiritual discipline. Yoga is the earlier word, being from Sanskrit; therefore, yoke is a (deliberate?) substitution during transliteration.

It is clear why the *Thomas* document would not be included by those bishops of so long ago. Although our current biblical archaeologists assign its writing to Thomas the disciple, one of the twelve, and date it as probably the earliest of the gospels, with its esoteric and metaphysical emphasis it would not support an agenda that wanted to give all power to a priesthood.

The reference list also includes a beautifully developed and presented book containing approximately one hundred parallel sayings of The Buddha and Jesus.

The third area, politics: I'm a Democrat. Surprise, surprise!

The fourth topic, biological evolution, Darwin's Theory. To start with, it has long ago moved out of the realm of theory. I've been studying and reading in this area for most of my life. It is of genuine interest to me. The evidence is manifold from multiple fields and cannot be reasonably denied. I'm not going to worry the point. Suffice it to say, after I first began to truly understand the concept, I saw that the miracle of biological evolution and what it has produced is far greater than any Adam and Eve story could ever be. Although "Lucy," Donald Johanson's incredible find (please see addenda), is an early branch off from our line, the first time I saw a mock-up of those tiny three-and-a-half-million-year-old skeletal remains in the San Francisco museum, I just stood there and cried. I probably embarrassed everyone around me. Our proto-ancestors always have been among the weakest creatures in the jungle. How was it possible that such a fragile, bitsy little lady and her kin lived long enough to reproduce? How Homo sapiens and our forebears on that complex family tree survived at all can best be explained by querying, as one of my anthropology professors at UCLA so aptly put it, "Was it a touch of the divine?"

As for our capacity for survival, we need only look across the millions of years and across the planet and think about what incredible, marvelous beings we are because of our tenacity and endurance in the face of seemingly overwhelming odds. These are qualities not in any way confined to any one time or place, one group or nationality. We hear the stories of the courage and doggedness of standout examples such as the Siege of Leningrad from September 8, 1941 to January 27, 1944. Indeed, those nine hundred days during World War II are a prime example of what people can and will do to survive and bring about a desired end. Congratulations to them. That siege was a headliner, but the same qualities are found among all kinds of populations under all kinds of adversities. We study it in our history books and in our anthropology texts. I have seen it and lived it. We are powerfully strong creatures when put to the test. We can lift ourselves out of the most devastating abysses, when we want to. That's the key...when we want to change, we can and will.

THE BEST OF THE BEST

And finally, the greatest human being I've ever had the privilege of being in the presence of is the Dalai Lama. He lectured for several days in Riga, Latvia, in the early summer of 2001, and I was able to escape from my assignment and travel to that city. My son, Gregory, had years before ended his relationship with Amanda and both had moved on with their lives. Since graduating from university, Greg had been living and working in Eastern Europe and had married the young Latvian woman, Jana, I mentioned earlier. They moved from Estonia to Latvia. Their first child was just three months old when Greg phoned me at my home in Russia with the news of the Dalai Lama's visit.

Although he believes himself to be a *simple monk*, to me, and many millions across the world, he is the epitome of a spiritual leader. He was scheduled to give a series of lectures and I was able to attend each one. Just being in his presence was an experience that moved me deeply; a truly inspiring model of goodness, radiating love and rich humor. I was even able to provide him with a word. I was sitting in the front row during his presentation to the medical staff at the children's hospital. He was commending the nurses on their care for those youngsters who were...not going to get well. He was searching for the correct word and I whispered to him from my front row seat, "terminal." He smiled slightly in my direction and inserted the word into his message. I was thrilled. (His translator was sitting directly behind him, but I was a bit quicker in responding. Trivial things make a big impact on me, I guess.) After the lecture, he walked down the farthest aisle to the exit. Jana had taken the baby and was standing at that doorway so that if the infant cried she would not disturb the gathering. The Dalai Lama stopped when he reached them and began to play with the baby...the whole kitchee-cooing small talk. A precious moment for my family.

The Dalai Lama's word is Compassion.

Yes...keeping in mind that compassion means compassion, it does not bridge over and mean that one's negative actions are cancelled out. Forgiving negative actions is one thing; it does not stand in the place of an obligation to atone for those actions. *Forgive them for they know not what they are doing* has been taken to mean that on a deathbed sins can be forgiven by a clergyman, thereby opening a path to some heaven, which Jesus had already admonished is not a location. Perhaps his message was to *judge not* but to *render unto Caesar* whatever it takes to keep a society functioning: clergymen have given themselves the right to forgive sins or to damn anyone to hell for eternity. That is aggrandizement in order to maintain a power base. Reincarnation is a far more exacting system; a system that calls us all to accounting; but does not inflict irreversible punishment and banish us to some nether region for eternity. There is no divine love in such a concept. Divine love is insisting that we keep on trying again and again until we get it right. I imagine a grand spiral highway winding upward with all of us on our paths. Sometimes we trip ourselves and fall backward, but we get back up...and some people even make a part of their trip facing backward... all because *we don't know what we're doing,* and then sometimes we hurry forward, but we're all moving along toward a goal of enlightenment. *Heaven—Paradise—Nirvana*: that level of supreme consciousness reached when negative karma has been eliminated through reparations; and human desires are naturally—not forcibly—extinguished And...if we put the comma after the word "day"...*I say unto you this day, thou shalt be*...then, finally, it all makes sense. Just give it time.

Atone now, or atone next time! It's all karma. It's all reincarnation. It's all God-consciousness. It's all up to us to avail ourselves of our inherent divinity. This is His compassionate and merciful and loving gift. So, come; let us celebrate the divine energy, the chi within.

Love,
Adair
Davis, California
22 November 2007 (Thanksgiving Day)

ADDENDA

Following the trail of the accumulating coincidences, there are clearly eighteen of them, listed below. Of the eighteen, nine can be said to be "cosmic in scope," in Norman's words. Cosmic due to the vast expanse of both time and space between the initiating events and the fulfillment of the coincidence, "merging together as two hands enfolding," again Norman's words. Whether cosmic or simple, each of the eighteen leads on to the next like one of those ever-expanding telescopes used in days of long ago.

I learned later that among the several American cities where the Fulbright advertisement for Cairo had been run, only one of the San Francisco papers had been selected, and the ad had run only on that one day. That was the morning when Barbara had offhandedly bought that particular paper. That coincidence made it possible for Norman to come to America and our marriage to take place. It opened wide those gates that I had always hoped for, the gates to our splendid future. Unquestionably, this coincidence brought into sharp focus the panorama on the tapestry. Considering again the details and ten-year time lapse between the Peace Corps meeting when I first heard the references to Teaching English to Speakers of Other Languages, Fulbright, USAID, and so forth, and the newspaper advertisement, it can be said without need for further validation that this coincidence was one of cosmic proportions. In many aspects, I had long been programmed for that particular Sunday.

LIST OF 18 MAJOR AND MINOR, UNPLANNED-FOR, LIFE-CHANGING EVENTS

Tbilisi, Georgia, USSR—Father suggests English for sons

Lake Tahoe, Nevada—Offhand suggestion by my son to join Peace Corps

Peace Corps—Unexpected cancellation

Peace Corps—Home of Victor's aunt for duration of tour of duty

Peace Corps—Island social meeting, learned about USAID, Fulbright, TESOL/M.A.

Peace Corps—Destruction of materials

Davis, California—Barbara's home, family social gathering, Greg meets Mandy

Application to American University, Cairo—Lost

Yerevan, Armenia—Tanya hired for university in China

Application to university in China—ignored, then

Alexander phones California, to phone Mandy, to phone me

Timing for teaching at university in China/Tiananmen Square massacre/Student demonstrations involvement

Sochi, Russia (Black Sea)—Tanya meets teacher from Tbilisi who knew Norman

Davis, California—Basketball game: Russia vs. Davis High/Russian chaperone

Yerevan, Armenia—Dropping by at AUA/meeting Jimmy Harris

Guadalajara, Mexico—Rescue after bus accident
Davis, California—Notified of death of former mother-in-law/collect from estate
Davis, California—San Francisco newspaper ad

REFERENCES

Bach, R. & Munson, R. (1970). Jonathan Livingston Seagull. New York, NY: Simon & Schuster.

Borg, M., & Riegert, R. (Eds.). (2002). Jesus and Buddha, the parallel sayings.

Chopra, D. (2000). How to know God. New York: Three Rivers Press.

Dalai Lama: everything he's written

Johanson, D., & Maitland, E. (1981). Lucy. New York, NY: Simon & Schuster.

Laszlo, E. (2004). Science and the akashic field. Rochester, VT: Inner Traditions.

Laszlo, E. (2006). Science and the reenchantment of the cosmos. Rochester, VT: Inner Traditions.

Online: (2 sites to initiate a search) Metagospels, http://www.metalog.org, Nag Hammadi, http://gnosis.org/naghamm/nhl.html

Yogananda, P. (1946). Autobiography of a yogi. Los Angeles: Self-Realization Fellowship.

Note: Dr. Laszlo is a distinguished scientist and recipient of the State Doctorate, the Sorbonne's highest degree, as well as multiple other degrees and awards. A scientist unafraid to cross over and think between two fields and to write reader-friendly texts.

3362996

Made in the USA